FOCUS: MUSIC AND RELIGION OF MOROCCO

Focus: Music and Religion of Morocco introduces the region and its history, highlighting how the pressures of religious life, post-colonial economic struggle, and global media come together within Moroccan musical life. Musical practices contextualize and clarify global historical and contemporary movements—many of which remain poorly understood—while articulating the daily realities of the region's populations in ways that rarely show through current news accounts of religious extremism, poverty and inequality, and forced migration.

As with other volumes in the series, *Focus: Music and Religion of Morocco* addresses large, conceptual issues though interwoven case studies in three parts:

- **Part I – Memories and Medias: Who We Are** highlights how issues of religion, colonialism, nationalism, and globalization transcend boundaries through music to create a sense of personal and national identity, whether hundreds of years ago or on today's satellite television stations.
- **Part II – Contesting Mainstreams: Where We're Going** explores Morocco's sacred and secular music practices as they relate to the country's diversity and its contemporary politics.
- **Part III – Focusing In: Fun and Faith in Fez** highlights Fez's sacred music industry by introducing musicians who navigate musical and religious expectations to appeal to both their own devotional ethics and their audiences' wants.

Links to music examples referenced in the text can be accessed on the eResource site www.routledge.com/9781138094581

Christopher Witulski is Instructor of Ethnomusicology at Bowling Green State University.

FOCUS ON WORLD MUSIC

Series Editor: Michael B. Bakan, Florida State University

The **Focus on World Music Series** is designed specifically for area courses in world music and ethnomusicology. Written by the top ethnomusicologists in their field, the Focus books balance sound pedagogy with exemplary scholarship. Each book provides a telescopic view of the music and cultures addressed, giving the reader a general introduction to the music and culture of the area and then zooming in on different musical styles with in-depth case studies.

Focus: Popular Music of India
Natalie Sarrazin

Focus: Music and Religion of Morocco
Christopher Witulski

Focus: Musics of the Caribbean
Sydney Jane Hutchinson

Focus: Music and Devotion in India
Jaime Jones

Focus: Choral Music in Global Perspective
André de Quadros

Focus: Scottish Traditional Music
Simon McKerrell

Focus: Music in Contemporary Japan
Jennifer Milioto Matsue

Focus: Music, Nationalism, and the Making of a New Europe, Second Edition
Philip V. Bohlman

Focus: Irish Traditional Music
Sean Williams

Focus: Music of Northeast Brazil, Second Edition
Larry Crook

Focus: Music of South Africa, Second Edition
Carol A. Muller

Focus: Gamelan Music of Indonesia, Second Edition
Henry Spiller

FOCUS: MUSIC AND RELIGION OF MOROCCO

Christopher Witulski

NEW YORK AND LONDON

First published 2019
by Routledge
52 Vanderbilt Avenue, New York, NY 10017

and by Routledge
2 Park Square, Milton Park, Abingdon, Oxon, OX14 4RN

Routledge is an imprint of the Taylor & Francis Group, an informa business

© 2019 Taylor & Francis

The right of Christopher Witulski to be identified as author of this work has been asserted by him in accordance with sections 77 and 78 of the Copyright, Designs and Patents Act 1988.

All rights reserved. No part of this book may be reprinted or reproduced or utilised in any form or by any electronic, mechanical, or other means, now known or hereafter invented, including photocopying and recording, or in any information storage or retrieval system, without permission in writing from the publishers.

Trademark notice: Product or corporate names may be trademarks or registered trademarks, and are used only for identification and explanation without intent to infringe.

Library of Congress Cataloging-in-Publication Data
Names: Witulski, Christopher, author.
Title: Focus: music and religion of Morocco/Christopher Witulski.
Other titles: Music and religion of Morocco
Description: New York; London: Routledge, 2019. | Includes bibliographical references and index.
Identifiers: LCCN 2018060312 (print) | LCCN 2019000758 (ebook) | ISBN 9781315106014 (ebook) | ISBN 9781138094574 (hardback) | ISBN 9781138094581 (pbk.)
Subjects: LCSH: Music–Social aspects–Morocco. | Music–Morocco–Religious aspects.
Classification: LCC ML3917.M68 (ebook) | LCC ML3917.M68 W58 2019 (print) | DDC 781.7/700964–dc23
LC record available at https://lccn.loc.gov/2018060312

ISBN: 978-1-138-09457-4 (hbk)
ISBN: 978-1-138-09458-1 (pbk)
ISBN: 978-1-315-10601-4 (ebk)

Typeset in Minion
by Deanta Global Publishing Services, Chennai, India

All photos by the author unless otherwise noted.
Visit the eResource: www.routledge.com/9781138094581

Contents

List of Map, Figures and Examples	vii
Series Foreword	x
Notes on Transcription and Transliteration	xii
Acknowledgments	xiii

PART I Memories and Medias: Who We Are — 1

1 Andalusian Memories — 7

   Morocco's Andalusian History 9
   Andalusian Music 13
   Musical Organization 17
   Religion, Class, and Music 20
   Notes 23

2 Global Popular Music — 24

   Global Exchanges 27
   The History and Practice of Islam 30
   Local Global Music 33
   Notes 40

Part II Contesting Mainstreams: Where We're Going — 41

3 Pop and Protest — 43

Political History Since Independence 44
A History of Protest 48
A New Generation of Protest 53
Notes 57

4 Gnawa Music and Ritual — 58

Slave Trade History 60
Ceremony and Beliefs 61
Rise to Popularity 68
Fusion Projects 70
Notes 75

Part III Focusing In: Faith and Fun in Fez — 77

5 Sufi Ritual — 79

Popular Sufism 80
Hamadsha History and Beliefs 84
Performing a Ritual in Meknes 87
Notes 95

6 Sufi Entertainments — 97

The 'Issawa and Their Ritual 101
Navigating Pop Careers 109
Notes 114

7 Malhun As Pop, Piety, and Local Pride — 115

Celebrating an Urban Identity 117
Malhun's History and Structure 121
A Wide Popularity 125
A Local (Sacred) Aesthetic 132
Notes 136

Conclusion: Who We Are and Where We're Going — 137
Resources — 146
Glossary — 149
References — 153
Index — 159

List of Map, Figures and Examples

Map

0.1	Map of Morocco and the Western Sahara with selected major cities	xiv

Figures

1.1	Ensemble leader playing the rabab	15
2.1	View from a rooftop terrace in Fez	25
2.2	A member of the Moroccan hip hop group Muslim performing in Fez in 2011	38
3.1	Omar Sayed and a member of a gnawa ensemble (see Chapter 4) stand on stage during a Nass El Ghiwane concert in Fez in 2011	51
4.1	Mʿallem Abd al-Rzaq and his brother Hamid each playing a tbal during a procession in Sidi Ali	64
4.2	Members of a gnawa group parading during a procession and playing quraqeb to open a major music festival in Essaouira	64
4.3	Mʿallem Allal Soudani playing the hajhuj and leading the ritual through the music for Sidi Musa and the blue spirits at the Zawiya Sidna Bilal in the city of Essaouira	66
4.4	Hamid al-Kasri performing in Essaouira with the American jazz group Snarky Puppy in 2018	70
5.1	Members of Abderrahim Amrani's hamadsha ensemble playing the guwwal during a ritual in Fez	88
5.2	Abderrahim Amrani playing the ginbri during a ritual in Fez	89
5.3	Ghita player performing during a procession in Sidi Ali	90

viii • List of Map, Figures and Examples

6.1	Abdellah Yâakoubi, a prominent ʿissawa muqaddim, performing at the Fez Festival of World Sacred Music	103
6.2	Nfar players and other members of Muqaddim Adil's ensemble parading into a wedding ceremony in Fez	104
6.3	A member of Muqaddim Adil's ensemble during a demonstration in Fez	105
6.4	Members of the two main jilala-focused groups collaborating to demonstrate their rituals in Meknes	107
6.5	Neighborhood youth from Amrani's ahl twat class practicing a stick dance	108
6.6	One of Abdellah Yâakoubi's VCD recordings	110
6.7	Screenshot from an undated video of Amrani casually singing with a group of other ritual musicians	111
6.8	A member of Amrani's ensemble playing ghita along with DJ Click, who is playing the theremin	111
6.9	Members of Muqaddim Adil's ensemble showing me (left, in sandals) and others from the study abroad group what to do during the ʿissawa procession	113
7.1	The venue where we were to perform outside of Mulay Yaqub	116
7.2	Part of the ensemble preparing for the performance, including Muhammad Soussi (in gray, next to the violinist) and the author (in the foreground, facing away from the camera)	117
7.3	Members of the ʿissawa ensemble dancing with guests during the concert outside of Mulay Yaqub	118
7.4	Muhammad Soussi (left) preparing for a malhun performance in Fez	122
7.5	The runway and crowd during Muhammad Soussi's fashion show performance in Fez	126
7.6	A model preparing for her trip down the catwalk	127
7.7	Soussi's ensemble and the models as they returned to the stage at the end of the show	128
7.8	Members of Amrani's ensemble sleeping in the van on the road to Casablanca	130
7.9	Amrani leading his hamadsha group through the Casablanca streets	131
7.10	Abderrahim Amrani (center) performing "Aisha Hamdushiyya" with Hamid al-Kasri (right)	132

Examples

1.1	Andalusi rhythmic patterns	19
1.2	Chiki version of the verse with published and ʿud melodies and highlighted syncopations	22
4.1	Some ostinato patterns that appear in Randy Weston's "Blue Moses"	73
4.2	Saxophone melody that appears during the "funk" section of Randy Weston's "Blue Moses"	73
5.1	Skeletal rhythmic clapping pattern used during al-unasa al-kabira	91
5.2	The guwwal pattern from the al-unasa al-kabira segment	92

5.3	A simplified version of the melody that Amrani and Calmus sang during a lesson (top line); an approximate transcription of what they sang that includes ornaments, syncopations, and other details (middle line); and the guwwal pattern that organizes the performance (bottom line)	94
5.4	Guwwal rhythms that are common during the hadra segment of the ceremony. Different players may add divisions that increase the overall density	95
7.1	Interlocking t'arija patterns combine to create the most common rhythm used in malhun music	125
7.2	The first and fourth iterations of the harba in Houcine Toulali's performance of "al-Shma'a," 3:10 and 8:30 in the example cited in the resources section, respectively	129
7.3	Melodic contours from Toulali's and Haroushi's performances of "al-Shma'a," excepting Toulali's final harba	130
7.4	The rhythmic transition from the majority of "Hakim al-Dhati" (a) to the insiraf segment (b), which is influenced by the flali pattern (c)	134

Series Foreword

Recent decades have witnessed extraordinary growth in the arena of ethnomusicology and world music publishing. From reference works such as the *Garland Encyclopedia of World Music* and *Grove Music Online* to a diverse array of introductory world music textbooks, and an ever-growing list of scholarly monographs and hefty edited volumes, the range of quality published sources for research and teaching is unprecedented. And then there is the internet, where YouTube, Spotify, websites, blogs, social media, and countless digital platforms for music delivery, multimedia production, and music-related metadata have fostered a veritable revolution in the realms of all things musical, from production and reception to public access, commodification, and practices of listening, reading, and viewing.

Yet for all that has come along and all that has been transformed, there has long been a conspicuous gap in the literature. For those of us who teach entry-level area courses in world music and ethnomusicology subject areas—the kinds of courses that straddle the divide between the introductory world music survey and the advanced graduate seminar, the ones that cater to upper-division undergraduates or to new graduate students who have a basic foundation in the field, but are not yet ready for the highly specialized studies of, say, a Chicago Studies in Ethnomusicology-based reading list—available options for appropriate core texts have remained slim at best.

It is to the instructors and students of these types of courses that the Routledge *Focus on World Music* series is primarily directed. *Focus* books balance sound pedagogy with exemplary scholarship. They are substantive in content, yet readily accessible to specialist and non-specialist readers alike. They are written in a lively and engaging style by leading ethnomusicologists and educators, bringing wide interdisciplinary scope and relevance to the contemporary concerns of world music studies. While each volume is unique, all share a commitment to providing readers with a "telescopic" view of the music and cultures they address, zooming in from broad-based surveys of expansive music-culture areas and topics toward compelling, in-depth case studies of specific musicultural traditions and their myriad transformations in the modern world.

When you adopt a *Focus* book for your course, you can count on getting a work that is authoritative, accessible, pedagogically strong, richly illustrated, and integrally linked to excellent online musical and multimedia supplementary resources. Threading the needle between pedagogical priorities and scholarly richness, these are texts that make teaching specific topics in world music and ethnomusicology meaningful, valuable, and rewarding. I am delighted to be part of the team that has brought this exciting and important series to fruition. I hope you enjoy reading and working with these books as much as I have!

Michael B. Bakan
Florida State University
Series Editor

Notes on Transcription and Transliteration

Systems of translation often fail to effectively represent the sounds and meanings of what they portray. This book uses two types of translation and representation: the transliteration of the Moroccan Arabic language and the transcription of musical sounds. Both are flawed, but I aim for simplicity by adapting the transliteration system of the *International Journal of Middle East Studies* and, for musical transcriptions, closely approximating the performances from my fieldwork recordings and other sources in musical notation. I omit all diacritical markings in proper names, but otherwise use ʿ for ʿayn (ع) and ʾ for hamza (ء) throughout the text. In the case of common English words or place names, I use those in place of a strict transliteration. In this way, I prioritize readability at the expense of some consistency. For example, the city is Fez (not Fas or Fès), but its residents are fassi. If a performer has an established transliteration of his or her name, I maintain that, though inconsistencies can still confuse the issue between different album releases or other mentions: Abdelah El Yâakoubi instead of Abd Allah Yʿaqubi or Abderrahim Amrani instead of Abd al-Rahim Amrani, for example. The ʿayn that opens many proper names (like ʿAbd or ʿAisha) has been removed for readability (Abd al-Rahim instead of ʿAbd al-Rahim). Plurals are constructed by adding an "s" instead of using the more complex Arabic system. Similarly, musical notation is meant to provide a rough outline of the sounds I describe. Rhythms and pitches are notoriously difficult to precisely reproduce in writing, and those moments of uncertainty are where many of the most interesting things happen.

Acknowledgments

I owe my sincere gratitude to many who have collaborated in so many ways to bring this project to its conclusion. This is especially true for those in Morocco who gave me the gift of sharing their time and expertise. *May God bless your parents.*

My thanks also go out to the many friends and scholars who have helped to inform these chapters as I worked to fill in the gaps in my knowledge. This includes Hicham Chami, Hamid Mountassir, Philip Murphy, Sadik Rddad, Kendra Salois, and Lhoussine Simour. Constance Ditzel's generous editorial work has been transformative. Foremost has been Michael Bakan's interest in making this project into a reality. I am grateful for his constant support, generous reading, and careful editorship. Of course, even with the help of these individuals, mistakes will make their way into this work. Any such errors are solely my own.

The project resulted from generous financial and logistical support from institutions including the Fulbright Student Grant Program and the Moroccan-American Commission for Educational and Cultural Exchange's wonderful staff, led by Jim Miller; the University of Florida's School of Music, Center for African Studies, and Alumni Fellowship Program; and the Department of Education's Foreign Language and Area Studies program. Thank you also to Philip Murphy and Sandy McCutcheon for sharing your photographs (see Figures 6.5, 7.9, and 7.10).

There were many who worked closely and patiently with me throughout my time in Morocco. They deserve special recognition for putting up with my constant questions. This includes M'allem Abd al-Rzaq; M'allem Aziz wuld Ba Blan; Abderrahim Amrani and the members of his ensemble; Muhammad Soussi, his son Yusef, and the members of his ensemble; Muqaddim Abdellah Yâakoubi; Muqaddim Adil; Fredric Calmus; Ahmed Chiki and his son Abd al-Salam; Fatima Zahra and the staff at Subul al-Salam; and so many others. To Mohammed Boujma' and his family, Abd al-Hafez and his family, Sandy McCutcheon and Suzanna Clark, and to my friends and neighbors in Fez, thank you for opening your homes and lives to me.

Finally, I want to thank Jessica, Madeleine, Julia, and Elise. Thank you for keeping me grounded and sane. Your faith and love are gifts from God.

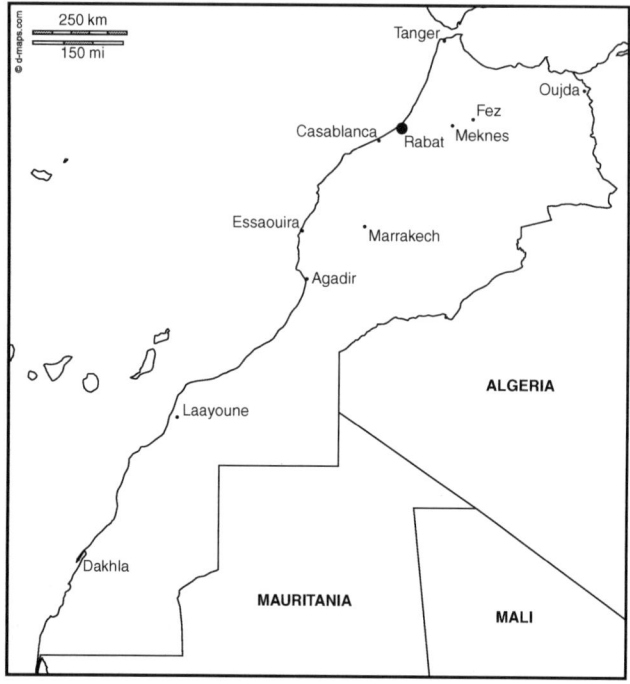

Map 0.1 Map of Morocco and the Western Sahara with selected major cities. © Daniel Dalet, http://d-maps.com/carte.php?num_car=22751&lang=en.

PART I

Memories and Medias: Who We Are

Like so many others, when I first visited the Middle East as a study abroad student in Egypt in 2004, I didn't know much about what to expect. I had been studying Arabic for a semester in the United States, which is really only enough time to learn the alphabet, how to ask for directions, and how to order food. Cairo was a surprise, but a big part of that surprise was how familiar it was. Just like any other big city I had spent time in, like New York, it was noisy and full of traffic. Signs were everywhere, advertisements sold cellphone plans, and the Pizza Hut delivered.

While Morocco is not Egypt and cities like Fez, Marrakech, and Tangier, where I spent most of my time, are not as big as Cairo, these major urban centers are global cities of roughly one million residents. Almost seven million people live in and around Morocco's largest city and economic center, Casablanca. Its urban population of about three and a half million puts it between Chicago and Los Angeles in terms of size. Morocco's cities look outward, making connections abroad, while also looking inward, creating their own identities. Fez, Marrakech, Tangier, and others have long histories of global cosmopolitanism, though it can manifest in different ways, both economic and cultural.

Global connections are not exclusive to cities, though. Especially today, when even the smallest rural homes have satellite dishes to pick up broadcasts from Morocco's news stations and from more far-reaching media outlets in Saudi Arabia, Egypt, or Qatar. Mass media plays an outsized role in Moroccan music and, despite the wealth of local styles that appear throughout this book, many stations' airwaves are dominated by the latest pop music from regional and global corporations. Their music videos play from television sets in cafés and restaurants, not to mention the cellphones of young people huddled around the latest hit.

These experiences came to define my understanding of music in Morocco, as well as how I started to see religion working. Just as Cairo felt familiar, I saw people working to live their lives in a familiarly confusing contemporary world. As we sat at cafés drinking coffee or waited for a gig to start, musicians and music fans frequently explained to me how they navigated their faith within a changing society. While it was important for me to remember the dramatic differences between my own experiences and theirs, these discussions showed me how similar today's concerns are for people trying to make a living while doing the right thing. Maybe it seems like a stretch, but talking about music—both sacred and popular—gave depth to these interactions. People have strong opinions about the newest pop trends, or how their fellow Muslims (or Christians, Jews, Buddhists, and so on) use music to bring their communities closer to or further from "the right path."

Music has a long history as a foundational part of the experience of religion. Around the world, religious activities have featured different kinds of musical performance to instigate or support worship. Ecstatic singing and dancing can enhance how humans understand the divine and supernatural, whether in prayer, ritual worship, spirit possession, meditation, or in any number of other spiritual encounters. Music can reinforce faith and help someone to live according to their morals, bringing believers closer to whatever the aims of that faith might be. This power has not gone unnoticed, however, as music also has a fraught history with religion. According to some, certain types of music like rock and roll in the 1950s or heavy metal in the 1980s might get connected with moral failure or even evil itself.

In most cases, the links between music and religion go beyond any explicit connection: they come out of social norms, or, more often, they come out of those moments when listeners don't follow those social norms. When they break the rules. But the aesthetics of music can play many roles within the spiritual or moral lives of listeners. As tastes change and the edgy loses its edge, musicians and listeners adapt. What was holy becomes bland or what was profane becomes sacred. Music-as-entertainment comes into contact with morality and, in some cases, like Evangelical churches fronted by rock bands, once-problematic tastes in music coincide with or even animate worship. It can become music with a mission. Religion and entertainment can inform one another to help someone navigate a difficult and confusing world. Or not.

Morocco, a country that sits on the northwest corner of the African continent, just a few miles south of Spain, has a diversity of both musical and religious practices that exemplify the wide range of connections between tastes, entertainment, and piety. While a similar book to this one could be written about any nation, region, or community (and many have), Morocco's history and prominence within the world's imagination make it particularly demonstrative of how music and religion work with and against each other. 99% majority of the country is Muslim (Central Intelligence Agency 2019), though there used to be a sizable Jewish minority. There are dramatic distinctions between urban and rural areas, between those who identify as Arab and those who are Amazight (Berber), and between an educated, often urban, elite and the poor. Gender dynamics are both significant and consequential throughout these discussions, but the nature of the male-dominated music industry and my own position as a man doing research largely with men forces me to omit far too much on the topic. A dramatic need for research on women's practices remains: I am all-too-aware that this book does not help to bring sufficient attention to the many women who are active as important performers, nor to those who are such a significant part of the listening audience. This book follows some of these lines—but not all—straddling them to explore how they came to be and how they hold up or fall apart when scrutinized by the debates surrounding music and religion. Sometimes the music is pop: they are products of the mass media industry appearing on the radio, burned CD mixes, or YouTube that are celebrated or derided for reasons of morality. In other instances, the music is part of religious practice that, itself, is either contested or held up as "authentic" by the community. In most situations, the line between these two is blurry, absent, or simply irrelevant.

About This Book

The aim of this book is to probe the intersection of music and religion. While this may lead to a better understanding of each, it also moves the focus onto how people incorporate their tastes and values into their morality. In the process, these pages may reflect concerns or conflicts that feel familiar. Questions about the appropriateness of incorporating the newest pop style into a worship service or engaging new followers through musical performance bring home the fact that music and religion are linked everywhere, not just abroad or within rituals that seem so far removed from my own experience as an American growing up in suburbia during the 1980s and 1990s. To this end, I often draw upon American or European public debates or musical styles that struggled with these same questions early in their own history to make points about Moroccan practice.

Similarly, the scope of these chapters is not meant to be exhaustive. To the contrary, they introduce the relevant history or political context that is necessary to understand the musical or religious questions that follow. We will move quickly through a host of styles, social movements, and religious practices to show a breadth of musical and religious identities. The focus moves from a national perspective—looking outward to make global connections and inward to create a national identity—to a regional one, where the country's diversity comes to the fore. The final section, Part III, goes deeper, reflecting my own experience doing ethnographic fieldwork over roughly two years in Fez. Here, the breadth is replaced by depth as a singular community of ritual musicians demonstrate some of the very questions that peppered the first two-thirds of the book, and their efforts toward finding answers.

This book is divided into three parts. Part I takes a wide view of Moroccan history and explores musical styles that look outward, reflecting national or global trends. Chapter 1 explores the relationship between Andalusian music, a celebrated "classical" genre, and Morocco's own Andalusian history. Firmly planted within today's world, the chapter explores how artists, listeners, and governments look outward and backward toward versions of music and religion from the past to build up a sense of tradition and culture today. In Chapter 2, musical tastes reflect similar issues of globalization in the contemporary world, as popular music looks outward for both influence and inspiration. Tastes from across the region and world come into conflict within the everyday lives of listeners who are left to think about how what they like relates to what they feel they should like.

Instead of looking outward, Part II refocuses on various regional communities across the country. Morocco is ethnically, linguistically, religiously, and geographically diverse, so it stands to reason that these distinctions extend to music and the arts. Chapter 3 looks more closely at the country's political history before, during, and following French colonialism during the 20th century. This perspective illuminates the important role that activist musicians play within national politics and as leaders of social movements, establishing the structures of power that inform musical and religious activity within the country. Chapter 4 introduces gnawa music as an example of a case in which musical and religious practices coming from the periphery instigate claims of moral decay or questions of proper Islamic practice. Social life, politics, arts, and entertainment are all tied into various perspectives on ethical behavior.

Part III focuses in on one city and the variety of religious musical performers who navigate its music scene. Fez was the country's capital for most of its history (before the arrival of the French) and it lays a special claim as a site of knowledge and piety. Chapters 5 and 6 introduce forms of ritual practice that are both celebrated and derided, depending on who you talk to. These mystical traditions have, in turn, become intertwined with popular music styles, wedding performances, major festivals, and the city's religious identity. They are ritual entertainment. The section closes with Chapter 7, a look at a form of semi-classical music related to Chapter 1's Andalusian styles and follows one performer who adopts these religious trends into his own music to demonstrate his piety, his city pride, and attract new audiences. Religion is celebrated and operationalized.

Each chapter in this book includes suggested listening and reading. The issues that come up throughout these chapters only touch the surface of the necessary larger questions, sacrificing depth for breadth. The resource listings will point toward accessible further scholarship on some of the main topics for interested readers. Furthermore, reading about music without listening to it is something of a farcical project. These chapters include lengthy discussions of individual artists and songs. The listing of resources following the final chapter includes recommended readings and links to playlists of recordings that are discussed within the text. In many cases, these artists—especially the older ones—did not work in an industry that focuses on preparing and selling complete albums. In these cases, I strive to provide links or suggestions for specific songs. They are worth a listen, both to firm up an understanding of the arguments in the text and as good music in their own right. Finally, a note about the structure of these chapters: I begin each with a short story, a narrative from my own experience living in Morocco. In these vignettes, I try to be honest, at the risk of sounding naïve or surprised (which, in many cases, I certainly was). These serve to make the discussions that follow more real, to give a picture of specific musical contexts, and to help flesh out a more three-dimensional image of the country and of those who were so generous in sharing their time and knowledge with me.

"Hips Don't Lie"

These pages present a broad outline of history, religion, and musical practice in a diverse North African country. The boundaries between communities and cultural practices are never as well-defined or concrete as they appear in a book like this. Religious groups influence each other, just as listeners listen widely. Tastes bleed from person to person, trends pick up and die away. The sound of Amazigh communities in rural areas appear in urban taxis while the latest international craze blasts through rural wedding celebrations. I remember my surprise at the ubiquity of Shakira's "Hips Don't Lie" during one of my visits to Morocco a few years ago. There is wisdom in those words: how people bridge what they believe, what they say that they want to do, what they say that they do, and what they do can bring important depth to understanding the practice of religion in the world today, whether in Morocco or elsewhere.

People are drawn to new sounds just as they are drawn to compelling and inspiring religious practices. For many, the line between entertainment and worship is not a clear one: listeners like what they like, and they want to hear more of it. The influence of aesthetic tastes on ritual practices show up early and often through these chapters, but they are especially present in the spirit possession ceremonies of the gnawa—a community that went from extreme marginalization to pop stardom—and the adaptations that Fez's Sufi musicians make in the three chapters that comprise Part III. Just as believers use music to orient their religious values and practices, musicians recognize the power of religion to bring them closer to their audiences. Faith-filled singers (and, likely, many opportunistic performers) present their works as moral, as righteous. The ethics of the music industry can take on a sacred hue, just as Christian rock can bridge seemingly insurmountable contradictions between the value systems core to many rock musicians (rebellion, anarchy, "sex, drugs, and rock and roll" mentalities) and those of pious listeners. That this is usually more than a veneer, but a way for young and old alike to operate within the contemporary world while adhering to a right path, may be unsurprising: it is not unique to Europe or the United States, nor is it unique to Christianity.

Yet, just as the relationship between music and religion in Morocco can be mutually reinforcing, it can also be a marker of difference. Religious perspectives hold powerful authority when criticizing musical trends or elements of popular culture. Within a conservative worldview (again, not unlike that seen in Christianity), the latest fads have substantial problems for the pious. Whether the drug-use common in EDM festivals in England or Morocco (Agadir hosts a major one), the occult references that pepper heavy metal, or the fun-focused lyrics of so much popular music, influences from the secular world can be hard to ignore. Even the most attentive moral reimagination of popular genres must tackle the question: what is innate to a musical genre? How can an artist or listener toy with these carriers of questionable lifestyles, of habits or contemporary norms that might pull the believer from the narrow path? Is the potential to reach more listeners, to satisfy a craving, or to engage an exciting new trend worth the temptation?

CHAPTER 1

Andalusian Memories

One afternoon in 2013, I went with a friend who was visiting me to see one of my teachers, a master musician named Ahmed Chiki. We wanted to discover, essentially, to what musical key our souls were tuned. Like so many of my previous lessons, Chiki invited us in and we sat on the couches that circled his living room. My teacher, who builds and plays a string instrument called the 'ud that likely inspired early guitars and lutes in Europe, has performed with the most renowned ensembles in the country. He has also played abroad in the US and Europe and teaches at Fez's main music conservatory. His quiet personality and depth of knowledge make it difficult not to feel a sense of weight in his presence. This was especially the case on this one particular afternoon.

Usually, our lessons involved me turning on my recorder before playing the song that we had last worked on. Ahmed Chiki would point out all of the problems (and there were many problems) and then play a new song. I would take my 'ud, recorder, and notebook, and head home with new music to transcribe and learn. One day, though, I had asked him about a story I heard about musicians using Andalusian music, one of Morocco's most celebrated classical traditions, to heal people. He basically said yes, that used to happen all the time, but no one does it anymore. Except him. I asked if he could demonstrate how it worked: yes, of course, but not today. Our lesson was ending, but I could not help wondering about this music's healing power.

Unlike most other performers, who stick to playing and singing, Chiki has spent a great deal of time collecting information and researching the practices of past generations, those who used their understanding of the musical modes (in Moroccan Arabic, tubu' or "natures") to promote healing and mental wellness in patients. He had mentioned to me that musicians used to move from room to room in the small psychiatric hospital adjacent to the Henna Souk in the medina, the walled "old city" of Fez. Their music would calm busy minds or assist those who were struggling to sort out their realities. Those with wild gestures—seizures, perhaps?—would be able to control their bodies for a few moments. It was not just listening that effected a cure, however. The music had to relate to both the diagnosis—the problem to be cured—and to the person who needed help. It had to connect with each individual's nature, so to speak. This reminded me of acupuncture or other forms of healing where discovering a patient's constitution is an important part of navigating an illness.

Much can obviously be said (and has been said) about music and the brain, music and wellness, or music's emotive qualities, but Chiki and a few others still practice a more specific link between these spheres. He helps people to identify their own nature and the corresponding musical modes. In doing so, they can better understand themselves and their personalities, and he provides them with a musical repertoire that will speak directly to their bodies and spirits. I wanted to learn mine.

We walked in and the quiet professor took out his ʿud al-ramal. This instrument is quite unlike the normal ʿud: it has four paired strings, like a mandolin, instead of the normal six. The string spacing is incredibly wide, making leaps between strings feel very large. Over time, another pair and a single bass string were added to the ʿud, and the ʿud al-ramal is rarely used in practice. The tuning is out of order; it is not sequential like a guitar. The strings are do (C), la (A), re (D), and sol (G), all within the same octave. Playing a scale requires an inordinate amount of movement across the instrument, not unlike the ukulele. Each pair of strings is colored. The colors, black, yellow, white, and red, respectively, reflect the natures.

These natures correspond to the four creations: earth (do, black), water (la, yellow), air (re, white), and fire (sol, red). Without each of these four, he explains, we cannot live. Later, he described to me that his nature is earth, trab (a word that also references dirt), which holds everything else. He therefore is slow to start and slow to stop. I notice this in our conversations: as we progress, I have fewer and fewer opportunities to direct his attention back toward my questions. These natures, he went on to say, were but one of many types of healing used by the learned men of Arab scientific history. Some doctors would give herbal medicine, and if that was not successful, people always had the opportunity to try a religious scholar, or a musician, in an effort to alleviate the symptoms of an illness. These men were specialists, and understood what they could and could not help. They would, he said, be quick to say "No, I cannot do anything for you. You need to go visit a musician." Just as the Prophet Muhammad was a doctor of Quranic healing and we have books on these practices, musicians had something to contribute to the mental and physical wellness of the community.

He brought his attention back to the instrument in his hand. Each of these four natures—earth, water, air, and fire—connects to a body part (this may sound familiar to people with experience in acupuncture or similar traditional medicines). These strings and the musical modes that they bring out speak to the liver, the spleen, the heart, and the lungs. Times of day, seasons, and personality types are similarly linked. He even connected the standard Andalusian performance dress, the white jellaba (a hooded gown of sorts), red tarbosh (hat) with a black tassel, and yellow balgha (slippers) to these strings, natures, and elements.

I don't know my blood type, which was a shame since it is a necessary part of this process. My second problem was that I didn't know what a Capricorn is. I used my iPhone to figure out that it's a goat, which gave me an odd sense of achronistic irony. We continued … The musical modes that sit at the end of December, around my birthday, are Rasd and Husayn. The beginning of January is Maya and Ramal al-Maya.

He started playing, warming the instrument up and toying with Rasd, a generally pentatonic mode (it's largely built on five notes, instead of the more standard seven that appear in a Western major or minor scale). It sounds different from most of the modes that I knew better. He played four pieces for me, one each from Rasd, Maya, Istihlal, and Rasd al-Dhil. Rasd and Rasd al-Dhil seem to hit me harder than the others. He explained some of the branches that come from these two modal families and how they fit together musically. Each articulation, every note, during these two songs gave me an abrupt twitch, as if the veins in my cheeks were pushing blood just a little bit faster than normal.

I learned that my nature sits between these two sets, between Rasd and Rasd al-Dhil. My modes are white and black, my nature is playful and melancholic. Both seem fitting. Rasd, the pentatonic mode, shares its pitch content with the music of the gnawa, which I spent most of my time in Morocco researching, and describe in Chapter 4. It also relates in subtle ways to much of the funk, R&B, and old-time banjo music that I play back home. I'm not sure if my experiences made this one sound more familiar, or if something shared, something musical, makes all of this music speak to me, but it felt appropriate. After he recorded a few more pieces from those modes for me to go home and learn, we departed. I learned the tunes and often found myself drifting back to them at night (my time of day, according to his natures), picking up my ʿud and improvising on some of the melodies. I can't help but admit that it's soothing.

Morocco's Andalusian music tradition spans much of the country's history, yet it has consistently changed to fit the needs of contemporary audiences, both then and now. It began as a courtly tradition that followed an emigration from present-day Spain to North Africa. Communities clung to this history as a symbol of the loss suffered by Islamic kingdoms during the Catholic reconquest of Iberia. From this place of nostalgia, it has come to represent a national history and nationalism that unites the arts and religion in Morocco. It also continues to exist, albeit in different forms, in Spain, Syria, Algeria, Tunisia, and Libya. While Morocco's variant of this tradition is unique, the memory that is embedded within the musical style spans the Mediterranean, linking the region.

This chapter looks closely at this music as both a marker of Morocco's Andalusian past and as a vibrant form of respected cultural nationalism today. It begins by using this music as a lens for introducing the history of the region and nation. It then moves to discussing how Andalusian music is performed today, by focusing on its instruments, contexts, and musical structures. The chapter concludes with a discussion of the relationship between Andalusian music and Sufism. Sufism is an umbrella term for a wide variety religious practices, diverse manifestations of the Islamic faith. These range from erudite scholarly approaches to ritual ceremonies of the urban poor that many decry as heretical. Questions of education, class, and appropriateness frequently enter into debates about how Islam works, and Andalusian music's devotional texts inform these interactions of global influence, governmental pressure, and local practice.

Morocco's Andalusian History

North Africa first enters into the history of western civilization when the Phoenicians colonized Morocco's coastline. Phoenicia was based in the eastern Mediterranean (the Levant, around current day Lebanon, Syria, and Israel) and began to spread across the sea, taking control of the southern coast and expanding trade routes, beginning around 1500 BCE. The Phoenicians are especially remembered for their alphabet, the oldest known to scholars, which links earlier systems like Egyptian hieroglyphics to later local derivations of Phoenician, including Arabic and Hebrew (via Aramaic), or Latin and Cyrillic (via Greek). These communities were primarily based around city-states like Carthage, one of the most well-known, which is near the modern city of Tunis, Tunisia.

There was a local population that was already in North Africa before the Phoenicians arrived, and they remained throughout. Early evidence of agricultural activity in the region, including cave paintings, comes from between 6000 and 2000 BCE. At times, these local tribes and kingdoms controlled major cities, while during other periods they remained inland or in other territories, outside of foreign control. The name Berber came to represent these populations, a probable derivation from Greek and Latin terms meaning "barbarian." Recent political movements have advocated for a change, and now these populations in Morocco call themselves Amazigh. Romans, and later the Byzantines, conquered these lands over the course of centuries because of successive political and military powers' desire to control the Mediterranean's valuable trade routes. Despite the changing authorities of major cities and ports, Amazigh populations survived and now comprise roughly 50 percent of Morocco's population.

Beginning in the 7th century CE, conquerors from the expanding Islamic empire further east brought the new religion to Morocco. When they took control of the area, they named it al-maghreb al-aqsa, the furthest west. Morocco symbolized the extreme distances that the growing military power could span. In doing so, however, it proved unstable. Maintaining control of the northwest corner of Africa from Damascus or Baghdad proved infeasible and the region experienced a great deal of political tumult. Local tribes had converted to Islam, but many maintained their own customs and practices, incorporating them into the new religion. This led to a series of revolts that were both political and religious in nature. Ibn Khaldun, a scholar from modern-day Tunisia who lived in the 1300s, wrote about this period of the region's history in what became one of the world's first works of sociology, anthropology, and political science. The *Muqaddimah*, the title of which literally means "introduction" in Arabic, was intended as an introduction to a larger history of the world, and describes a consistent cycle of overthrow. Rural tribes following puritan readings of Islam gain strength and invade the cities, the centers of power. After generations, their descendants become weak, losing their "grit" with the comforts of wealth and urban life. New rural tribes rise, take over, and continue the cycle.

This reality fragmented the region between concurrent kingdoms. One of these North African militaries campaigned north, entering into the Iberian Peninsula (present-day Spain) by crossing the Strait of Gibraltar, which is named for one of the commanders (Gibraltar derives from Jabal Tariq, the mountain of Tariq, referencing Tariq ibn Ziyad, the military leader who brought the first soldiers across the strait in 711 CE). New Islamic city-states based in Cordoba, Granada, Seville, and across Andalusia resulted. Their independence from Middle Eastern politics solidified when the Umayyads, based in Damascus, were defeated by the ʿAbbasids, who moved their capital to Baghdad in 750. One family member from the Umayyad dynasty, Abd al-Rahman I (731–88), escaped to the distant lands out west and solidified a new, firmly independent Umayyad caliphate in Andalusia.

While battles between rural and urban areas continued throughout this history, the cities of Andalusia hosted a cultural and intellectual society that was somewhat rare during Europe's Middle Ages. Conversion to Islam opened social, political, and economic doors for the Iberian population and many took advantage. Intermarriage led to an expansion of the number of people who could claim Arab lineage. The Arab minority became a majority after a few centuries had passed. The relative stability in the region over time increased agricultural production and economic success.

The religious texture of social life was similarly dynamic. Christians, who had been the majority on the peninsula, learned the Arabic language and adopted new cultural norms. The same went for the Jewish minority. Members of these populations who chose not to convert to Islam could continue to practice their religion while paying a tax. The social integration of these three communities, called "La Convivencia," is frequently romanticized in contemporary literature and past scholarship, but it does represent a period in the Middle Ages where a cultural hybrid achieved great heights. During this time in Andalusia, when scholarship in Europe was largely relegated to the copying of texts by monks in monasteries, dramatic discoveries from math and the sciences changed architecture and other fields; poets and musicians enjoyed close relationships with high-level patrons and were afforded the opportunity to create; and many Greek and Latin texts that would have otherwise disappeared were translated into Arabic, to be translated back again in Europe during the Renaissance. These successes in knowledge production were enabled in part by relative stability, but more recent historians have noted, violence—including assassinations and martyrdoms—still punctuated relationships between religious and ethnic communities.[1]

The trajectory of musical creativity in Andalusia during this time led to a variety of celebrated genres across Spain, Morocco, the rest of North Africa, and Syria. Just like the Andalusian manifestation of the Umayyad caliphate, this music exists as both an outgrowth of what was going on in the Middle East and a sharp departure from those very same influences. In fact, there is a more distinct parallel between the narratives of the caliphate and the musical style that grew within its palaces. Like Abd al-Rahman who escaped when his family was killed in Damascus and consolidated power within the far west, Andalusian musical style is born of a man whose own history involves a new start after a long forced migration.

Ziryab's story is, to use Carl Davila's phrase, "semi-legendary" (2016, 7). He was a court musician in the 'Abbasid court of Baghdad before he left, likely because of a growing rivalry with his own teacher. He traveled to Qayrawan, in present-day Tunisia, to join the court there before he was forced out once again. These travels appeared to serve him well, however. When he arrived in Andalusia, he rose to prominence and became a cultural and musical marvel. His style of dress and even his haircut are said to have incited fads across town. But his musical prodigy was what stood out in the standard narrative of his life. He knew 10,000 songs and composed many more of his own, allegedly thanks in part to his relationship and communication with spirits. He manipulated the ʿud, a central instrument within Arab music, by adding a fifth string, and is often cited as the source for the entirety of Andalusian music (Reynolds 2008, 155).

As scholars of this tradition describe, however, the genre's history is far more complex. It is based in the various Andalusian city-states' support of the arts over centuries, the common use of singing slaves for entertainment, and the cultural and religious diversity that flourished in the region. Dwight Reynolds compares different historical mentions of Ziryab, for example, to note that he may have been one of many court musicians and prone to conflict and competition, as

> a black slave ... who was a gifted musician, but who was also temperamental, a spoiled favourite, a lavish spender, at times publicly mocked because of his skin color, the butt of crude sexual jokes, and frequently caught up in court rivalries.
>
> (2008, 156)

Aside from changing the mechanics of the ʿud, Ziryab is cited as having organized the formal structures of his court's musical performances. By beginning with an instrumental or vocal prelude and song called a "nashid," then continuing into three song forms that likely referenced the rhythmic patterns that accompanied the melodies ("al-basit," "al-haraka," and "al-hazaj"), Ziryab may have outlined the slow-to-fast structure that organizes each movement of today's Andalusian music in Morocco. In describing this potential innovation, Carl Davila explains that "al-hazaj," for example, was "a very old term for a rhythmic mode that originally contrasted with thaqil, 'heavy' (see Farmer 1929, III), which would suggest that Ziryab was recommending concluding one's performance with an up-tempo song" (Davila 2015, 151). He goes on, however, to note that the term "nuba," the main organizational structure of today's Andalusian music in Morocco, does not appear for another two centuries.

Abd al-Rahman III had declared himself caliph of a united Andalusia in 929 CE. From this point, the emirate's stability at home and abroad triggered the economic, cultural, and scientific prosperity that still symbolizes the era today. After roughly 100 years, however, external and internal disputes overcame the centralized government based in Cordoba. Major cities continued to flourish, but they did so independently, as smaller states dotting the Iberian Peninsula. Some local leaders worked closely with nearby Christian kingdoms to combat their Muslim neighbors. The lack of unity opened an opportunity for rivals and in 1085, Toledo fell to Alfonso VI. The Christian reconquest of Spain was underway.

Other city-states looked south, back across the Strait of Gibraltar, to Morocco's Almoravid dynasty for support. The Almoravids slowed, but were unable to stop, the advancing Christian armies. During these efforts, they themselves fell to a reformist movement back home in Morocco, being replaced by the Almohads. By the 1200s, facing pressure from the Christian armies, the unity fell apart again. By 1248, Cordoba, Valencia, and Seville had been lost. Granada continued under Muslim rule until 1492. Jews were expelled from across Spain, and by the 1600s, Muslims had been forced to convert to Christianity or emigrate (Hendrickson 2009).

Those who eventually left did so as refugees. They went from being an untrusted minority within Spain to living a similar experience in the Islamic world. Those who came to Morocco lived in tight-knit communities as minorities within major cities. Many went to Tetuan, a city on Morocco's northern coast that later was a part of a Spanish colony and whose population continues to speak Spanish as much as (if not more than) the French that pervades education, business, and politics across the country. A large enough population came to Fez that half of today's "old city" is called al-Andalus, named after the Arabic term for Andalusia.

Both of these cities, and many others with substantial populations of exiles from centuries ago, house significant ensembles and communities of listeners for Andalusian music. In poetry, devotion, and song, these contemporary performers and audiences look back to the beauty and prestige that Andalusia represents with nostalgia. Ziryab serves this sense of longing and loss, standing in as a mythical symbol for musical genius and creativity, for artistic excellence. In his book *Performing al-Andalus: Music and Nostalgia across the Mediterranean*, Jonathan Shannon (2015) outlines how different countries look back to this time in diverse ways. Tunisia, Algeria, Syria, and Spain each have their own traditions that link to a memory and sense of loss. The musical traditions that animate these memories differ, however. From Algeria, during France's colonial rule, Andalusian histories resulted in new forms of popular music across Parisian radio and cabarets (Glasser 2016). It comprises the repertoire of some of Syria's most famous performers, both popular and sacred (Shannon 2006). In Morocco, Andalusian music fuses elite tastes and religious devotion. Its version of this Andalusian tradition is called al-ala, which literally means "the instrument."

Andalusian Music

During the time I spent living and doing research in Fez, I often stopped in a small shop run by a man named Hamid. Hamid sold music, and his store, as is the norm, was an alcove of sorts, a stall built into the wall of the old city. His decor made it obvious that he sold music: small shelves built into the wall displayed CD cases and posters of famous Moroccan and Egyptian musicians were taped onto the display case that he stood behind. But during the many hours that I spent drinking tea and listening to music with Hamid, I never saw him pull down a CD and sell it. Instead, he burned discs of MP3s from his computer, making mixes and collections for his customers. When someone wanted a new track, he went to YouTube and used software to download the latest hits.

This form of buying and selling music, of pirating the latest craze, is not new to Morocco. It has been going on since the days of cassette tapes.[2] Just as I remember friends sitting by the radio with blank cassettes waiting to hit record and capture a favorite song to a mixtape (it was always friends, I was never cool enough to make mixtapes), cassettes, and later CDs, enabled new modes of musical distribution and circulation within Morocco. With advancements in internet upload and downloading speeds, fans of bands like Phish and Dave Matthews Band were able to trade their recordings of live shows. Everyone could be a collector. This same logic played into music collecting and listening in Morocco.

While Hamid was making "mixtapes" on CD for his neighborhood customers, another shop owner from across the alleyway was selling watches. He bought them from estate sales, repaired them, and sold his antiques to local customers and tourists alike. His shop was equally tight, but it was a space where you could step inside and turn around, admiring the floor-to-ceiling display cases full of beautiful ticking time pieces. At one point, the owner asked me why I spent so much time listening to music in Hamid's shop. When I explained that I was studying Moroccan music, his eyes grew excited and he opened up a drawer behind his small counter. It was one of many that was full of cassette tapes in neat rows. This shop owner, whose name I sadly don't remember, was a connoisseur of al-ala. He spent his life collecting and listening to tapes from all types of venues. He quickly gave me a few to borrow. I had to find an electronics shop and buy a used cassette player to listen to them. Days later, I returned them, thanking him for his generosity. I was struck by the winding melodies and dense textures, but I just couldn't get into the music. It didn't catch my attention the way other Moroccan styles did. Since I was engaged in fieldwork research on other topics in Fez, I put the experience aside, only to come back to it a few years later, after having played other styles of Moroccan music like malhun (see Chapter 7) that draw heavily on Andalusian traditions.

There are two elements of Andalusian music that made it difficult for me to "get" it right away. The first is the appearance of melodic simplicity: trying to sing along exposes an extraordinary degree of complexity as melodies consistently evaded my expectations. The second is the importance of poetry within the tradition. Both of these revealed themselves to me one Ramadan night in 2012 (Ramadan is a month of spiritual renewal and celebration accomanied by fasting during daylight hours). Despite the watch seller's proselytizing about al-ala, it was when I experienced a live performance in a home celebrating the holy month that it started to click.

Philip Murphy, my friend and colleague who was doing research in Morocco on sung devotional poetry known as samaʿa, invited me to the home of a wealthy connoisseur of this music. He was pursuing connections between the religious poetry and Andalusian styles in Fez and had been working with some of the musicians who had been hired to perform that night. I had seen this music on concert stages where it represented Morocco's intellectual heritage within southern Spain, but this event was different. The main room of the home and two that broke off of it were filled with chairs, the kind you would rent for a wedding reception. They were in rows, facing couches that were arranged in a U-shape around a number of microphones where the ensemble sat. The hosts had set up a sound system and printed booklets of the poetry so that their guests could sing along, full-throated, while still hearing the group clearly.

The booklets were not short; this was an evening of singing and socializing that extended well into the night. It was a chance to see friends and family, to celebrate Ramadan, and to listen to and sing some special music. In a way, it reminded me of the cliché that references old movies where families gather around the piano and sing Christmas carols together, drinking eggnog, as a gauzy camera frame fades to the credits. But this was more raucous. The room was packed and hot—it was August in Morocco. Men wore their finest white shirts and slacks under white jellabas (long hooded garments) and women dressed in exquisite kaftans, ornate (and heavy) traditional gowns. They clapped and sang, some following along in the booklet, others knew all the words by heart. Children, up well past their bedtimes, clamored through the rows, playing and watching. Instead of something sterile to be enjoyed from afar, this experience placed Andalusian music (and the watchmaker's tapes) in a new context for me, it was something to be a part of.

But that was still hard to do. Phil and I sat right next to the ensemble, behind the percussionists. We were enveloped by the loud music, but I didn't know the songs. I tried to sing along, following the words, but the melodies were deceptive. They sounded so repetitive and simple. Whenever I thought I got it, though, they changed. Sometimes they turned in an unexpected direction, while other times they repeated a phrase from the middle of the line over and over before concluding. There's a point in Bob Dylan's "Mr. Tambourine Man," an American folk song from the 1960s, where he adds phrases in the middle of a verse to complete his idea. The text drives the musical structure and, since he's playing alone, he can be as flexible as necessary to fit his music to his poetry. Al-ala does the same thing, but it's a large ensemble. The text is central and the music bends to fit it, usually.

The musical ensemble that animates this poetry is made up of a number of instruments, some of which are unique to the tradition. Others, however, appear across the Middle East or the world. The group's focal point is the rabab (see Figure 1.1). This is a bowed string instrument that the ensemble's leader plays. It has two thick strings made out of gut. The body is constructed from hollowed out wood and covered with leather. The bow is rounded, more like a small archery bow than a contemporary violin bow. The term rabab appears across the Middle East and elsewhere to reference various older styles of bowed string instruments more generally, but here it carries a specific meaning associated with Andalusian music. This is not the kind of instrument that can play fancy ornate melodies. Instead, the leader of the group will use it to ground what everyone else is doing. It cuts through all of the sound in the room with its unique tone color, outlining the main melodic idea and directing the ensemble, letting them know when to repeat a section or go on, when to begin or end.

Figure 1.1 Ensemble leader playing the rabab.

The ornamentations that add density to the sound of this music come, in large part, from the violins and violas. Most ensembles have at least one or two violinists and many include the larger viola. Both of these are the same instruments that appear in the western symphony orchestra, but instead of holding them up on a shoulder, these musicians prop them upright on their knee. Violins and violas, with four strings, a wider range, and a much quicker response time than the rabab, follow the older instrument's skeletal melody, but take liberties. They jump up and down into different octaves and play phrases that quickly dance around the main idea. Each musician does this a little differently, turning a musical style that features one central melody into a thick bed of sound, supporting the sung texts.

One or more Middle Eastern 'uds, like Ahmed Chiki's from this chapter's opening, also appear within these ensembles. Historically, according to Chiki and the narratives of Ziryab's life and innovations, the Andalusian 'ud had four doubled strings, like those on a mandolin or 12-string guitar. The pear-shaped fretless guitar-like instrument also had a higher "action;" the strings were further away from the neck of the instrument than they are now. This made it harder to play fast, but the 'ud was able to emphasize the sung melodies loudly and accompany the rabab. Now, however, you see 'uds that mirror the construction that is popular elsewhere in the region. They are made to be quick so that performers can join the violins in their decorative ornamentations. With the help of microphones, they can still be loud enough to hear.

A pair of percussion instruments, two drums, carry the mizan, the underlying beat for each section of an Andalusian music performance. The first, a small frame drum with cymbals built into the frame, is called a tar. In its construction, the tar is similar to a tambourine, but smaller, thicker, heavier, and with larger cymbals. In terms of how it's played, though, it is quite different. The player holds the tar upright in his left hand (most, but not all, percussionists in Morocco are men) and uses his right hand to hit the center or edge of the drum head to get different tones. He also uses his right hand or left fingers (the ones that are not holding the drum upright) to click the cymbals. The wealth of subtlety to the range of sounds that a master musician can bring out of this small instrument makes it one of the most difficult to learn. The other percussion instrument, the darbuka, is an hourglass-shaped drum that the musician holds across his lap. This, which shows up in popular and classical music across the Middle East, is a more recent addition to the al-ala ensemble.

Beyond these mainstays within the tradition, some groups add other instruments to change their sound. There are recordings with trumpets; many use electric keyboards to mimic organs, pianos, or the Middle Eastern qanun (a string instrument that is similar to the hammer dulcimer in construction, but which uses finger picks in place of small "hammers"); and the group that was performing in the home in Fez had a cellist to give the sound more depth.

These heavily ornamented performances of a melody exemplify a musical texture called heterophony. Listening to other styles of Middle Eastern music, American old-time fiddling, or an Irish music session at a pub can provide other examples of this texture, where a number of instruments play the same melody, but they play it differently. Instead of having a single line melody or a group of musicians each acting independently (as you might have in a rock band, where the bass plays one line while the singer sings another and the guitar has interesting, but supportive, backing chords), these players and singers are roughly following the same melodic path. In most performances, that path is outlined by the rabab and, when people sing, the crowd of singers (a vocal soloist may take his or her own virtuosic departures, like the violins or other instrumentalists).

Musical Organization

Within Morocco's al-ala, the melodies themselves are strictly organized. This is not a repertoire where someone can compose brand new songs and introduce them within a concert to a receptive audience. Andalusian music elsewhere works this way, but Morocco's version of it is more bounded by history and tradition. The nostalgia that winds through these songs prioritizes learning older music over creating new pieces. That is not to say that this music is static: to the contrary, the innovations in instrumentation described above and the virtuosity that comes out of the heterophonic texture can build exciting and dynamic performances.

In this way, Morocco's musicians work to recover older songs. Many are believed to have been lost, but the ones that remain are organized into groups, each of which is called a nuba. Each nuba contains a fixed number of songs. Rasd has just over 100. Ramal al-Maya has more, others have less. The nuba orders these songs into five sections. Each section is known by its dominant rhythmic pattern, the mizan. In a performance, a group may choose to perform songs from one or more mizans from one nuba (depending on the length of the event). Some may choose to perform one mizan from one nuba and then jump to another from a different nuba to mix up the evening. Very rarely, however, does a performance include a song or two from scattered selections of mizans or nubas. In this way, songs are meant to progress in a certain fixed order. They are not like songs on a band's album that can be reconfigured in a new order (a setlist) for concerts on different nights.

One reason for this rigidity is the melodic system that underlies this music. Al-ala is a modal music, meaning that melodic motion has certain unspoken expectations. Western classical composers spent much of the early and middle parts of the 20th century pushing their tradition to its limits, creating music that breaks away from the norms of the previous centuries. Despite those efforts, many of those norms still exist. An untrained ear can usually tell that some performers on early seasons of reality shows like American Idol are better than others. Some music speaks to wide audiences, while other pieces come across as boring, dull, or weird, perhaps because they fail to navigate listener expectations (even if the listeners cannot articulate what those expectations are). When beginning musicians take their earliest lessons, they often learn about scales as sets of ascending and descending notes, but in reality, there is much more embedded within them. Pedagogically, it may be helpful to learn them in this simple form, but in everyday life as a listener, we hear melodies, not scales. And when they don't go where we expect them to, we can be disappointed or excited, depending on the skill and daring of the composer or our own tastes.

Al-ala's nubas are conceived of as complete works that explore this progression. On one hand, they are fairly simple to ease singing and, on the other, they are constantly shifting, exploring different modes. These modes have distinct pitch collections, subtle changes that help to maintain interest in these long performances, and different melodic expectations. Some will go up where others might go down. Each mode is called a tubuʻ, a "nature." Nubas take their name from the dominant tubuʻ, and some of them only contain one tubuʻ within them. Nuba Rasd al-Dhil is made up entirely of the tubuʽ named rasd al-dhil. The same is true of Nuba al-Maya, which contains only al-maya. Others have two, three, or four different tubuʽs within them. Nuba Rasd, contains the tubuʽ called rasd, the one that I connected with so powerfully when I went to visit Ahmed Chiki. As the nuba continues, though, it moves from rasd to al-husar and al-zidan, before concluding in a tubuʽ called al-mazmum. In total, there are eleven known nubas, but between them there are 26 tubuʽs (Shami 2009, 104). It is worth noting that the limited amount of music that is known and regularly performed today makes it difficult to know exactly how these modes worked, or if the ways in which they are understood by performers now match how they progressed in the past, when newly composed pieces could still enter into the repertoire. And while new music does not show up in al-ala concerts, there are examples of musicians from within this tradition composing new songs that carry on their own lives outside of the bounds of the Andalusian performance context. Some, for example, appear on the radio as popular music inspired by this well-regarded elite tradition (see Chapter 2).

Returning to musical organization, the mizan is the central structure. Each nuba is divided into five. If a group were to perform an entire nuba, they would begin with a piece called a bughiyya. This is in free rhythm; there is no underlying pulse, and the percussion instruments do not play. The rest of the ensemble has a melody that winds through the tubuʽ, introducing it with a combination of quick passages and long notes. It almost sounds improvised, except everyone follows the same general outline; they know where they are going. The leader, often playing the rabab, will nod or otherwise signal to the group that they are moving from one long note, or one section, to the next. After the bughiyya, an instrumentalist or vocalist may perform an improvised solo. There is a flexibility before and after various sections. A group may feature some of its best performers or stick closely to the songs by going directly from one to the next.

Then, they enter the first mizan, called basit. The mizan is a set of individual songs, called sanʽa. Most mizans, and some individual sanaʽis, have a prelude called a tushiyya. These tushiyyas are upbeat and can be exciting and, unlike the sanaʽi that follow, they are in a simple duple meter. This separates them out, they sound different than the surrounding music. After this prelude, the group moves into the sanaʽi. Each mizan in each nuba can have a different number of sanaʽi, and even then, not everyone agrees on how many there are. Or what order they go in. Or which sanaʽi goes in which mizan. This music is an oral tradition, but knowledge about its poetry has lived through the recent past in written collections. Often, these collections do not completely agree (Davila 2013).

Within a mizan, the sanaʽis begin slowly. As the group progresses through the music, it gets gradually quicker. Each mizan has a rhythmic feel that is central to the music. As it becomes faster, the feel changes. Music that was patient and meditative in the beginning is exciting and full of energy by the end. Example 1.1 shows this change. The core rhythm for basit is a slow pattern with six beats, six consistent underlying pulses. The melodic phrases are long enough that it is actually imagined in two halves, a four-beat phrase followed by a two-beat phrase (pictured with the dotted bar line). Because a number of musicians play percussion instruments and each has a degree of independence on how he or she performs this core rhythm, these representations are better understood as rhythmic outlines, core grooves. Just as the rabab outlines the melody and other instruments dance around it, everyone in the group imagines a core groove and performs with accents, fills, or other decorative patterns that make it

Example 1.1 Andalusi rhythmic patterns.

more interesting in performance. The "dum" and "tek" syllables are standard to Middle Eastern music. Dum usually references a low note, perhaps a stroke in the middle of a drum head. The tek is a higher-pitched note, usually a "rim shot" effect on the edge of a drum head. But with many different instruments, a musician can get a range of dum and tek sounds to make their groove more interesting.

In basit, the slow "dum - dum - tek tek - - dum -" (where dashes indicate rests or pauses) simply gets faster as the music increase in speed. Instead of hearing this pattern extended over six beats, the notes get closer together, and the "fast" version that appears toward the end of the mizan is the same thing compressed into three beats. For other mizans, however, the faster variation is rhythmically different. The slow version of the darj groove, for example, almost feels flipped backward when it speeds up. After going from slow to fast, a group concludes the mizan with a vocal flourish and, depending on the context, the crowd may be on its feet clapping along. Then, after a short break, they will proceed to the next mizan, beginning again with a tushiyya and slow, pensive sana'is.

These structures—the modes, the organization within individual nubas, and the progression of an event from slow to fast through the various mizans—give this music a sound that is distinct from classical traditions from elsewhere in the Middle East. Even so, listeners in Morocco know the most famous musicians and songs coming from places like Egypt, especially those who thrived during the middle of the 20th century, the so-called "Golden Age" of Arabic music. The history of that tradition will inform the discussion of other styles of Moroccan popular music in Chapter 2, but it is worth a moment here to note that these systems overlap in contemporary performances of al-ala. The moments of confluence illuminate the opportunities for innovation that musicians enjoy within what may otherwise appear to be a strict tradition.

The nuba system that features individual modes, tubu', is different than the modal system that underlies so much music across the Middle East. The maqam system presides over much of the Arab classical music and extends back centuries. While the tubu' system of modes originated from in and around Andalusia, it likely derived from these other styles. Remember that the dynastic tradition itself broke away from a history located further east and, because most of these musical genres grew out of courtly traditions, the relationship between political power and cultural production is strong.

The maqam system is structured around modes comprised of smaller segments. These sets of three, four, or five pitches combine to create larger scalar patterns. By swapping out halves of the larger scale, composers and improvising musicians can weave their way through a musical progression from one mode to another.[3] Composers can write new songs based on these underlying norms and expectations. They may be two-minute pop tunes or 45-minute epic poems. Unlike Morocco's al-ala, the system is widely used to create material. And in Morocco, vocal and instrumental musicians frequently borrow the modes, combining them with al-ala's own norms, to develop unique musical phrases and go in unexpectedly creative directions.

Religion, Class, and Music

Morocco's diverse forms of religious devotion reappear throughout these chapters. In many cases, the practice of worship, how people pray and celebrate their faith, closely aligns with what region they are from or, in the case of the gnawa, their community's racial history (see Chapter 4). More often, however, the lines coincide with economic class. The uneducated poor who live in makeshift slums or poorly cared for urban neighborhoods—many of whom are from families that moved to the city from the rural outskirts—practice their faith in community events that raise questions, criticism, and eyebrows from the educated elite. These divides inform the local forms of Sufi devotion and entertainment that comprise the final 3 chapters of this book, as well as the popular music styles that pervade Chapters 2, 3, and 4.

When they are not in beautiful homes during Ramadan, al-ala performances often happen in expensive hotel ballrooms or athletic clubs that operate like country clubs do in the United States. Thick programs with the texts have glossy color photographs on the cover. Men in suits, sometimes with jellabas over them, and women in expensive kaftans sit around tables full of juices, tea, cookies, and other snacks. Or the event may be in a theater, celebrating an elder musician with well-produced short documentary snippets playing on televisions to either side of the stage during breaks. This music carries a symbolism of Morocco's elite Andalusian heritage. When it shows up on television, the recordings are from ornate rooms that feature beautiful plaster carvings and detailed tile work on the walls. It has the trappings of elite society.

This music also carries devotional purpose. In many cases, it is a devout form of religious practice that is intimately related to Sufi traditions. Some of the poems come straight from Moroccan Sufism. While many forms of "popular" Sufism in Morocco use musical instruments, few that are linked to more elite communities do so. Instead, these more esoteric and literate forms of Sufism look to the long lineage of scholarship on the Islamic faith. These Sufis memorize long poems and recite them together, using the words and melodies to achieve a state of union with Allah and each other. Al-ala, in turn, uses some of the same melodies—though often with different words—to act on its own audiences. It is a form of religious entertainment that can profoundly impact the men and women of faith who listen to it. It also directly connects the notion of Andalusian heritage to religious piety. One example of this also happens to be one of the most famous songs from the genre's repertoire. "Shams al-'Ashiyya," a song about a lover departing as the sun sets (the title means "the evening sun"), gets reconfigured in many Sufi gatherings. New lyrics praising the Prophet Muhammad instead dance along the well-known melody.

Beyond these melodic borrowings that stretch between al-ala and Sufism, other linkages solidify the relationship. The Sufi lodges, called zawiyas, that served communities of Andalusian migrants in Morocco's cities also helped to preserve the music through periods of changing religious fervor of successive governments. For those who came to Morocco from Andalusia, the music was a mark of their own history, a celebration of their own community's past. The music grew through the centuries after the Catholic reconquest of Spain, expanding with new nubas like al-istihlal during the 18th century (Davila 2016, 8–9).

Ahmed Chiki told me of another role that the zawiya played. He showed me two different sets of written texts for one nuba, ramal al-maya. He described how some of the successive governments that controlled Morocco throughout its history were more puritan than others. They pushed back against Islamic practices that they deemed heretical or outside of those that were described in the Quran, Islam's holy text. In order to save the musical tradition, which included some texts that were not explicitly religious, they changed the words. Songs that were about love or nights of drinking wine shifted to become praise for the Prophet or for Allah. Texts about love and drink are not uncommon in Sufi traditions across the Islamic world. To the contrary, scholars generally interpret them as poetic metaphors for one's intoxication with the faith, the experience of falling into God's love. With stricter interpretations of the practice of Islam gaining credence across the country at various times in Morocco's history, however, less controversial texts helped the Andalusian communities to hold onto their musical traditions.

Ahmed Chiki held that second version, the older book of problematic poems, closely. During our short series of lessons, he did not share its contents with me, though I hope to have the opportunity to see what the differences might be at some point in the future. He did, however, teach me some songs from ramal al-maya, now one of the more pious nubas that frequently appears on religious occasions. Two performances of one of these songs, "Fi Rida w-Amitnan," show the breadth of what al-ala can sound like.

Chiki recorded the song for me. His version features only his ʿud and his singing. He chose one verse. According to Carl Davila's translations of the nuba (2016, 199), it reads:

Li-nabi al-rasul haja shawq al-ʿabdi
The longing of the servant for the Prophet, the Messenger stirs[4]

Yunis al-Shami, a Moroccan scholar, published musical transcriptions of these pieces (Shami 1984). Compared to his versions, which are transcribed from a performance by another famous musician named Sheikh Ahmad Zituni, Ahmed Chiki's are similar, but he syncopates some moments, adding rhythmic energy in his solo performance. His ʿud playing adds an extraordinary amount of forward movement through more syncopation and his quick octave leaps (see Example 1.2).

Contrasting this with a recorded version of the same song from Muhammad Large Temsamani's Orchestre du Conservatoire de Tétouan, the differences between the intimate solo setting and the large ensemble version that is so much more common on

Example 1.2 Chiki version of the verse with published and 'ud melodies and highlighted syncopations.

Morocco's stages becomes stark. Instead of just a voice and an 'ud, an entire group interacts to create a lively full sound.[5]

The full poem for this piece of music speaks to the longing of the devout worshipper. There is a sadness here as the poet, a Sufi named al-Shushtari who lived in the 13th century, "laments the distance" between himself and his God. Nowadays, it could speak to a longing for a place, a history, or just a memory as this music continues to reflect Morocco's Andalusian history.[6] Again, as translated by Carl Davila:

In contentment and favor and lofty rank,
His character is the best, with (its) banner and glory.
The longing of the servant for the Prophet, the Messenger stirs
My Lord, bring (his) arrival close to one who laments the distance.
Perhaps the east wind brings me close to my aim.
Time in love of one whom we know oppressed me.
I fasted from him for a time and made him my fast-breaking.

Notes

1. For more on La Convivencia and how it impacted the social and intellectual lives of Andalusia's residents, see María Rose Menocal's *The Ornament of the World: How Muslims, Jews, and Christians Created a Culture of Tolerance in Medieval Spain* (2002) and *Convivencia: Jews, Muslims, and Christians in Medieval Spain* by Vivian Mann, Thomas Glick, and Jerrilynn Dodds (2007).
2. See Peter Manuel's *Cassette Culture* (1993) for a discussion on how this technology changed musical communities and the global industry.
3. See Shumays 2013 and Marcus 2001 for examples of how improvisation and modulation work within the maqam system.
4. My recording of this demonstration is available on through the playlists outlined in the Resources section.
5. This recording from *Anthologie al-ala, Maroc: Nuba ramal al-maya* is available through the playlists described in the Resources section.
6. See Shannon 2015 and Menocal 2002 for more on longing and memory within Andalusian music and contemporary culture.

CHAPTER 2

Global Popular Music

There's an image that invariably surprises visitors to Morocco's old cities. After walking, almost, if not completely, lost, through open-air markets, snaking around horses carrying propane tanks and donkeys with construction supplies strapped to their backs, and dodging mopeds that race up and down the tight alleyways, tourists come upon a small wooden door and enter into a beautiful open space with a courtyard that looks into a bright blue sky. Ornate tile-work, delicately carved plaster, and hand-painted wood adorn the walls while colorful pillows on couches and chairs surround a fountain or garden. The serene peace is startling after the cacophonous clatter of the streets outside. Morocco's tourist destinations highlight this respite from the modern world in hotels, restaurants, and travel shows. But there is a twist. Hotel rooftops often feature cafés overlooking even more picturesque views of the city, a chance to look down on those winding streets from above. You can see women hanging clothes to dry, cats jumping from one place to another, the minarets of mosques calling Muslims to pray.

You can also see satellite dishes. So many satellite dishes. Every home has one, if not two, three, or four (see Figure 2.1). The vista is covered with parabolic dishes pointing up into space. They don't just dot the view, they blanket it. This reality may strike some as anachronistic; in a world where donkeys carry supplies around town, these satellite dishes seem out of place. But the truer story is that this is a connected world less unlike the cities of the United States and Europe than the hotel courtyard might show.

Going back to those same streets, the signs of connection and technology are everywhere. Just around the corner from that open-air fruit market might be a very different market, one where cellphones and cellphone chargers are on sale in stall after stall. Cheap ones piled in boxes sit alongside the newest iPhones which in turn are next to poorly manufactured knock offs. I remember being very confused one day when I picked up a new iPod, turned it on, and saw a screen that was just weird. The insides had been taken out of what was probably a broken iPod and replaced with some other small MP3 player.

Figure 2.1 View from a rooftop terrace in Fez.

The outer shell could trick someone who had only seen Apple's expensive gadget on a commercial into overpaying. Many of these are stolen, others are bought and sold by men and women who want the latest and best tech that they can afford. Other boxes have piles of random phone chargers and some carts even sport long strings of power outlets for people to charge their latest purchase.

Communications technologies, including cellphones and satellite dishes, connect Moroccans to each other and to all sorts of national and international media. These cities are not the enclaves of the past that they might seem to visitors. They are global, and their residents are both creators and consumers of global popular culture.

This chapter describes the globalization of Islam through its relationship to global media forms like satellite television. There is a certain power that comes from the ability to pipe your ideologies into living rooms across the world. There is also a power that comes from wealth, as oil-rich countries like Saudi Arabia invest heavily in building schools and mosques across the Middle East and in Africa. These charitable works spread specific readings of the Islamic faith, readings that often seek to reform local practices, bringing them more closely in line with those seen in the Arab East. More recent, and perhaps more dramatic, examples include the role of social media in instigating the 2011 uprisings across the region that came to be known as the Arab Spring that are described in Chapter 3. Similar occurrences regularly follow elections or other dramatic political events. And, of course, the news over the past few years has been rife with examples of the Islamic State (also known as ISIS) using slickly edited and well-crafted violent propaganda videos (and music) to spread a harsh reactionary ideology to followers across the world. Without any specific connection, they inspire "lone wolf" terrorists who are nearly impossible for governments and police organizations to catch ahead of time. The spontaneity of these acts is largely enabled by the very media formats that are so often celebrated as instigators of democracy. And, though they are less often reported, the targets of these attacks are most often Muslims living in Muslim majority countries. While their reach may be global, in part because of their use of music and media, they remain despised as unwelcome extremists throughout the Islamic world.

With access to global media, Morocco, like everywhere else, becomes a media market. And, just as the United States is struggling with the partisanship enabled by social media, the internet, and the "filter bubble"[1] as people look to disparate sources for their news and entertainment, not all views coming into or moving through Morocco agree. Globalization has enabled a whole range of diverse perspectives to take hold within the country. It has given rise to conflicts, some of which have long been a part of Morocco's history. Some, however, are new, or at least have taken turns in stark directions thanks to the opportunities provided by today's communications technology.

Globalization and nationalism in Morocco are wrapped up into a political history that moves beyond the military engagements described in Chapter 1. Under colonialism, Moroccans were simultaneously within and outside of European society. Since independence, three different kings have been using different strategies to balance stability against freedom. The religious implications and pressures that come out of this balance have shifted back and forth. It is difficult to overstate the role of popular culture and mass media within today's political debates. Satellite networks and the internet bring conservative ideologies into conflict with popular culture. The lines between musical taste, entertainment, and religious piety that might seem quite predictable are blurred.

The fluidity that makes popular culture both unpredictable and difficult to contain is not a new phenomenon in the Islamic world. This chapter tells a story of Morocco's post-colonial history through the lens of globalized popular music. It explores some technological and political changes that situated the country within Europe's orbit as colonialism came to a close, while noting the importance of an ideological Arab unity and identity that came through Egyptian popular music at roughly the same time. The simultaneous success of different strains of popular culture show how a national identity can be pulled in multiple directions at once. More recent examples demonstrate how changing technology bring these pressures into focus today.

In the introduction to his edited volume titled *Music and Media in the Arab World* (2010), Michael Frishkopf describes two broad types of debates that play out through popular culture.[2] The first is nationalistic. Popular culture and popular music are central to defining who we are and what we do as modern citizens. How are Moroccans of any era going to be modern? In what ways will citizens maintain local or national traditions and, conversely, in what ways will they leave those traditions behind to join global trends? Individual choices about dress and language are important here. Some faithful complete their prayers in traditional clothing, while others might choose to do so in jeans and t-shirts, making these considerations familiar ones to attendees of Christian services or other religious worship around the world. Similarly, collective choices can stake out claims to religion's place in the modern world: should Friday be a business day (like it is in Europe) or a day off to allow people to go to the mosque? In terms of music, this may involve questions about whether the symphony plays European music or celebrates Arab composers, or whether the radio plays local music or the latest hits from the United States.

The other perspective that informs so many debates around mass media and contemporary music scenes is also not particularly foreign to American or European audiences. It asks questions about the morality of so much global mass media of the type that appears on television and the radio, in magazines, and, more recently, on cellphones across the country. In Morocco, concerns align with Islamic values, but those values are quite close to the ones that criticize EDM culture, heavy metal, or hip hop in the United States. Just as the morality of rock and roll was a concern in the 1950s and jazz frightened conservatives in the 1920s, Morocco's relationship with popular culture is fraught with debates about appropriate behavior within youth culture. Whether it's scandalous music videos or song lyrics, hits often bring out condemnation and celebration. "Liberal" and "conservative" are both political terms and moral ideologies.

The conflated nature of nationalistic and moral arguments surrounding popular culture can be difficult to pull apart. Both reflect efforts to create and mold today's Muslim citizens, though the efforts can come from different authorities. Some are religious, some are political, some are economic, and many are all three. While this chapter provides more of an overview than an in-depth analysis of these pressures, keeping the national and moral debates in mind while reading about and listening to Morocco's popular music gives it another layer, one that extends through the sacred and secular music in the chapters that follow.

Global Exchanges

Alongside this moral and nationalistic duality, another relationship is threaded through Morocco's popular music and popular culture: the influence of Western styles. Many ethnomusicologists and cultural critics have theorized at length about how globalization impacts local communities. Others note the powerful role of the global music industry in circulating ideas among and between different regions.[3] "Global" styles—musical genres like rock or hip hop—often have origin stories that arise from specific artists or spaces: hip hop arising from the public neglect and street dances of the Bronx or heavy metal's growth out of a disenfranchised working-class youth in English cities. These genres are, and in most cases, always have been, global, however. Hip hop grew out of diverse communities in New York and Los Angeles and, even at the outset, artists were drawing on musical and philosophical ideas from Jamaica, West Africa, and further afield. Similarly, heavy metal was a musical and countercultural social aesthetic long before it had a name and communities from around the world have gathered around it.[4] What ethnomusicology and, more generally, listening to the latest hits tells us is that popular music styles are rarely, if ever, exclusively rooted to a single place and time.

Morocco has been a major part of the global exchange of ideas for quite some time. While much of this chapter and the ones that follow show a history of adaptation, of borrowing from genres that come from somewhere else, Morocco's musical style also has a fascinating history of influence on global popular music, or at least on the American musical styles of different times and places. If a wide view of "Moroccan music" is used—if music made by a Moroccan musician is, in fact, Moroccan music—than it is notable that Lady Gaga's producer, Nadir Khayat (known as RedOne) was born in Morocco before moving to Sweden. He had a hand in "Poker Face," "Bad Romance," "Alejandro," and many other hits as a producer or co-writer.

During the 1960s and 1970s, when countercultural movements in the United States were protesting the Vietnam War, many looked eastward for inspiration. George Harrison of the Beatles, who worked closely with Ravi Shankar, famously included Indian musical instruments, styles, and musicians in some of the era's big hits, but other artists came to North Africa instead, including Jimi Hendrix and Crosby, Stills, and Nash, a famous folk rock group. Crosby, Stills, and Nash followed their visit with a hit song called "Marrakech Express." In 1969, it reached number 28 on the Billboard Hot 100 charts. In the song, which describes the train from Casablanca to Marrakech, the band evokes what Brian Edwards calls "hippie orientalism" (2005): drawing on romantic (mis)understandings of unfamiliar regions, especially those in the Middle East and North Africa, they float through exotic imagery, bringing it back to their audiences. But, as Graham Nash describes in an interview with Rolling Stone magazine,

> In 1966 I was visiting Morocco on vacation to Marrakesh and getting on a train and having a first-class ticket and then realizing that the first-class compartment was completely fucking boring, you know, ladies with blue hair [presumably, older women] in there — it wasn't my scene at all. So I decide I'm going to go and see what the rest of the train is like. And the rest of the train was fascinating. Just like the song says, there were ducks and pigs and chickens all over the place and people lighting fires. It's literally the song as it is — what happened to me
>
> (Greene 2008)

I've been on this train and, while some surprising things can go on, I can attest that ducks and pigs are more likely to appear on Morocco's long-range buses nowadays. Through all of this imagery, however, comes a larger effort to "get away" and find oneself, a hope that ran through much of the hippie movement. Nash's lyrics describe how, as he rides through "clear Moroccan skies," he was reflecting on his understanding of himself, searching for something new, and questioning those who seemed to have all of the answers:

Sweeping cobwebs from the edges of my mind
Had to get away to see what we could find

Morocco was, in fact, a hotbed for artists and writers who wanted to "get away." It served as both a muse and a refuge for many who were pushing the edges of various artistic movements during and just after the colonial period. As such, it comes through as a powerful force within different streams of the arts, influencing literature, poetry, popular culture, and the cultural nationalism of the American Civil Rights movement. The most prominent setting for these efforts was Tangier in northern Morocco. A city just 20 miles south of Spain, Tangier felt like it was worlds away.

While the rest of Morocco was under colonial rule—mostly by the French, but with some areas controlled by Spain—Tangier remained unique. Between 1924 and 1956, when it rejoined Morocco after the country gained independence, Tangier operated as an "international zone." It was governed by an association of eight European countries that included France, Spain, Belgium, and others alongside the United States. This complex system—the local and foreign populations had differing rules of law—largely meant that the city was left alone. Enforcement was relatively minimal, leading those who were on the edge of licit society to make their way to its shores. Within the arts, this notably brought writers who were associated with the "beat poetry" movement, including William Burroughs. Other authors who made a home in Tangier or the nearby area included Paul Bowles and Tennessee Williams. Morocco pervades Burroughs's *Naked Lunch* and most of Bowles's works: the sounds and smells of the country's old cities operate almost as characters in works like *The Spider's House*.

Artists like Brion Gysin and musicians like Randy Weston also made their way to North Africa via Tangier. Paul Bowles, himself a composer, spent time traveling the country and recording Moroccan performers for a collection that long resided in the US Library of Congress before its recent release as a CD box set (Bowles 2016). Other jazz artists made their way to the country as well. Some of the various resulting collaborations will come up throughout this chapter and within the ones that follow.

These global interactions, whether appropriations or collaborations, left an influence on both Morocco and the rest of the world. The degree to which these kinds of exchanges can happen has continued to intensify and, thanks in no small part to communications technologies like the satellite dishes that opened this chapter, the world increasingly feels both smaller and larger. It is shrinking as trends, ideas, and ideologies spread quickly. It grows as those ideas come from a huge diversity of sources, leading to an array of smaller, but interconnected, communities.

Mass media, in this sense, is not a force so much as it is a tool. While discussions of "the media" permeate political discourse, especially in the United States, it is important to recognize that the media itself is a platform. Those who control the levers of that platform—whether the leadership of massive corporations or the individual authors of popular blog posts and YouTube channels—are not a singular monolithic force. Instead, the media is a space for debate, for the presentation of these diverse ideas. Taken this way, the mass media, especially the digital and satellite media formats that are so pervasive in Morocco today, play a significant role in music, religion, and the confluence of the two.

Alongside subtitled films coming from America's Hollywood and India's Bollywood, satellite television features a host of music video stations: think MTV and VH1 before they replaced much of their music with television shows. These stations, like Rotana and MBC, are part of larger corporate interests. They sign artists, record them, create the music videos, and own the stations that play those videos. Because of rampant piracy and the prominence of websites like YouTube, this vertical integration allows the companies to control other revenue streams. They are largely stationed in the Gulf region of the Middle East, far from Morocco, but their reach extends across national boundaries (Frishkopf 2010, 14). Artists like the Lebanese singer Nancy Ajram demonstrate the importance of these alternative sources of income: her success as one of the most famous singers in the Middle East has led to major endorsement deals with Coca-Cola, Samsung, Ericsson, Nissan, and many other major companies. Her Coca-Cola deal includes a number of songs that work as hybrid music videos and advertisements, many of which are major hits like "Moegaba" (Admirer). The song's video features the brand's bright red and white amidst a circus full of flamethrowers and jugglers. The music is a mix of Arab styles produced to work as a dance club track. One advertisement from the larger campaign has the singer enjoying a Coke before stepping down from the audience to sing the song with the circus.[5] In a world where record sales are not a dependable source of income, tie-ins of this sort and tour dates become even more important.

Global popular music, whether from the Middle East or elsewhere, plays a substantial role within debates about religious piety as well. Not unlike the concerns that seem to appear with every generation of youth culture—debates about rock and roll in the 1950s and 1960s, punk and heavy metal in the 1970s and 1980s, or hip hop in the 1980s and 1990s, for example—parents and religious leaders get worried when they see what their kids are watching and listening to. Arab music videos often highlight an upper-class or upper-middle-class lifestyle with all of the trappings that go along with wealth: beautiful homes, lush landscapes, and, of course, fast cars. Scantily clad women rolling in bedsheets or wearing expensive gowns often sing about love and life. In a world where news images show the most conservative elements of Muslim communities, the most popular videos that blare through television sets across the region can be surprising.

They also lead to backlash and heated debates. One moment involving a Rotana artist named Haifa Wehbe from 2010 illustrates this well. The Lebanese singer and actress was known for outspoken songs including "Ana Haifa" (I am Haifa) and "Bus al-Wawa" (Kiss the Booboo). Both include seductive imagery of the type that regularly appears in music videos worldwide. To emphasize her image and success, when she married for the second time in Beirut, guests included Kim Kardashian and Sean Combs. Conservative politicians have criticized her and attempted to ban her shows.[6] Her record label, responding to some of these political and social pressures, went so far as to publish a news item stating that the singer, who was recently voted to be the sexiest woman alive, was given a Quran, kissed it, and declared it "the most precious gift she'd ever received." It went on to describe how she knows verses by heart and regularly reads the holy book because "it soothes and calms her" (Rotana 2010). The photo that accompanies the article shows the singer wearing a head-scarf, an image far removed from what appears in her music videos. The tension between popular culture and religious devotion—between entertainment and piety—threads through the work of many of Morocco's own artists. As we move toward a discussion of popular genres that carry distinct linkages to global styles—and in Part III, where religious artists are navigating the music industry to find popular audiences—these negotiations should begin to feel familiar. That it plays out differently with many of the examples that follow also demonstrates the heavily gendered nature of these debates: female artists, even those who push back against conservative religious norms, overwhelmingly need to play by a set of rules that are generally much looser for their male counterparts.

The History and Practice of Islam

These concerns demonstrate the wide range of intersections between musical and religious practices in a global society. In some cases, these are closely aligned or one and the same: singing in ritual ceremonies, for example. Elsewhere, the relationship is more tenuous or subtle, like the ways in which musicians use their art and popularity to speak out against politics by invoking piety. This book focuses on music, though history and religious practice are important to telling these stories. And since Morocco is a Muslim majority country, a cursory understanding of the Islamic faith is central to understanding where these figures and their audiences are coming from. Islam is not a singular faith: there is no "head," no Pope-like figure. Being Muslim in Morocco may look (and sound) different to being a Muslim in Pakistan, or Indonesia, or Detroit, Michigan. There are, however, some core tenets that are worth knowing before moving on.

Islam's earliest history began in two cities in present day Saudi Arabia, a region that was then populated by primarily nomadic tribes. This was in the 7th century CE, not long after the European era known as "antiquity" shifted toward the early Middle Ages. Christianity was well-established in Europe: the Roman emperor Constantine had converted roughly 300 years earlier. Islam, like Christianity, follows in the Jewish prophetic tradition, though its holy book, the Quran, revises many well-known Old Testament histories. That book came from the central figure of the Islamic faith, the Prophet Muhammad. God, Allah, revealed the poetic verses that make up the Quran to Muhammad through the angel Gabriel and he, in turn, preached the scripture as a "messenger," the last in a long line of prophets that include Abraham (Ibrahim), Moses (Musa), and Jesus (Isa). Islam's kinship with other "people of the book" like Christians and Jews is described in the Quran, though over 1,000 years of military, social, economic, and political conflict certainly show their influence in today's world events.

Islam, as an Arabic term, means "submission." Most note this meaning as a sign of its inherent move toward peace and terms of war like "jihad" are often interpreted to be internal struggles against encroaching temptations both historically and in today's world. Without a clear hierarchy, however, very different leaders and teachers find congregants who follow them in diverse readings of the faith, its history, and its place in the contemporary world.

Structural similarities continue, however. The faith is built upon five "pillars," for example. Daily prayer (salat) is an expectation for all Muslims, with Friday afternoon prayers necessitating a trip to the mosque, a place of worship. Of course, as many self-identified Christians do not attend masses or services every week, not every Muslim succeeds in meeting his or her spiritual obligations. Many drink alcohol or eat pork, two things that are forbidden or discouraged. A second pillar is charity (zikat). A third involves fasting (sawm) from food, water, smoking, sex, and other things during daylight hours in the holy month of Ramadan. A fourth, for those who can afford it, is the expectation to make a pilgrimage to the religion's birthplace in Mecca, the hajj. Upon returning, a pilgrim takes on an honorific title, Hajj or Hajja, before his or her name. Arguably the most important pillar of the faith is faith itself: the core of Islamic conversion involves honestly stating an intention or testimony (shahada):

La ilaha illa Allah
Muhammadun rasulu Allah

There is no god but God [Allah]
Muhammad is the messenger [prophet] of God

Beyond these and other unifying factors, Moroccan Islam has some important distinctions. The country is at the far West of the historic Islamic empires, putting it far out to the periphery in some ways. As an example, the Quran is written in Arabic and represent the actual words spoken by the angel Gabriel when revealing the text to Muhammad. While versions in other languages exist, they are not understood as being particularly accurate because of the difficulty in translating language. Most of the Muslim world speaks Arabic, but with such a vast expanse over three continents, it is unsurprising that local versions of Arabic can be quite different. A Moroccan speaking daraja (Moroccan Arabic) on the hajj, the pilgrimage to Mecca, may struggle to be understood in Saudi Arabia. Consider how different Spanish and French are, despite being related romance languages in adjacent regions of Europe. Religion can work the same way.

The idea of "Moroccan Islam" has fascinated anthropologists and religious scholars for decades, partially because of its difference from what so many consider to be the "norm."[7] This mainly refers to the strong presence of Sufism, an umbrella term that encompasses a wide range of local religious beliefs and practices. Roughly linked as "Islamic mysticism," Sufi practices can be the most erudite and elite forms of scholarly faith seen in Fez's long-standing religious university and library. They can also be the illiterate, improvised, and adaptable forms of faith that appear in the poorest neighborhoods of the same city. Further, different forms of Sufism have a history within Morocco's nationalist movement under French colonialism or link to political access in today's government. Despite these vast distinctions, most forms of Sufism share a handful of commonalities. There is some type of hierarchy, unlike in Islam as a whole, as adepts follow leaders and scholars, sheikhs, on "paths." These paths, called tariqas, are similar to religious denominations, though they can be very large or small and can be closely related to each other. Most groups have a zawiya, a lodge or meeting place that can serve as a mosque and might hold some other types of historical import. There is generally a belief in an idea of "blessing" or "grace," known as baraka, that can imbue a holy man or object and be transmitted in different ways (especially during ritual or by touching the folds of someone's clothing). Many of these tariqas involve music in their religious practices, and some appear throughout this book.

The earliest years of Islam were a time of political and religious changes. The Prophet Muhammad was an adept commander and those who followed him quickly expanded their territory, building their religion with new converts along the way. During the ten years from 622 to 632 CE under his leadership, the Muslim community grew from one city in present-day Saudi Arabia (Medina). They took control of nearby Mecca, where they cleared out false idols from the Ka'ba, a stone building that, according to the Quran, was built by Ibrahim (Abraham). Not only is this site the focus of the hajj, the main pilgrimage that is one of the five pillars of Islam, every Muslim faces it when praying, even when he or she is on the other side of the globe. Very quickly, the community's expansion included much of Western Saudi Arabia and present-day Yemen, converting the nomadic tribes who lived in the Arabian peninsula.

Muhammad had a daughter, but no male heirs. Following his death, leadership went to his friends and relatives. Four successive leaders each served for a short period during the next thirty years. These figures were known as the "Rightly Guided Caliphs" and extended the reach of the Muslim community beyond the Arabian peninsula, through today's Syria, up into Turkey, Iran, and Afghanistan, and west through Egypt and halfway across North Africa. In about 40 years, the Muslim world grew to be significantly larger than the major European empires of the time. Following the death of Ali, Muhammad's son-in-law and the last of the Rightly Guided Caliphs, a leadership and doctrinal dispute instigated a split between Sunni and Shi'a Muslims that extends to today's sectarian strife between Iran and Saudi Arabia, and the political influence that each has in other countries around the region.

The empires that followed moved administrative capitals to Damascus (in present-day Syria) and then Baghdad (in Iraq). The first, which remained in power for 90 years, until 750 CE, continued the conquest of the North Africa, and eventually took hold of the Iberian peninsula, present-day Spain. This empire, known as the Umayyads, eventually lost control to the ʿAbbassid dynasty, but their legacy continued in Spain, which provides the background for Chapter 1. The ʿAbbassids, in turn, controlled the region for 500 years during the so-called "Dark Ages" of European history. They, along with the Andalusian dynasties in Spain described in Chapter 1, were known for maintaining and advancing Greek and Roman knowledge during a time when Europe lacked the central institutions to do so.

With control of the Indian Ocean and the Mediterranean Sea, the Islamic world eventually ran across North Africa, up into Europe, through the Middle East, down East Africa, through Persia and much of India, and covered many of the islands in and around Indonesia. It was, and is, truly global, even if the difficulties of sustaining a large empire meant that it was not necessarily politically unified.

By the advent of the modern era in the 19th and 20th centuries, most of North Africa had come under colonial control. Egypt was British territory, while much of the rest of the southern coast of the Mediterranean belonged to the French. The Ottoman Empire, based in Turkey, continued, but was weakened compared to its past heyday, when its militaries threatened the gates of Vienna and controlled much of what we know of as southeastern Europe today (including Greece, Bulgaria, and the Czech Republic). After the Second World War, many of these countries, like other colonies across sub-Saharan Africa and Latin America, demanded and won independence (see Chapter 3). Some, like Egypt, rose to prominence by navigating the hostilities of the Cold War, playing the United States and Soviet Republic against each other. Movements to re-unify—in the sense of collaboration, not as part of a larger political project to create a single state—under a feeling of Arab nationalism played an important role in developing individual countries' own nationalistic sentiments. Music played a similarly large role within this process, as seen with Egypt's primacy (described later), and the intellectual debates that orient protest within Morocco (see Chapter 3).

Beyond the level of "nation," music and religion interact to bind Muslim communities across the region and around the world. This is especially the case in the "web 2.0" era, where social media and video-sharing sites like Facebook and YouTube and those media stations coming from further east can quickly spread new sounds and ideas. Some groups operationalize these relatively new forms of communication to build a following, while in many other cases, the spread of religious perspectives, musical creativity, or political movements are more "grassroots"; they bubble up from individuals going "viral."

Local Global Music

Keeping this global dynamic in mind, the remainder of this chapter introduces a handful of musical genres that look outward from within Morocco's borders, connecting to styles coming from elsewhere. While the major pop artists described above are piped into the country through digital media technologies, the following examples include music that brings foreign styles into conversation with local ones.

One obvious example of this derives from the country's Andalusian history described in Chapter 1. While that musical tradition has clear boundaries and exists as a symbol of memory for that past, it influences creative artists who innovate in other ways. Andalusian-flavored popular music abounds in Morocco. Much of this was performed by the country's substantial Jewish population before and during the French colonial period. While those communities left the country, fearing political and social persecution under the previous king (Hassan II), the musical legacies that they left continued.[8] Partially because of its historic linkages to Spain and partially because of the cosmopolitan experiences of the musicians, this Andalusian popular music has been a vehicle for national pride and international collaboration.

Abdessadeq Chakara was a prominent performer of Andalusian music who also composed new pieces that drew on that genre's style. One of his songs, "Ya Bint Bladi" (loosely, "Girl from My Country"), has been performed by a number of artists working in collaboration between Spain and Morocco. By invoking Spanish flamenco, a musical style and dance that has roots within the same Andalusian geography as Morocco's al-ala, these efforts serve to promote international efforts toward peace and understanding (see Shannon 2015).

Some of the strongest international connections, however, are with the music that came out of Egypt during the middle of the 20th century. Before satellite television, there was broadcast television and radio and, in these modes of mass media, Egypt was dominant. The sounds coming from Cairo adapted the classical Arabic systems from centuries past to meet the needs of the day's audiences. They also aligned closely with social and political trends that were consuming the region during and just after the Second World War.

Just as Andalusian music harkens back to the courts and palaces of al-Andalus, Arabic music from further east developed from the sounds of courts and palaces in the capitals of previous empires. These cities included Baghdad, in contemporary Iraq, and Damascus, in Syria, among others. The musical system that organized this music was based on a system of modes known as maqams. This was a type of chamber music and featured a small ensemble that could include an 'ud, nay, qanun, riqq, voice, and violin. The 'ud is similar to the one used in Andalusian music. The nay is a wind instrument made out of a reed. It works somewhat like a flute, but instead of holding it out to the side and blowing across a hole, the musician holds it at and angle and blows across the end, almost as if trying to get a sound out of an empty soda or beer bottle. The qanun is the instrument described in Chapter 1 that uses sets of three plucked strings for each pitch stretched across an angular flat box with small levers to one side that allow the musician to subtly alter the pitch when the music shifts between maqams. Groups usually featured an instrument similar to the violin, though the modern instrument has long become the standard. Percussion instruments generally include a riqq (an instrument that resembles, but is heavier than, a tambourine) and a goblet drum known as a darbuka, though other names like tabla are also common. Finally, one or more singers may join this small ensemble, which is known as a takht. The goal of performance is helping audience members—knowledgeable connoisseurs called sama'i—reach a state of tarab, a sense of enchantment within the music (Racy 2003). This experience relates to the ecstasy that can feed religious musical listening known as hal. Whereas tarab relates to the feeling of falling into musical listening, hal means "the condition" and generally refers to the experience of mystical connection with Allah that appears within Moroccan Sufism and which also influences religious practices elsewhere, including in Egypt (Frishkopf 2001).

The sound of tarab changed dramatically over the course of the 20th century, however, as audience tastes and mass media opportunities shifted. Gamal Abdel Nasser, a soldier who became Egypt's first president in 1956 (the same year that Morocco won independence from France), leaned heavily on Cairo's media industries while making a claim to lead the Arab world. His argument that Arab countries needed to unify to succeed in the post-Second World War world order, invoked a sense of "pan-Arabism" or "Arab Nationalism." With Egyptian films broadcasting across the Middle East and North Africa, singers who starred in movies were able to align with some of Nasser's policies, broadening his appeal outside of Egypt's national borders. One figure who exemplified this trend, named Umm Kulthum, did so using her film stardom, roots within the "authenticity" of rural Egypt, and her religious devotion (Danielson 1998). Her Thursday night radio concerts were major events every week, with families and friends tuning in on the radio to listen to the newest compositions from Egypt. Notably, her music makes other changes within the aesthetics of Arab music clear as well. During this same period, musicians and audiences were working to incorporate the "modern" sounds that they heard coming from Europe. While striving to maintain their own musical identities and traditions, they looked outward for inspiration as composers like Sayyid Darwish and Muhammad Abd al-Wahab utilized compositional elements of opera, jazz, and American popular music (Danielson 1997).

Egyptian styles, especially those that were broadcast to Morocco during this period, were heavily influential on local tastes across the Middle East. Many artists incorporated the styles of famous Egyptian artists including Umm Kulthum, Muhammad Abd al-Wahab, and others. Abd al-Halim Hafez, an Egyptian Frank Sinatra-like figure who made use of new microphone technology to sing intimate love songs (Stokes 2009), inspired many artists to take up this mold. One example of a Moroccan artist who was heavily influenced by these aesthetic trends was Abd al-Hadi bil-Khayat. An ʿud player who went to Cairo to train, Khayat was an artist who very intentionally worked to sound like his Egyptian "Golden Age" predecessors. This is audible in his songs, though he sings in the Moroccan dialect of Arabic, instead of the Egyptian version that was so prominent thanks to the film and music industries. Biographical narratives about his life focus on his move away from music. In the 1980s, he completed the pilgrimage to Mecca and devoted himself to his faith, leaving his vocation behind. At the request of the king, Hassan II, he returned to the stage with a new-found ethical focus, though his music carried the same Egyptian influences.

The song "Mataqshi Biyya" (I have no trust for her) shows how Khayat incorporated these influences into a song that also keeps up with popular tastes. Structurally, the song has the complexity of previous Egyptian singers. The recording that a CD shop owner in Fez (where Khayat is from) gave me is over 12 minutes long. It begins with two and a half minutes of instrumental introduction. There is little rush to get to the poem. Alternating strings, and ʿud, an accordion, and other melodic instruments carry a feel that is familiar to listeners of Abd al-Halim Hafez's work with other pop styles. The addition of a saxophone and some other backgrounds, along with a beat that elides Arab patterns with a Western pop-oriented drum set give the music a feel that, despite its Egyptian-ness, has hints of 1970s disco and soul.

When Khayat enters, he sings about the pain of love. The song's title plays on a grammatical structure to roughly mean "there is no trust within me." He has been hurt by his love, despite the obvious and pure (wadah wa bayn) nature of his heart's desire. As is usually the case, poetic elements of a poem translate somewhat awkwardly. This text is no exception as it utilizes a standard practice in Arab poetry, using male grammatical forms for female subjects. References to "she" and "her" appear in brackets here where they are "he" and "his" within the text. While there are artists who push against normative sexualities across the region, Khayat is not one of them. The refrain that begins the song articulates the singer's sense of loss and despair.

Ah ah ma taqshi biyya ash nʿaml ma taqshi biyya
ʿAlash ʿalash yakadabni wash maʿndu taqa fiyya
Wa ana hubbi ya nas wadah wa bayn wadah wa bayn
Wa duh al-shams fi nhar jamil wadah wa bayn wadah wa bayn

Ah ah, I have no trust for her, what am I to do? I have no trust for her
Why, why did [she] lie to me? What can [she] do to make me trust again?
My love, oh people, is clear and obvious, clear and obvious
As clear as the sun on a beautiful day, clear and obvious, clear and obvious

Beyond the tortured poetry and discotheque sound, the verses are structurally complex. When the refrain returns throughout, it is rarely identical to previous versions. Sometimes the text is the same, but the melodies have shifted. Elsewhere, the title line itself is missing. Verses move through modes in ways that resemble the popular versions of Egyptian tarab music. This song is not unique; he and other artists like Abdelwahab Doukkali represent a movement in the 1950s and 1960s where a developing genre known as "al-ughniya al-ʿasriya" (modern song) relied heavily on Egyptian trends. Within Khayat's own repertoire, other songs like "Al-Qamar al-Ahmar" (The Reddest Moon) show that this is not an isolated interest in "al-ughniya al-sharqiya" (Eastern/Egyptian song). That Khayat was an entertainer himself, appearing in movies like so many of the Egyptian singers who were so famous, further emphasizes this inspiration.

Morocco's neighbor, Algeria, is the source of another global style that found a comfortable home within Morocco's popular music scene. This one, however, is more recent and is arguably more present on today's radio stations. Rai music originated as an adaptation of local genres, most of which were exclusive to private settings. They pushed the boundaries of what was acceptable behavior in public. This music was first named in the bars of Oran, Algeria, a city that is about 100 miles East of Oudja, Morocco. Despite the closed borders between these two countries since 1994, the global popularity (and local smuggling) of rai music keeps it relevant in Morocco. Since their respective independence movements, Morocco and Algeria have had a strained relationship. The most pressing issue for Morocco was Algeria's recognition of the Western Sahara (a piece of land extending down the African coast that roughly doubles Morocco's geographic size) as independently governed by the separatist Polisario Front. Algerians, in turn, argue that Morocco has a history of supporting rebellions and terrorism against their government. Under French colonialism and before it, however, these two regions were closely linked. The Islamic empires and Amazigh communities who lived there extended across today's national boundaries. Cultural, religious, and musical ties continue to breed a sense of familiarity, especially between cities like Oujda, Oran, and Tlemcen, places that are now cut off from each other by the closed border.

At weddings and nightclubs, some of the early scenes for rai music, performers engaged in elaborate wordplay that "praised and teased the audience" (Langlois 1996, 261).

It was improvised and humorous, albeit in a vulgar tone that has since offended religiously conservative leaders. Further, this music was distinctly part of a female domain. It would appear within the homogeneously female portions of a wedding, for example, as entertainment by and for women.[9] Once it shifted into bars and nightclubs in Oran, which was a major port of trade under French colonialism, attitudes toward the music shifted and it came to be known for its associations with brothels and other seedy elements.[10] When Algeria fell into a bloody and ideological civil war in the 1990s, many rai artists fled, though one famous artist named Cheb Hasni is still remembered by his compatriots after being killed by Islamist forces.

The music was such a touchstone partially because of its roots within youth culture. Young (increasingly male) singers took on the title "Cheb," or "Cheba" for a woman. The term refers to youth as a whole and, as such, these performers were differentiating themselves from the generations that preceded them. They sang about the concerns of young people: most of the music was sentimental, and love songs and dance tracks dominated (and continue to dominate) the repertoire. But the use of youth vernacular also provided an opportunity for coded protest. Before independence, this meant that singers occasionally added the struggle for liberation from the French to their repertoire of songs about "wine, love and the problems of marginal life." After winning their freedom, the "state-sponsored puritanism" of the new Algerian government pushed the music back toward the margins. It was in the 1980s, however, that looser government restrictions and easily shared cassette tapes gave what was now called "pop rai" a chance to take off (Gross et al. 1992, 12–13). In their discussion of Algerian rai history, Joan Gross, David McMurray, and Ted Swedenburg highlight lyrics like these, from Cheikha Remitti:

> *Oh my love, to gaze upon you is a sin,*
> *It's you who makes me break my fast.*
> *Oh lover, to gaze upon you is a sin,*
> *It's you who makes me "eat" during Ramadan.*

Another colorful example that they give is her line, "People adore God, I adore beer" (quoted in Gross et al. 1992, 13). The music was constantly eliding between being a closed-door entertainment for private settings and an outspoken public statement against political or religious authorities (whether French or Algerian). These three scholars continue by describing how rai, especially in its newfound pop rai form, gained popularity within the North African communities that lived in the banlieues, the impoverished "suburbs," that surround France's largest cities.

Looking at a map, Oujda and Oran are fairly close. The 100-mile span is similar to the distance between New York and Philadelphia in the United States. They are closer together than London and Birmingham in the United Kingdom. The closed border eliminates much of the commercial and cultural exchange that would otherwise move between these two countries. Smuggling, a major industry on the border, certainly bridges that gap (see McMurray 2001), but it is rai's global spread to France and beyond that truly enables the genre's popularity within Morocco. Before the border closed, Moroccan artists like Muhammad Rey, Rachid Beryah, Cheb Kader, and Mimoun el Oujdi (whose name actually cites the border town of Oujda) found success bringing rai to their country's audiences. Since then, however, it has been international stars like Cheb Khaled and Cheb Mami, Algerian expatriates to Europe, who have become the names and faces of rai. Cheb Mami, for example, brought the genre to English-speaking audiences in a collaboration with Sting, a British bass player and singer (and past member of The Police). The song, 1999's "Desert Rose," featured Mami's voice over an electronic dance beat that could easily appear within a pop rai tune from the time. The string parts following the vocal lines further emphasize the North African sound. Other pop collaborations of his are more regional in scope, including one with Samira Said, a prominent singer.

It might be hip hop, however, that has become the most present globally-oriented genre within Morocco's airwaves. The music that came out of urban neglect in New York City, in the Bronx, has come to be a dominant force in popular music worldwide. It has inspired new social movements, cultural organizations, and genres of entertainment. While this chapter concludes with a reflection on how global religious trends influence politics and popular music, it is in the next, Chapter 3, where we will see how protest music—and hip hop especially—encapsulates the breadth of attitudes that Moroccan artists hold about their government, society, and religion (see Figure 2.2).

During one of my visits to Morocco, I remember being struck by signage that I had not noticed before. Large posters appeared on storefronts and cafés, though the one I passed most often was on the papered-over windows of a liquor store that I walked by every day. The posters featured an outline of a giant palm held upright, as if to say "talk to the hand." The hand was red with a green outline, mirroring the colors of the Moroccan flag (a red flag with a green star), the national soccer team's uniform, and so

Figure 2.2 A member of the Moroccan hip hop group Muslim performing in Fez in 2011. He is wearing a shirt with the colors and symbols of the Moroccan flag: a green star on a red background.

many other patriotic symbols. The symmetrical shape of it, with three fingers upright and two outward, almost as if there were a thumb on each side, was also very much a familiar symbol: the Hand of Fatima. The use of an open-palmed right hand to protect against evil has roots within ancient Greek and Egyptian communities and has spread throughout the Islamic world (Apostolos-Cappadona 2005). Women, especially, use the hand to ward off the "evil eye," spiritual attacks from neighbors, enemies, or supernatural beings. Pregnant women and children are especially vulnerable, making this a common symbol throughout everyday life. This hand shows up in jewelry, on clothing, around homes, and hanging from mirrors in taxis. The open hand—likely representing the daughter of the Prophet Muhammad, named Fatima—can also feature an open eye in the palm, making it a symbol that reflects back to Buddhist roots as well.

These signs that I had not noticed before use color to fuse this popular religious symbol of protection with national pride. In place of the eye, in the center of the palm, read the words "Matkish Bladi," "Don't touch my country."[11] Some versions underlined the message by repeating it in French along the bottom of the palm: "Touché pas à mon pays." The phrase was an explicit statement to Islamist movements in response to recent terrorist attacks in major Muslim cities across the region, but more specifically, it was pushing back against incidents within Morocco's own borders. In 2001, the same year in which the September 11th attacks hit the United States, Moroccan security forces found an al-Qaʿida cell within the country and jailed a number of religious leaders during the investigations that followed. While the country had new leadership under Muhammad VI, this triggered fears of repression similar to those that had marked his father's reign (see Chapter 3 for more on the political relationship between the crown and religious groups since independence). Members of the terrorist-linked group had carried out bombings in Casablanca, killing 45 people, in 2003. A year later, bombings in Madrid, Spain were allegedly planned and executed by Moroccans (Miller 2013, 224). One result was the signage that I was noticing on my walks around Fez.

But people agreed the popular tide was flatly and resolutely against terrorist efforts. Friends and colleagues, even men at cafés or wives of musicians who would host me for lunch, expressed disdain for what they saw as a foreign intervention. Terrorism was against Islam, it was a misreading of holy texts and a deliberate misunderstanding of religious teachings. Plus, as they saw it, it had no home in Morocco. It was part of a war that Moroccans did not want to be a part of and, for many, it was just a play of power and politics. I was reminded of the types of conversations surrounding America's own hyper-partisan political (dis)engagement in a time of frequent mass shootings and racial strife. As we will see, the revolutionary and nationalistic attitudes that come out of Morocco's contentious political history unfold within popular culture. That hip hop artists take these questions on and use their music to make statements or demands is unsurprising; not only is it a part of the country's past, it's a central element of the musical genre's own embattled narratives. In Chapter 3, we see various perspectives on these intersections of music, nation, religion, and activism.

In this section, local musicians have shown an adeptness at bringing styles of music from outside of Morocco's borders to communities of listeners within the country. They have also influenced the efforts of musicians from elsewhere: musicians and audiences are looking outward as well as inward as they innovate new styles and sounds. Mass media in the 20th and 21st centuries—whether radio, the film industry, satellite television, private radio stations, or social media—plays a role in this, but it enables the efforts of real people, of artists and listeners who search for new ideas and engage with local and global trends. These actors, especially in the case of media conglomerates based elsewhere, push all types of agendas. Many of these are religiously oriented, forwarding or resisting various ideologies. With this dynamic in mind, it should not be surprising that religion, politics, and economics intertwine within media and popular culture, in Morocco and everywhere else around the globe.

This chapter's focus on the interactivity of global and local aesthetics (both musical and religious) foregrounds the pressures that animate the next chapter. Global religious ideologies—just like global musical styles—play a major role within local religious practices, debates, and the politics that surround them. Music responds in kind as artists and audiences express opinions about their communities, country, and world. Where Chapter 1 described some dominant historical narratives in Morocco today and Chapter 2 looked more closely at the workings of internationally engaged forms of popular culture, Chapter 3 outlines the often uneasy relationship between outspoken musicians, powerful governmental forces, and the Moroccan citizens who listen to, follow, and resist each.

Notes

1 The filter bubble refers to the algorithmic sorting of internet search results and social media posts that contributes to confirmation bias among users (see Pariser 2011, Bozdag and van den Hoven 2015).
2 Also see Tarik Sabry's *Cultural Encounters in the Arab World: On Media, the Modern and the Everyday* (2010).
3 For examples of ethnographic accounts of local communities encountering and responding to global trends, see Guilbault (1993), Klein (2007), Turino (2003), or innumerable others. For examples focused on the circulation of musical tastes and ideas, see Erlmann (1996), Meintjes (1990), Novak (2013).
4 On the origins of hip hop, see Chang (2005), on metal's history, see Walser (1993). For an account of the globalization of hip hop, see Morgan and Bennett (2011) and, regarding metal, see Weinstein (2011).
5 See the Resources section for a link to playlists that include these videos.
6 One example involved an effort by Bahrain's parliament to prevent her from performing in the country (Ya Libnan 2008).
7 See, for example, seminal works from Clifford Geertz (1971), Dale Eickelman (1976), and Abdellah Hammoudi (1997).
8 While Morocco's Jewish community is described in some detail in Part III, this book's scope and focus does not fully address the community's important contributions to Moroccan musical history and style.
9 It has since become a male-dominated genre where young artists articulate various types of masculinity. This has been a major focus of scholarship on rai and popular youth culture in North Africa (see Schade-Poulsen 1999, DeAngelis 2003).
10 An article by Tony Langlois (1996) describes this history in some detail while focusing on the trends toward globalization and its influence on production choices that artists made in the studio.
11 Cristina Moreno Almeida includes a photograph of one of these signs in her book, *Rap Beyond Resistance: Staging Power in Contemporary Morocco* (2017, 66).

PART II

Contesting Mainstreams: Where We're Going

The previous chapters told a history of Morocco while exploring the relationships between music, religion, media, and power. These four concepts are closely linked and the connections between them remain important today. Political power within the country rests largely in the hands of the monarchy. It spreads through state-run media, is contested by oppositional political parties, and resisted by still others who sit further from the "center," whether in rural areas or marginalized communities. The union of religious and political authority within the person of the king strengthens the bindings that consolidate religion, media, and power, but it also creates a vulnerability that protesting groups exploited: perceived moral failures or attacks on the government's piety open opportunities for alternative voices. As we will see in Part II, the monarchy supports different types of religious activity within the country in an effort to control and maintain a specific Islamic identity for the country and its people, but the population is more diverse than these top-down efforts imply. The country's identity is varied with dramatic regional, ethnic, and class-based distinctions.

In Part II, Chapters 3 and 4 explore marginalized musical and religious identities. Whereas Part I focused on various forms of mainstream or elite cultural and religious practices, Part II focuses on important ways in which music and religion across the country are distinct from and oppose those overarching narratives. I hesitate to say "minorities" here, since each of the traditions represented in these two chapters are important in significant ways. While much of the country, especially in urban areas, identifies as Arab, the reality is that Morocco was, and still is, Amazigh. The people who were native to this part of the world before the arrival of Islamic empires 1,500 years ago still hold tightly to their language and culture. Within the past few decades, Amazigh language and cultural identities have come to the forefront of political debates as many within the population argue for the recognition of this cultural history in today's infrastructure and educational systems. The religious practices that fused with Islam and the large-scale social music that animates major events within small villages continue as important markers for people's identities, for who they are. While fewer may self-identify as Amazigh nowadays, the number is still around half of the population and the actual racial makeup is probably much higher. (As noted in Chapter 1, Amazigh is a native replacement for "Berber," a term seen by many as foreign at best and offensive at worst). The idea of Amazigh language and culture as a minority or special interest is something that developed over a long moment of Arabization and Islamization; it is a distinction that was created and cultivated during the colonial period and that is breaking down today.

Chapter 4 moves on to a different type of minority, a racial one. The gnawa practice a musical ritual ceremony that is simultaneously well outside of the norms of mainstream Islamic practice and also representative of the diversity of Moroccan Islam. In various ways, it is derided and celebrated by the state and the country's population. This is a minority practice that has become one of the most important markers of distinction for the country as a whole, separating it from the Islamism of other Middle Eastern countries as the nation represents itself to the rest of the world. By revisiting regional popular culture styles that have spread across the country to create national genres, and by specifically exploring the ways in which faithful performers and audiences lace their entertainment with their own approaches to piety and spirituality, this segment serves to introduce groovy music while touching on themes that will permeate the final three chapters of this book.

CHAPTER 3

Pop and Protest

Much of doing fieldwork research involves asking questions and trying to make sense of the answers. While musical and anthropological training can help when working to decipher the nuances of what people are doing and how they are using music to build communities or identities (among other things), more basic issues can present larger barriers. One of these is finding people and places in the first place. Much of my time in Morocco was spent trying to figure out who or where people were. One of these experiences led me to a suburb of Casablanca, an area of the city where I had never been, to hear what was allegedly a concert featuring a band who is arguably the most famous in Morocco's history. Having seen them perform a handful of times before, this gig caught my attention because of who was playing with them: Victor Wooten, an American bass player whose virtuosity and musicality had gotten me into playing bass years ago when I saw him perform with Bela Fleck and the Flecktones while I was in high school.

I was intrigued by the lineup, which brought together four artists who have little in common. Besides Wooten and Nass El Ghiwane, Safi Boutella, an Algerian composer and arranger, and Saida Fikri, a Moroccan singer and composer, were involved in the collaboration. But to see the concert, I had to find it. Morocco hosts a wide range of major music festivals, many of which are geared toward exactly these types of collaborative efforts. They promote tolerance and diversity within the country while simultaneously performing those values for international festival audiences. This is most apparent within the major festivals in Fez, Essaouira, and Rabat. The first two appear in discussions in later chapters, but the third, Rabat's Mawazine Festival was the instigator of this event, so far as I can tell. Many of these huge concerts draw crowds to city centers, but each is increasingly likely to "share the wealth" by putting stages in poorer neighborhoods or towns. At the time, I did not know about the performance in Rabat, but I was in Casablanca, where these four artists were setting up. I gave the neighborhood's name to a taxi driver, got in, and hoped for the best.

We drove around a bit, looking for a big crowd. I had no details to help in our search. When we found it (amazingly), the stage was nestled between large apartment buildings in an empty grassy space alongside a hill. It was dark, but I got the feeling that this unkempt, rocky field served only the most informal purposes: a makeshift soccer field or hangout, perhaps. It was around the corner from shops, but not on the main road, where I would have expected a major concert from well-known artists to be set up. When the music started up, the gathering crowd went wild. Nass El Ghiwane's songs are the type of music that nearly everyone knows. Whenever I would play the beginning of one on my banjo, everyone around would sing along. They also represent the protest against the oppression of the 1970s in Morocco. Their music and outspoken lyrics made them arguably the first nationally popular band in the country. That they were now collaborating with these artists and rearranging their songs to incorporate musical elements from today's popular music struck a chord. I have since found some YouTube videos of the main performance that year, the one that took place in Rabat during the Mawazine Festival. The comments tell the story well:

Lhayha04: c quoi ça??????????? hchouma tssma3 had chi au nom du nass l ghiwane [...] [What is this??????????? Shame, delete this thing in the name of Nass El Ghiwane!]
Karim Use: Vaut mieux supprimer cette video [Better to delete this video]
Koussai Schuldiner: victor wooten l'un des meilleurs bassiste au monde, a commi une faute de participer à ce merde [...] [Victor Wooten is one of the best bassists in the world, he made a mistake in participating in this shit]
Marrakechmusique: @Mojjitous non ,elle a chanté en harmonie ,juste le son ,dans cette video n'est pas terrible . sur la tele ,j'ai entendu ,c'est bien . [@Mojjitous, no, she sang in tune, it is just that the sound in this video is terrible. On TV I was able to hear it well.]
Samira Elyousfi: En tout cas la chanson reste et restera legendaire. [In every case this song remains and will remain legendary.][1]

To agree with Marrakechmusique, the sound in the video is rough and does not do Saida Fikri any favors. But the larger defense against manipulating Nass El Ghiwane's music shows how powerful it remains (and will remain, to use Samira Elyousfi's phrase). In this chapter, the country's political and social history come into conversation with music and musical activism. The protests that extended through the 1960s and 1970s found a voice in music and popular culture. They continue today as foundational groups like Nass El Ghiwane inspire more recent controversial singers like Saida Fikri in the 1990s. The chapter concludes by revisiting hip hop artists from Chapter 2 who articulate conflicting viewpoints about today's concerns, things like terrorism, women's rights, and the Arab Spring.

Political History Since Independence

The outspoken activism in this chapter's music protests the economic, social, and political inequality and injustice of the day. The most recent examples, however, carry the country's history within them by situating their own words within those of artists who came before and maintaining an (often unspoken) critique of past wrongs. Partially because of the lack of recordings before the mid-20th century and the importance of oral tradition within these types of music, our understanding of these critical musicians only begins during the country's colonial period, though there was certainly a culture of governmental distrust during various periods before the arrival of the French. In fact, Morocco's precolonial history leading up to their subjugation by European powers reflects the strife that had marked its earlier Andalusian history. In this case, however, the ruling dynasty was able to maintain control against encroaching rural tribal leaders.

During the second half of the 19th century, the Alaouite dynasty had been in power for roughly 200 years. After a series of battles that ended in failure, successive Sultans attempted to enact a series of reforms. Military losses to European powers including the French and Spanish demonstrated the weakness of the army and treasury. France had taken hold of most of North Africa by this point, leading Morocco to enter into free trade agreements and other arrangements with the British. Some of the leaders during these decades steered the central government in making effective structural reforms, while others were criticized for losing touch with the Moroccan people. Rural leaders increasingly felt alienated by new taxes while hearing rumors that, for example, one sultan in the early 1900s spent lavishly on new European technologies like bicycles, videocameras, and steamships. Revolts dotted the landscape and, as the 1800s turned over to the 1900s, regional leaders and frustrated members of the upper classes began to see the inevitability of France overtaking the struggling kingdom. They signed deals that put them in positions of power under colonialism, either showing tremendous foresight or an ultimate betrayal of their country, depending on one's perspective.

During the years just before 1912, when France officially took hold of the Moroccan military and government, the literati and religious scholars engaged in heated debate about European influence. Many saw the encroaching infidels as debasing Islam and the increasing acceptance of European habits and goods as a sign of Morocco's "moral decay" (Miller 2013, 48–9). The king, even when weak, became a symbol for the country in a way that proved important when a national independence movement began to gather steam later in the colonial period.

Once the protectorate took hold in 1912, French administrators began to establish a dual government. Hubert Lyautey became the head of the colonial administration until 1925. During his time, he worked to carry out the literal mission of the protectorate: to protect and develop Morocco. In his eyes, the country was neither a colony nor was it ostensibly part of France, as neighboring Algeria was. He worked to respect tradition, though he did so according to French expectations. Through new construction projects, educational initiatives, and military advances, Lyautey and his administration built up and maintained a strict sense of hierarchy, partially because of his avowed royalist leanings (Miller 2013). School systems for Muslims, Jews, those who were not from the cities, and other ethnic, religious, and linguistic groups reinforced clear class distinctions: they trained people for specific roles with little opportunity for mobility between social levels. Importantly, his entire administration was built on an alleged role of service to the sultan.

The duality of governance came out of this respect for hierarchy. Lyautey exiled the defeated Sultan Mulay Abd al-Hafid in 1912 and replaced him with his younger brother Yusef. The sultan maintained court in a way that created a sense of authority and consistency with the past, while the French administration continued on as a "service" to the "native" government. Yet, the sultan's authority quickly dwindled to encompass little outside of the realm of religion. Taxes, infrastructure, social issues, trade, and most other workings of government were carried out under the growing French bureaucracy. The sense of pride in the sultanate, despite its relative weakness, helped to mobilize a sense of nationalism in the later decades of French rule.

The French invested substantial sums of money in Morocco, rebuilding cities and constructing new ones alongside the old Arab quarters. The ville nouvelle (new city) outside each major urban area is now the center of town. The medina (old city), on the contrary, is often under disrepair, though many throughout Morocco are being revitalized or celebrated as heritage sites. Populations were shifting, as well. People from the countryside were moving to these old cities, just as the wealthy from the old cities took up new residences in the new ones. Like elsewhere during the early 20th century, industry and changing demographics had a profound impact on Morocco. That most of the popular music described below comes from major cities while drawing on rural traditions reflects these earlier changes.

Through the colonial period, the French administration worked successfully with local rural chiefs, known as the "Lords of the Atlas," referencing the name of the Atlas mountain chain. This strategy was a common and useful one that helped colonial powers across the world to "capture" indigenous power structures. While some rural areas proved difficult to conquer, many heads of families saw colonialism as an opportunity. By working with the French, they stood as powerful intermediaries. As tax collectors, they kept a cut or were able to extort local communities for more than was required, keeping the rest for themselves. The practice led to further distance between urban intellectuals and rural communities because of this corruption and other vast disparities in how Moroccans across the country were treated by the French. It also reinforced social, religious, and musical distinctions between urban and rural areas.

As Europe fought the First World War and the Second World War, colonial realities shifted. Moroccans were spending more time in France. Many fought bravely in the Second World War as part of the Allied forces, though they increasingly experienced racism; they were never afforded the opportunities of French soldiers, despite their valor and sacrifice. Others were learning more about independence movements in Egypt, Algeria, and elsewhere. Some were drawn to communism or Europe's growing labor rights movements. In the end, urban intellectuals were able to engage global powers like the United Nations to put pressure on the French for independence. The postwar years of the 1940s and 50s were a time when independence movements were gaining traction across the colonial world, and Morocco was fully a part of this moment.

Eventually, a war for independence broke out. The French administration made the decision to exile the Moroccan sultan, Muhammad V, to Madagascar. He had increasingly been seen by the population as a symbol, a link to Morocco's pre-colonial past. With his exile, the movement hit a fever pitch and, thanks in part to independence struggles across North Africa and East Asia that were drawing France's attention, after a few short but bloody years, they allowed the sultan back into the country, now as a king. Independence came shortly thereafter, though the new country kept—and still maintains—a close relationship with France.

The new government was set up to be a constitutional monarchy with the sultan, Muhammad V, now a king, sharing power with the political parties that had been so instrumental in bringing about independence. What happened, however, was different. The king was able to outmaneuver the politicians while quickly consolidating authority over the central levers of power: military, the police, and the intelligence sector. When

French settlers left, the monarchy purchased their land and either kept it or doled it out to supporters, further reinforcing its own control over agriculture. The "center" and "periphery" system of government that had been the organization of Morocco's empires in the past continued. Instead of a clear power-sharing, the elites with access held sway, though now the "Lords of the Atlas" had some level of access from their rural homes as well.

The king's son, Hassan II, took over in 1961, four years after independence. His father passed away during a surgical operation, making his ascent to the throne sudden. He had been Mohammad V's right-hand man for a while, however, so he came prepared. His reign was marked by his heavy-handed policies. Political dissidents were regularly "disappeared," and musicians were often subject to an atmosphere of fear, as we will soon see. Multiple assassination attempts were made on his life and he reacted strongly. One of his leading ministers was quickly killed and his family was sent to a secret prison in the desert, for example.[2] He simultaneously cultivated the role of "commander of the faithful" in the person of the king, despite his penchant for "fast cars and sleek women" (Miller 2013, 162). Demands for loyalty and the heavy-handed punishments for those who questioned the king's authority gave his reign a name: "les anneés de plomb," the years of lead.

When Hassan II's son, Muhammad VI, ascended the throne in 1999, he continued reforms that his father had begun during the last decades of his reign. Despite, or more likely making up for, a long history of human rights abuses, Hassan II had made cautious overtures toward improving conditions within the country. Muhammad VI took starker measures by firing leadership and opening commissions to look into lingering questions about political prisoners and other abuses, though never in a way that allowed for criticism of his father's name. Additionally, the new king was renowned for his business acumen and his pro-capitalism stance, giving him the opportunity to more closely align with European and American governments and commercial interests. After the September 11th terrorist attacks in the United States, a 2003 terrorist bombing in Casablanca, and instances of Moroccans being involved in similar incidents in Spain, Muhammad VI solidified his engagement with the war on terror, making Morocco one of the most active Middle Eastern states in fighting Islamic extremism within its borders. The country has been home to cells of various groups, but the crackdown against them was swift. This has made for a stable country, but it also stoked some fears that, despite openings in democratic opportunity since the "years of lead," autocratic tendencies were still very much a part of the monarchy's relationship with its people.

Equally notable within these years was the new king's shrewd navigation of major women's issues and cultural politics. A rising frustration with the outdated legal exclusion of women's rights came to a head when the king created a commission to revise Morocco's rendering of Islamic law regarding things like divorce, inheritance, and property ownership. Choosing the most liberal of the options presented to him, the king successfully headed off a potential source of discontent among the population and put the country on course to be a leader for women's issues in the region (though, in practice, conservative local governments and judges have hindered the actual implementation of revisions to family law, called the mudawana). In a similar move, he quelled protests during the Arab Spring of 2011 (see later in this chapter) by adopting a new constitution that recognized the status of Amazigh as a language and cultural component of the Moroccan people. While the protesters were unsatisfied with these moves—which also included important, but not necessarily effectual, changes to the political system—the population accepted them resoundingly in a referendum. This style of coopting certain issues to prevent larger anti-government movements show that, despite being a very different leader than his father, the current king is also adept at outmaneuvering his opponents. The following section returns to this historical period with a focus on musical activity to show how musicians and the various administrations each used popular culture, religious ideologies, and artistic trends to navigate the country's defining political struggles since independence.

A History of Protest

In a remark about the Arab Spring, the political uprisings that conclude this chapter, John Philip Rode Schaefer states that "mass-popular singers are not structurally positioned to speak to the current moment" (2015, 503). His reference is to Egyptian artists who supported the falling regime and have, as a result, struggled to maintain a following in the years after the social and political upheaval. American artists experienced similarly difficult moments during the Civil Rights movement, a period that will return later in this chapter. Without economic stability within the music industry, black artists were largely unable to make overt political statements during the 1960s. White artists like Bob Dylan, however, were able to speak from a more powerful position, taking strong stances during the volatile moment in American history (Garofalo 1992). An artist's ability to be outspoken is, in many ways, a direct function of her ability to maintain a position within the industry. The ease with which a record label can drop a performer for being controversial circumscribes the opportunity for protest. A superstar who is too valuable to lose or a performer who works outside of the mainstream industry, however, may enjoy a bit more maneuverability.

Schaefer goes on to note that "the most significant forebears of the 2010s" [the current period of musical activism] are not the stars of the past. Instead, he argues, "we must look to the early folk singers who also had smaller audiences and played 'off the radar'—artists from before the 1940s who were not classical and pan-Arab but popular and local during their lifetimes" (2015, 503–4). One of these, he notes, is Morocco's Houcine Slaoui.

Slaoui lived and performed during the first half of the 20th century, passing away in 1951 in his early 30s. His short career left a mark on the sound of Moroccan popular music, informed the role of musicians within social life, and contributed to the tension between local, national, and cosmopolitan influences in popular song for the generations that followed. His career began in city squares. Semi-professional and professional musicians continue to set up and perform in market spaces today, where audiences will form circles (singular: halqa) around them, watching and giving money. These street performances can be lucrative enough to live on for the most entertaining of artists and the live music requires performers to be quick-witted, often improvising jokes and stories within and alongside their singing. They have also been an important inspiration for other kinds of Moroccan theater and music (Amine and Carlson 2012). Not unlike the major Egyptian artists mentioned in Chapter 2, Slaoui's fame spread through recording and the radio. He traveled to Paris after label executives noticed him and his 20s and 30s involved touring widely, both nationally and across North Africa.

His music was innovative and foundational for a handful of reasons. He was one of the first to incorporate classical instruments into a popular song tradition by playing 'ud, primarily, within the halqa. Aside from recording, he also welcomed new technologies in the shape of western instruments like the accordion (Fuson n.d., Karl 2012). In songs like "El Mirikan" (The American), Slaoui uses humor to deride both incoming American soldiers who, during a 1942 operation against the German military, were bringing foreign influences into Morocco, and his own compatriots' eager acceptance of new influences. Jamila Bargach's persuasive translation and analysis of the song (1999) place it as a subversive and ironic twist on both Andalusian musical norms (the song is organized as if it were from the Andalusian tradition) and social perspectives on the colonial experience. The refrain, adapted here from Bargach's translation (1999, 62-3)[3] show the narrator's despair when reflecting on his degraded society:

Zin wa al-ʿain zarqa jana bkul khir
Al-yum yimshiwu bil-firqa al-bnat nafkhin
Shhal man hi maʿshuqa daru l-ha al-shan
Al-mirikan
Tsmaʿ ghir okay, okay, hada ma kan

Blue-eyed and beautiful, they brought all kinds of bounties.
Girls today walk in packs, arrogant.
How many loved ones [lovers, likely sarcastic] are made to feel self-important.
Those Americans!
All you hear is "Okay, okay." This is what happened.

While the sexist lyrics decry Moroccan women—both young and old—for debauchery and consumerism when faced with the blue-eyed beauty of the Americans, Bargach argues that Slaoui's words come from a place of deep irony, like so many of the other characters that dot his repertoire. Instead of an overly simplistic rant against opportunistic women, the song forces Moroccan society to confront its own relationship to the French. Later lines describe how these Americans distribute candy and give out dollars, a metaphor for how the French "protectorate" infantilizes Morocco and Moroccans. The narrator laments his own lack of value, saying that his words are meaningless against growing consumerism. Taken this way, the song fits into Houcine Slaoui's support of a national movement during the colonial period while also setting a standard for ironically subjecting traditional Moroccan musical genres to subtle forms of social and political protest.

One famed group that came to prominence during the next generation was Nass El Ghiwane. During the 1970s, Nass El Ghiwane took diverse regional music from across Morocco and successfully turned it into what could arguably be the country's first "popular" music (Simour 2016). Their subtle protests against an oppressive and closed government during the second half of the 20th century also landed them firmly within a budding and outspoken counterculture.

The group's various members lived in a poor neighborhood of Casablanca. They each came from families that saw different parts of the country as "home." Casablanca was a growing city, full of economic opportunity. It drew workers and families from the north, the south, and the mountains and deserts of the interior. Urbanization was connecting previously isolated regions, or at least that was the case for citizens from afar who settled into new communities after leaving the towns where their families had been for generations.

In some ways, the members of Nass El Ghiwane effectively represent the range of musical styles that dot the national landscape. That this band was the first to bring those styles together to create something new is notable. The germination for the group that would continue performing for decades (and still headlines gigs today, like the one that opened this chapter) came out of an amateur theater group in the 1960s. During this time, they learned about Morocco's poetic and artistic traditions. This "heritage" was a part of history, but it was a folkloric version of that history, not something that was actively present within the artistic movements and popular culture of the day (Dernouny and Zoulef 1980, 5).

The four founding members, each of whom were a part of the popular theater community, were Larbi Batma, Boujemaa Ahgour, Allal Yaala, and Omar Sayed. Yaala was an 'ud player who adapted his knowledge of the Andalusian tradition to the banjo, an instrument that was both louder and easier to maintain on stage. He came from an artistic family, having grown up in the country's south with a father who led a group that played music from the area. Abd El-Aziz Tahiri joined the group in the early 1970s on the hajhuj, a gnawa instrument described in Chapter 4. After he left to join a different band, Nass El Ghiwane eventually added Abderrahman Kirouj, known as "Paco." Paco came from Essaouira where he was a master gnawa musician and his presence brought that spiritual tradition's influence into the band's sound. One of their albums, *Chants Gnawa du Maroc* (Nass El Ghiwane 2009), exemplifies the ways in which the band brings regional sacred music styles into a popular music aesthetic. There are no guitars and drum sets, as might be expected with a group that was so heavily influenced by the global pop styles of the 1960s and 70s, but the revolutionary attitude, styles of dress, and stage presence come through in their live recordings. *Chants Gnawa*, furthermore, adopted sacred songs and instruments, but not with the intention of creating faithful renditions. They blend in their own instruments—mostly hand drums and Yaala's banjo—to create an aesthetic that matches that of their other major hits.

Nass El Ghiwane eventually became known worldwide after they were featured in a documentary film called Trances, released in 1981. It won prizes in Rabat and internationally and a restored version caught the attention of famed American film director Martin Scorsese, who referred to the band as Morocco's Rolling Stones, referencing the 1960s-era British rock group (Sayed 2011).

Some of Nass El Ghiwane's most famous songs demonstrate their subtle push back against the oppressions of Morocco's "Years of Lead." They speak to the celebration of tradition that coincides with a concern for the struggles of contemporary reality, especially as experienced by the poor. One of their most famous songs, "Essiniya," laments changing society through a metaphor of gathering around tea, a central ritual within everyday Moroccan life. By asking where the beautiful clothing, companionship, and the neighborhood community of the past has gone, the song mourns the additions and pained bitterness of its day (see Figure 3.1).

"Fin Ghadi Biyya Khuya" similarly questions the present by remembering the past. The title translates to "Where are you taking us, brother?" It questions leadership, though it does not point to the government by name. The repetition of the phrase with a simple melody makes the song an easy one to sing along to, and therefore it became an effective force within live performances. Successive lines ask for forgiveness, or at least understanding, as the singer claims that he has not forgotten his past, his tradition, despite his

Figure 3.1 Omar Sayed and a member of a gnawa ensemble (see Chapter 4) stand on stage during a Nass El Ghiwane concert in Fez in 2011.

steps away from it (and their catastrophic results). Some representative lyrics show this pain and longing:

Fin ghadi biyya khuya? Fin ghadi biyya?
Daqqa tab'a daqqa, shkun yahad al-bas?

Where are you taking us, brother? Where are you taking us?
Moment after moment, who can end the misery?

The song continues as the band claims to remember the bendir (a type of frame drum) and the qasba (a flute). They have not forgotten the celebrations and running horses that bring their Moroccan brothers and sisters out into the street during the summer. Moreover, they declare that they remember their people, their family, while they lament how their current lives have become catastrophe.

"Mahmuma," another one of the many songs that are still widely recognized today, speaks more directly to the conditions of life. The title, which means "troubled" or "oppressed," alludes to the lyrical content. The refrain, also quite repetitive and therefore singable conveys the message in no uncertain terms:

Mahmuma ya khay mahmuma
Mahmuma had al-duniyya mahmuma

Troubled, my brother, troubled
Troubled, this world is troubled

The verses go on to explain the struggles of the people, again in metaphorical terms. Nothing particularly specific implicates the current government, but the implications are strong enough to have led to the police knocking on the group members' doors multiple times over the course of their careers. They sing that the people's souls are becoming controlled just as they are blamed for the world's problems. They become slaves. Special attention goes to the poor, who swim in pools of depression.

These are not "cherry-picked" examples. To the contrary, these metaphoric themes of lament and unrest thread through much of Nass El Ghiwane's music. That the songs continue to resonate, even as the band stands on the country's biggest stages, sponsored by the very government that they once resisted, highlights the continued relevance of their message. It also shows that the memory of this band, like the Rolling Stones that they are so often compared to, is powerful within the music industry. Some members have passed away and relatives have taken over in key spots. Omar Sayed, one of the founding singers and songwriters, continues to perform, leading the band in concerts like the one in Casablanca that opened the chapter. A new generation has picked up on their ideals to use music to push back against what they see as more contemporary forms of injustice. The "Years of Lead" are over, but that does not mean that musicians have stopped resisting.

One of the keys to understanding the role of protest music within Morocco involves the relationship between religion, politics, and social life. As is the case around the world, a value-based worldview drives much political activity and feelings of injustice can give rise to unrest. In religiously conservative areas, whether in the Islamic Middle East or the Christian world, power and piety can coincide to present an equally moral high ground for the status quo. Religion, whether conservative or liberal in ideology, can play a role on both sides of political and social debates. This chapter will close with some examples of how this plays out within contemporary (post-Arab Spring) hip hop, but it first explores this relationship between piety and protest a little closer as it exists in Morocco.

Islam holds a non-hierarchical structure at its core: all are equal in the eyes of God. Any practicing Muslim can stand and lead prayers at the mosque. The term imam, a "leader," in fact means "in front of" and is related to terms for maturity and cleanliness: it's not a signifier of training, class, or bestowed title. It just references the person who stands in front of the others, reciting aloud. To contrast this with Catholicism, for example, a priest requires a great deal of training. Even deacons (who also have dedicated their lives to their vocation) cannot carry out some of the duties that are reserved for the priest, like the consecration of the bread and wine into Jesus Christ's body and blood. The divides are clear and there are many of them. Some are gendered (women cannot become priests), while others are vocational (laypeople cannot carry out sacraments like marriage or baptism).

Within Islam, these lines don't exist, or at least they are not supposed to. There is no "pope," no singular religious authority. While this is supposed to lead to equality, it also allows for extreme views to go uncontested within specific communities. In Moroccan Sufism and elsewhere, charismatic or well-read leaders can gain significant followings. There are classes of religious scholars who have a strong influence on the discourses surrounding faith and piety. Economics come into play as certain individuals, companies, or entire countries can support their own readings of the religion. This is the case with Saudi Arabian investment in ideological schools and religious centers across the region. It is also, of course, a part of politics.

To make matters even more clear, Moroccan Islam has a specific political connection. The king himself is the "Commander of the Faithful," according to the country's constitution. Unlike the United States—but very much like other places around the world—religion and governance are not distinct, they are inherently linked together. Religious leadership comes from the king and, therefore, using religious values or a different reading of the Islamic faith as part of a protest carries an added connotation: it undermines the religious (and therefore political) authority of the king himself.[4] Listening to Nass El Ghiwane's calls for religious, social, and political leadership, then, shows why the band caught the attention of the government. Despite this threat to past artists, many continued to speak out against injustice. Nass El Ghiwane was not alone, and they spawned movements since.

Again, connecting religious piety to political protest is hardly unique to Morocco. Dr Martin Luther King Jr, a foremost leader within the American Civil Rights movement, was a Baptist preacher. Malcolm X, another Civil Rights leader, converted to Islam and was a part of the Nation of Islam, a political religious organization in the States at the time. One of the most extreme and notorious organizations to oppose that social movement, the Ku Klux Klan, was also (ostensibly) religious in nature, growing out of Protestant communities to oppose civil rights, Catholics, and Jews. Both laid claim to proper religious (and, in most cases, Christian) values. What those values were, however, were quite different.

In connecting religion and politics so clearly, the Moroccan constitution raises the stakes of protest. Unlike that moment in American history—a moment that continues to resonate—Moroccan artists protesting the status quo often run up against a united political and religious front. But values are still individual, or at least social, and singing them maintains a certain power to enact change.

A New Generation of Protest

The music of protest in Morocco has found a common thread with that of America and elsewhere throughout the globe. Since the 1990s, hip hop has become something of a lingua franca for outspoken critique; it provides a voice and an avenue for powerful reflection on economic inequality, social ills, racial injustice, and politics. But, as described by Marcyliena Morgan and Dionne Bennett, it can both serve this form of protest and build up new community ideals (2011). This was the case well before the "Arab Spring" movements that spread across North Africa in 2011, but, as these scholars (and many within journalism) describe, hip hop crystallized a narrative to go along with these political uprisings.

The protests that were soon enshrined under the name "The Arab Spring" began in Tunisia, and hip hop was right there with them. A Tunisian rapper by the name of El Général, who had earlier been banned from the radio by the government, released a new song to YouTube in 2010 called "Rais Lebled" (Head of State). It went viral. Shortly after this, in December of 2010, Muhammad Bouazizi, a small-time street vender, burned himself alive. Local officials regularly confiscated the food that he was selling, but without recourse to any other job opportunities, he continued to buy and sell food from his cart. As described by Time Magazine reporter Rania Abouzeid (2011), this harassment eventually led him to desperation and a public suicide, in protest:

> But on Dec. 17 his livelihood was threatened when a policewoman confiscated his unlicensed vegetable cart and its goods. [...] Not satisfied with accepting the 10-dinar fine that Bouazizi tried to pay [...], the policewoman allegedly slapped the scrawny young man, spat in his face and insulted his dead father.
>
> Humiliated and dejected, Bouazizi, the breadwinner for his family of eight, went to the provincial headquarters, hoping to complain to local municipality officials, but they refused to see him. [... Bouazizi] poured fuel over himself and set himself on fire. He did not die right away but lingered in the hospital till Jan. 4.

The suicide sparked massive protests in Tunisia. Within 10 days of Bouazizi's death, Tunisia's leader, Ben Ali, ended his 23-year rule of the country. This movement eventually spread across the region and resulted in Hosni Mubarak, the long-standing president of Egypt, stepping down. It also played a major role in bringing about civil war in Syria. But the speed with which it toppled Tunisia's president, the "Head of State" referenced in El Général's song, was the first signal of the movement's power.

El Général, a rapper who had long idolized Tupac Shakur, had written prophetic words just before the uprisings. As described in another article from this historic moment, lyrics within "Rais Lebled" include:

> *Mr. President, your people are dying*
> *People are eating rubbish*
> *Look at what is happening*
> *Miseries everywhere Mr. President*
> *I talk with no fear*
> *Although I know I will only get troubles*
> *I see injustice everywhere*

He was right; troubles followed quickly. According to the rapper, "After that my mobile phone was tapped and my Facebook account was blocked" (Walt 2011). Shortly afterward, however, he wrote a new song celebrating the growing protests, and within a few short months he was able to perform a concert commemorating the president's removal from office (Thuburn and Mouelhi 2011). His music spread to Egypt, where it inspired similar artists (Morgan and Bennett 2011, 178). Tunisia, located in the middle of North Africa, just south of Italy, was instigating dramatic movements elsewhere. Morocco's artists were listening, the government was watching, and the country was responding.

Hip hop in Morocco, especially before this revolutionary moment in neighboring Tunisia, played a different role; at least, of course, the hip hop that was featured in a centralized media system did. Many artists took advantage of opportunities provided by the government to act as a form of "soft power," a type of cultural activism that supported institutional narratives of patriotism and pride. These bled into narratives of development and faith as the king, the nation, and religion were consolidated as one ideal sense of "Moroccan-ness." Two groups whose work appears throughout the scholarly literature on Morocco's hip hop scene serve as examples: Fnaïre and H-Kayne.

Christina Moreno Almeida describes how Fnaïre, a group that got together in Marrakech in the early 2000s—a decade before the Arab Spring—labeled themselves with the term taqlidi rap, "traditional" rap (Moreno Almeida 2016, 116). In their biography,[5] the group (or their marketing directors) place them directly within a lineage of Nass El Ghiwane by stating that they are "often compared to" the famous ensemble. That the three came together through hip hop to create a group during a moment of success for fusion bands in Morocco may be part of the cause for this claim. Many groups from major cities across the country were combining rock, funk, alternative, and jazz groups with various Moroccan genres during the early 2000s and many were gaining traction with local audiences (see Callen 2006). Some were touring Europe and finding other work internationally, as well.

Fnaïre's use of "tradition" (the "taqlid" of taqlidi rap) comes largely through the sound of the backing musical production, though some tunes are more overt in their nationalism and patriotism. For example, after the Casablanca bombings described at the end of Chapter 2, Fnaïre released a song that coincided with those anti-terrorism posters that I had seen around town: "Matkiche Bladi" (Don't Touch my Country).[6] The video begins with a spinning 33⅓ record whose label matches the Hand of Fatima from the signs. In it, the three rappers perform in Marrakech, criticizing the acts of violence as "haram," forbidden within Islam. Kids, older men, and veiled women each hold their hand up, pushing back, refusing these acts. The underlying music features a hip hop beat, but the sample includes both a lotar (a string instrument from the country's interior) and a synthesizer performing the melodic material. Other songs carry a similar strategy: "Attarikh" samples Andalusian music (see Chapter 1), while "Mogador" sings with pride of the gnawa music that permeates that city, now known as Essaouira (see Chapter 4).

H-Kayne, a group whose name roughly translates to "What happened?" or "What is this?," made their mark with an early hit called "Issawa Style" (2006). As Moreno Almeida (2016) notes, the song promotes a specific local religious brotherhood called the ʿissawa (see Part III) by both singing about the group, wearing traditional ʿissawi dress, and performing with a brotherhood. The group is from Meknes, one of the most important cities for the ʿissawa brotherhood. By emphasizing this group and its link to Moroccan identity, the band is similarly codifying a specific type of nationalism, one that aligns closely with the goals of the government. Just as support for global variants of Islamic faith can serve as a protest against the king (who is, after all, the "Commander of the Faithful") promoting local ones can be read as a form of support. In a time when Islamist political parties were carrying out these very strategies—criticizing local forms of Islamic practice as a proxy for the current government—this music for youth reinforced the royal ideology.

Hip hop is rarely so straightforward, however. H-Kayne has caught the attention of a number of scholars. One of these, Aomar Boum, is an anthropologist who reflected on the group's lyrics during a pair of concerts he saw in 2004. The second of these concerts was in Ifrane, a city in the mountains that is home to an English language private university that educates many middle-class and upper-class students. He writes:

> I wondered how the student population, largely from the middle and upper class, would respond […] H-Kayne not only protests the economic inequalities

in the country, but sometimes attributes their misfortunes to the parents of these students, some of whom are key decision-makers in the government.
(Boum 2012, 162–3)

Boum cites the lyrics of the song "Fil-Houma" (In the Neighborhood) to demonstrate how H-Kayne aligns themselves with a narrative of protest, calling out injustice. Houma, a term for neighborhood, might be better understood here as "the hood" in the sense of "ghetto," as it appears in so much American hip hop. This space of poverty, along with the hopelessness that leads to crime and addiction, comes through in the song. Adapted from his translation (Boum 2012, 163):

> *I'll tell you what's up: in the 'hood you see everything*
> *There are those who are unemployed and those who struggle to make ends meet*
> *It wears at us and the people of the neighborhood*
> *Our life is misery, addiction becomes a coma*
> *Nass El Ghiwane said it, brother: troubled*

The last line's reference to Nass El Ghiwane cites one of the songs from earlier in the chapter. H-Kayne, like many other hip hop groups (some of which Boum introduces and translates in this same article) connects themselves to a larger political and social struggle by quoting Nass El Ghiwane's poetic lyrics. In this case, a simple mention of the band's name and the title of the song "Mahmuma" is enough to make the link explicit.

Groups like H-Kayne—and there is a growing number of hip hop crews across the country—embody a form of protest that orients them within Moroccan history through connections to Nass El Ghiwane and concerns about social and economic inequality. They also celebrate their country, homeland, tradition, and fellow Moroccans, as seen in "'Issawa Style." Lest this sounds too binary, Kendra Salois describes a performance in Meknes where H-Kayne "hides a teach-in on public protests in plain sight." They demonstrate a gesture depicting handcuffs by crossing their arms at the wrist, high above their heads. Whereas a single person doing this "would mean little, a sea of people raising their arms in the same gesture electrifies everyone at the sight of their combined strength" (Salois 2014, 1039).

The difficulty comes in navigating a delicate balance. Outspoken lyrics that stray too far may limit a band's opportunities in the music festivals and on national television, two things that are important for finding and expanding audiences. Adhering too closely to the aims of the government may draw criticisms from other artists. Christina Moreno Almeida gives an example from another Moroccan rapper, Mobydick (known as Lmoutchou). In his 2011 song "Checkmate," he sings "Fuck patriotic rap." As she writes: "Between humorous lines in the song are direct attacks on rappers like Fnaïre, H-Kayne and Don Bigg whose lyrics avoid any meaningful criticism of the country's political elite, Moroccan authorities, or official institutions" (2017, 95).

Despite these narrow threads of opportunity that activist artists have, it's difficult to overstate the change since the "Years of Lead." Elder Moroccans listening to musicians openly criticizing the workings of government (even if they may avoid mentioning the king directly) might feel a shudder of shock, or perhaps a tinge of offense. Nation, religion, and king are so closely intertwined in Morocco that these statements of protest require either an extraordinary degree of nuance or an extreme disregard for convention. Anything else might fall on deaf ears. In a way, I am reminded of how "patriotism" gets used in a polarized America: what one side counts as an act of loyalty to what the country can and should be, the other sees as a degrading slap in the face of the nation's ideals. Pride is in the eye of the beholder.

The religious ties that have been a part of political protest since Moroccan kingdoms held Andalusia continued into, through, and after the colonial period. A failure to repel European non-believers held sway as a powerful testament toward a government's alleged failures and, therefore, as a compelling reason for people to change their allegiances and side with a revolt. The bourgeois religious leadership in and around the government often worried that the sultan or king (depending on the era) was ignoring the spiritual health of his subjects, again inspiring critique. Shrewd leaders throughout these decades knew how to cultivate a sense of moral authority, using it to inspire loyalty. In this way, it's not surprising that musicians, even the most activist ones, developed a similar sense of nuance when speaking out. They, like their government, knew and respected their own lineages of faith and morality.

Notes

1 These comments are from a video of the song "Fin Ghadi Biya Khuya" that is available at www.youtube.com/watch?v=xYeMZqZSA1o.
2 Malika Oufkir tells her family's story in her memoir, *Stolen Lives* (Oufkir and Fitoussi 1999).
3 Thank you to Hicham Chami for sharing his own translation of the song, parts of which are reflected here as well.
4 This political relationship has been a common subject of study for anthropologists and political scientists. See, for example, Abdellah Hammoudi's *Master and Disciple* (1997) and Henry Munson Jr's *Religion and Power in Morocco* (1993) for more.
5 Available at: www.fnairemusic.com/fna%C3%AFre/biographie.
6 The Resources section has links to playlists that include the videos described here.

CHAPTER 4

Gnawa Music and Ritual

The Jamaaʿ al-Fanaʾ is an open marketplace that serves as both an entrance and a focal point for Marrakech's old city, its medina. Swarms of tourists arrive by bus and taxi, they walk past gardens, horse-drawn carriages, and enter into the square. In the morning, when so many tourists are up and exploring the city's markets, the square is full of snake-charmers and women who will cover your hands with henna. Later, musicians of a different type—groups of men dancing and playing iron castanets—overtake sections of the space. As dusk falls, food stalls fill the area in neat tight rows. Crowds form circles—some large, some small—around storytellers, more musicians, acrobats, children's games, and other entertainments. These circles of crowds, called halqas, are illuminated by small lanterns or motorcycle headlights, among other things. Moroccan and foreign families, teens, and young children cycle between the smoky smells of the makeshift kitchens on one side and the wide range of entertainments on the other.

I had visited Jamaaʿ al-Fanaʾ many times. It's a first stop for tourists visiting the city. But in May of 2011, I had a more specific purpose. I had been studying gnawa music for a few years, but made most of my efforts in Fez, a city far north of Marrakech. It was time for me to make a more concerted effort to learn about gnawa musicians in what so many people viewed as the tradition's central city. Marrakech was a major stop on the slave trade route, making it a landing point for many gnawa as they were brought to Morocco from West Africa in previous centuries. This is a population whose history of marginalization weaves through its ritual music.

So I arrived and, after joining a colleague for a coffee on the square and noticing the return of the bustle after a recent terrorist attack in the Jamaaʿ al-Fanaʾ that rocked the country's news and politics,[1] I walked toward one of the groups of young men who were singing and dancing in the mid-afternoon. Rachid saw me and, as is the standard practice for these groups, he came toward me, sang, danced, and held his hat out for a tip. I told him that I was interested in learning more about the gnawa in his city. After some yelling back and forth over the loud cacophony that defines the square, he invited me to join his group for a ceremony the next day.

I met his group early the next morning. They were loading a pair of grand taxis—old Mercedes-Benz sedans that serve as inexpensive transportation between major cities—with their drums, amps, and gear for the ritual. We packed in, four stuffed into the back seat and two jammed into the passenger seat as is the norm for these car trips, and made our way to the mountains outside of the city. We were headed to Mulay Brahim, a pilgrimage site during other times of the year that, this weekend, was empty despite the beauty of the views.

After watching members of the group tie a large tarp over the courtyard of the hotel that we were going to be using for the night (it was threatening to rain) and just generally hanging around for a few hours drinking tea and chatting with the younger members of the ensemble while waiting for things to get going, we were all called downstairs for the sacrifice. The youngest member of the group, a boy roughly ten years old who was apprenticing, held one of three goats by the horns. M'allem Abd al-Kebir Merchane, the elder leader of this ensemble, lit a burner of incense in the middle of the room and gathered bottles of blessed rosewater. Members of the group stood in a circle and began to recite prayers. Hicham, the m'allem's son who directed the ensemble for stretches of time later in the evening, grabbed one of the three goats, flipped it over, and held it down while his father cut its throat in two quick strokes as directed by halal rites.[2] They repeated this with the other two goats while a small crowd of friends and family looked on, some through the screens on their phones as they recorded. The women chanted short prayers, M'allem Abd al-Kebir Merchane circled the room, spraying rosewater on the dying animals and on us as we watched. Hicham and his father took turns rhythmically blessing the hosts, the ensemble, the guests (including me), the sky, the land, the nation, the gnawa, thanking Allah, thanking the Prophet Muhammad, and so on. The group's chanted prayers punctuated these improvised blessings as the sacrifices continued with chickens and the m'allem prepared the rest of the coming evening's ritual paraphernalia needs.

The gnawa are an historically marginalized population within Morocco's religious sphere. But they are an important minority, one whose music has gone from heretical to symbolic of the nation itself. The story of the gnawa begins with the history of Morocco's slave trade. West Africans who were brought to the country maintained elements of their previous beliefs and fused them with local Islamic practices. This combination took the form of an all-night ritual healing ceremony that used music to invoke spirit possessions among listeners.

These practices were far outside of the bounds of "normal" Islam in Morocco, which led to the population's marginalized status. Racism and claims of religious heresy forced the gnawa to keep their rituals secretive, lending them a mysterious reputation. Their power over the spirit world, and their ability to heal those who could not find relief from the country's doctors and hospitals made them famous, or at least infamous. Over time, especially since Morocco's independence, gnawa musicians increasingly performed in public. First, this happened in spaces like Marrakech's Jamaa' al-Fana', where the open market could lead to new ritual clients or tips from intrigued tourists, Moroccans and foreigners alike. Later, these openings led to opportunities within the world of popular music, staged festivals, and musical fusion projects.

The music's grooves burst from its clandestine roots and now appears at the country's largest venues alongside hip hop, in collaboration with major international jazz artists like Wayne Shorter, and in trendy Brooklyn bars. Not only has the music of the gnawa ritual become a hit in its own right, the spiritual side of the tradition will reappear as an influential part of other local religious traditions in Part III. In this chapter, we move from this history of slavery into the ritual's spiritual and musical context. We then explore how these sounds became so dramatically popular by returning to some artists that we met earlier, before listening to more recent projects that bring the music of the gnawa ritual into conversation with more contemporary styles.

Slave Trade History

The Sahara is a sea of sand, one that is nearly as impassable as an ocean. This did not prevent ample trade routes between North Africa and areas of the continent south of the desert, however, and caravans of camels have been trading between West Africa and what is now Morocco for centuries. While parts of Europe were fighting the Crusades around 1000 CE, the Moroccan empire of the time, the Almoravids, were consolidating trade routes to the south by extending their kingdoms into parts of contemporary Mali, Mauritania, and Senegal (M'bokolo 1998). This increased trade in gold, salt, and slaves between major cities like Timbuktu in the south and Sijilmasa in southeastern Morocco. From there, they could be brought further north to the Mediterranean and sent elsewhere or brought to Marrakech, a nearby hub and the capital of the Almoravid dynasty.

Many of the slaves who were brought to Morocco were used as domestic servants or concubines. Male slaves had various other duties. Many were farmers, though Mulay Ismail, an early sultan in the Alaouite dynasty (and an ancestor of the current king) who ruled from the late 1600s to the early 1700s used slaves to form the "Black Guard," an army of slaves. This type of proximity to power mirrored the use of slaves in other Middle Eastern countries, like the Janissary military in Turkey or the Mamluks, who were purchased slaves primarily from Turkey and southeastern Europe and who rose to rule Egypt from the 13th to 16th centuries.

The West African men and women who were brought to Morocco through the slave trade did not forget their beliefs, languages, and cultural practices during the trans-Saharan voyage. Instead, these vestiges of their previous lives—and for children, those memories of their parents and grandparents—became important markers of identity and community. While many incoming slaves were Muslim, others converted after they arrived and maintained previous beliefs by combining them with Islamic practices. This led to "Afro-Islamic" rituals like those of the gnawa that reflect similar processes in the New World. Santeria in Cuba (Hagedorn 2001), voodoo in Haiti (Largey 2006), and Condomble in Brazil (Matory 2005) are all examples of "Afro-Catholic" religious practices that grew out of African slaves converting after their arrival in South America and the Caribbean. These traditions carry musical, spiritual, and linguistic symbols of each community's past, but they do so in a way that is vague and difficult to pull apart. This is, in part, due to the fact that communities of slaves are rarely all from the same region. They are brought together as shipments, they are purchased "goods," moved from place to place as necessitated by markets. These mixed communities often find meaning within their commonalities, and after generations of slavery, rare reminders of a specific past become even more blurred as the new manifestations of community, the rituals that are "native" to the new world, grow in importance.

These same processes are at play in the trans-Saharan slave trade as communities like the gnawa struggle for new identities. West Africa was—and still is—home to a diverse collection of ethnicities. Communities like the Fula, Bambara, and Songhay not only spoke different languages, they featured a range of governmental structures, political conflicts, religious differences, and languages. Much like what happened in early American slavery (Epstein 1977) or in the Afro-Catholic traditions mentioned above, new practices emerged in Morocco that bore relationships to many of these cultural memories.

In the gnawa ritual, the past continued through musical style and the spirits themselves, which we will return to in more detail below. Lyrics also maintained this history in powerfully symbolic ways. My primary teacher, M'allem Abd al-Rzaq from the city of Fez, once told me a story about a concert that he played in West Africa. He performed one of the songs that opens the ritual ceremony, called "Vangara Vangara." In it, the singer and ritual leader calls out to these ethnic groups, remembering them as central to gnawa identity. "Ah Fulani," he sings, referencing the Fula, a region of West Africa that stretches across northern Nigeria and Niger. "Vangara Vangara," responds the members of his ensemble. "Ah Hawsawi," he continues, singing to Hausa ancestors from the same general region. "Vangara Vangara … ." Abd al-Rzaq was in West Africa singing directly to an audience comprised of some of these ethnicities, not just metaphorically referencing a communal memory from before the time of slavery during a ritual in Morocco. This moment was even more surprising for him, though. These songs often contain words (like "Vangara") that are not Arabic. They come from this distant time and place and are carried through the gnawa ritual as a reminder of who the gnawa were and are. But his crowd could understand the words that he was singing. The experience made this history of slavery and displacement even more real for my teacher.

Despite the placement of some within royal palaces, most slave communities remained in urban poverty well after slavery itself was officially abolished in 1925. Racism and marginalization continued and still exists today in various guises. In 1970, one scholar described sub-Saharans in Morocco by saying that they "might be reasonably termed a scheduled caste," referencing India's strict social system and referring to prohibitions in marriage between black Africans and white Arabs (Grame 1970, 79). The binaries of race described in Chapter 3 regarding the country's Amazigh population are equally present—or perhaps even more so—between "white" Arabs and "black" Africans. While Morocco is on the African continent, the "sea" that is the Sahara links the country's identity more closely with the Mediterranean, the Arab East, and, especially since the advent of colonialism, Europe. This distinction effectively makes the gnawa and other sub-Saharan communities outsiders, though processes like the popularization of gnawa music and the widening acceptability of their ritual practices, thanks in part to tourism markets and the music industry, are changing this reality for some. Commercial opportunities increasingly lead to exposure which has the effect of generating both interest in this minority's cultural products and a backlash against a religious practice that critics can easily decry as outside of proper Islamic belief, demonic, and therefore dangerous for the population.

Ceremony and Beliefs

The animal sacrifice that opened this chapter is a prelude to an evening ritual. It prepares the space, the host, the ensemble, and the spirits for the events that follow. That afternoon, some family and friends who had experience with preparing meat helped a few members of the ensemble to skin, drain, and butcher the animals. Other musicians returned to a balcony overlooking the small hotel's courtyard to rest and drink tea. Some napped, including Rachid, who had invited me, knowing that they would be awake all night long. One of the musicians collected the intestines from the goats, pulling them from a bucket, and twisted them into a tight strand. He tied them between two posts in the balcony so that they would dry. It was only the next morning that I realized what he was doing: he was making new strings for the hajhuj, the central string instrument within this tradition.

The ritual ceremony is comprised of three main sections, though one is substantially longer than the other two. Each section can differ across the country and the order of the three is not the same everywhere either. In Fez, where I spent most of my time, groups begin the ceremony outside, inviting neighbors and spirits. Then they move inside to bless and prepare the space while playing music that was both celebratory and entertaining. These two sections of the ceremony are preludes to the final part, which lasts through the night and into the next morning, where spirits take over the trancing bodies of listeners, healing them. Elsewhere, including in Mulay Brahim where this event took place, the first two sections are reversed. A long evening of entertainment ends before the ensemble, hosts, friends, and family gather their things and move outside to announce the event to the neighborhood.

The outdoor procession announces the presence of the gnawa to neighbors. Morocco's urban streets, especially those in the older medina sections of cities, wind through paths of tightly knit homes. Tall walls with few—if any—windows shield homes that may be small, divided between a number of impoverished families. They may also house palatial homes with wide-open courtyards, trees, gardens, and fountains. In either case, the sound of a gnawa group will travel up, around, over, and through these maze-like streets. It flows into courtyards and onto rooftop terraces. While they move through the neighborhood, crowds grow around the ensemble and hosts. Many in this crowd are invited, though it can occasionally grow to include men and teenagers who are drunk or smoking hashish, making it necessary for a family member to act as an informal bouncer when the crowd is re-entering the home. These are community events and, despite the history of this tradition and population's marginalization, people are curious. They want to see the trances, hear the music, and enjoy the social scene that coincides with the religious ritual of a gnawa lila.

The event is called a lila, a daraja word meaning "night," because it begins one evening, lasts through the night, and only ends after the sun rises the next morning. According to elders within the tradition, the lila used to extend across multiple evenings, each focusing on a different activity or set of spirits. More recently, however, the cost of these events has become prohibitive for hosts, many of whom are poor. Inviting guests into the home for a full evening involves more than just paying for the increasingly professional musicians. A host must feed guests meals—both dinner and breakfast—while providing tea and cookies, renting chairs, and working around government ordinances. In many cities, loud noises are regulated after a certain hour of the evening, just as bars must generally close by a specific time in most US cities. Hosts have to arrange for permits to have loud music beyond these hours and any engagement with the police can turn expensive because of both fees and, in some cases, bribes. As a result, not only are lila ceremonies confined to a single night now, hosts often choose to begin them after dinner instead of later at night. They shorten the event and conclude it at midnight or two in the morning. These shorter rituals are sufficient for many spirits, but the musicians may complain that they are rushed and, in a criticism of a younger generation of performers that we will return to below, they claim that the music is turning into a series of "hits." A well-worn collection of pieces become standard while so many others are forgotten.

There are three central roles for practitioners, those who carry out the gnawa ritual, whether a lila or the shorter ʿashiyya (a term meaning "evening" instead of the lila's "night"). The first is knows as a muqaddima. These roles are heavily gendered; while there are counter-examples, almost all muqaddimas are women. The other two roles, both musicians, are almost exclusively men. The muqaddima prepares the event. When someone needs to host a ceremony, either because of a new illness or in an effort to maintain a positive relationship with a possessing spirit, the family hires a muqaddima. Many muqaddimas have exceptionally powerful relationships with the spirits, which aides them in their efforts to foster a productive ritual. But they have practical duties as well: the muqaddima brings a whole range of goods to the ceremony, including a bag of brightly colored cloth and clothing that she will use to help incite trance for those who become possessed. She also arranges for all of the other necessary services, acting, in a way, like an event planner.

Aside from arranging for food and service, she hires the mʿallem, the ensemble leader who will provide the music that animates the ceremony. The mʿallem, in turn, hires drari, a word that literally refers to dependents, and is generally used for children. The drari are ensemble members. Some are professionals who work for a number of mʿallems. Others are learning: they are apprentices making their way through their training by working closely with a teacher.

During the dakhla procession and, in some regions of the country, other moments of the ritual, the mʿallem and one of the drari play a drum, called a tbal, that is slung over the shoulder with a strap like an older-styled marching drum. Using two sticks, one curved and one straight, the accompanist plays a consistent pattern on his tbal while the mʿallem improvises rhythms on the other. The two increase their energy, intensity, and speed while the rest of the drari beat out another rhythm on iron castanets called quraqeb. These instruments are made of two flat barbell-shaped pieces of metal that are fashioned together at the bottom using a metal ring or strap of leather. A player holds one set in each hand and alternates clapping them together to play a series of loud notes. During the dakhla, these contribute to the loud atmosphere of the street. Once the group moves inside, however, the quraqeb echo through the house in a way that you can feel reverberating through your body (see Figures 4.1 and 4.2).

As the crowd grows around the procession, the ensemble will occasionally stop to perform. Sometimes these can span a great deal of space, but often, the procession will extend only from the nearest corner to the entrance of the home. When the drari extend into a straight line, the mʿallem and another tbal player will increase their speed and build rhythmic complexity. The rest of the group dances while assistants or family members hold large candles that have been blessed. The host, if the event is off to an auspicious start, will fall into a trance, writhing until the possessing spirit fully takes hold. Once the spirit is finished, having overtaken the host's body and danced, the intensity drops, the music will stop, and the mʿallem will chant a series of blessings, the crowd shares in dates and milk that have been blessed, and everyone enters the home.

Figure 4.1 M'allem Abd al-Rzaq and his brother Hamid each playing a tbal during a procession in Sidi Ali.

Figure 4.2 Members of a gnawa group parading during a procession and playing quraqeb to open a major music festival in Essaouira.

Inside the home, whether before or after the dakhla procession, the gnawa ensemble has two roles before the ceremony can fully begin. First, they must prepare the ritual space, blessing and purifying it for the events to come. Second, they entertain the crowd in a way that both celebrates gnawa history and welcomes the spirits. While there are a few institutionalized spaces dotting the country, the most prominent of which is in the coastal town of Essaouira, the gnawa are unlike other religious traditions in Morocco in that they rarely enjoy access to a centralized building like a mosque or zawiya. Because every neighborhood has a mosque, though some are quite small, men and women have a place to go to pray together. Most other Sufi traditions have a zawiya, a lodge of sorts, in major cities. The gnawa's history of marginalization has kept the lila ritual more clandestine. It happens in homes, in the same rooms where families gather to eat meals, watch television, and welcome friends. Therefore, the space needs to be protected from inappropriate spirits who may be there already and sacralized for the desired spirits who will possess and heal trancing bodies.

For wealthy families, homes may have a courtyard with lemon or orange trees and a fountain. For others, this all happens in a family room. In either case, Moroccan homes are usually tiled, both on the walls and the floors. Long couches with large pillows encircle the room and, when hosts expect many guests, there may be rented chairs filling the middle of the room. The ensemble sits on a carpet on the floor, leaning back against one wall. The mʿallem or muqaddima prepare incense for the evening, placing different varieties into small bowls in front of the musicians. Next to these sits a burner, often a terracotta or ceramic pot filled with lit charcoal. Other necessities not central to the ritual like small glasses of coffee, cigarettes or thin pipes, cellphones, and other things are also scattered around the carpet.

While part of this blessing of the space involves similar dances to what happens outside, for much of it the mʿallem puts down the tbal and picks up the tradition's central instrument. Variously called a ginbri, hajhuj, or a sintir, this string instrument sounds like a string bass but works like an old-time clawhammer banjo. It features a rectangular hollowed-out wooden body covered by an animal skin. In expensive instruments, this might be from the neck of a camel, on instruments that appear in tourist marketplaces, it may be made of goat. A long dowel extends from the base of the instrument through the far end, making a neck that works like that of a guitar. A major difference, however, is that where a guitar's neck is flat and covered in frets, this is rounded. Leather straps or tuners drilled through the far end of the neck hold strings that stretch along the instrument, over a wooden bridge, and are tied to the far end of the long stick (see Figure 4.3). Newer players use nylon for these strings—they tune more easily and have a clear tone—but in rituals, gut strings remain the norm. After the sacrifice that opened this chapter, one of the ensemble members who was twisting and stretching the blessed goat's intestines across a balcony, leaving them in the sun to dry, was making new strings for a future event.

After a series of blessings, songs, and dances that enact the gnawa community's history of slavery in Morocco, the living room or courtyard has effectively transformed into a sacred space. Following a short break, with time for a smoke while hosts pass tea and cookies around the room, the musicians begin singing to invite the first of the mluk. In Morocco, and within Islam more generally, there are a variety of types of spirits. Just the Christian Bible recognizes angels who deliver messages and fight wars or demons who take control of children, just as there is both a God and a Satan, the Quran

Figure 4.3 M'allem Allal Soudani playing the hajhuj and leading the ritual through the music for Sidi Musa and the blue spirits at the Zawiya Sidna Bilal in the city of Essaouira.

references the presence of spirits who are both holy and unholy, of a clear God (Allah) and Satan (Shaytan). The question of who and what these mluk are, these spirits who join the gnawa ceremony, is central to whether this tradition is an appropriate practice within Islam or a heretical ceremony that invites evil into the body.

The term mluk itself means "owners." The king of Morocco is the "malik"; he reigns over the land and its subjects. Similarly, the mluk have ownership over the bodies that they possess. This is not an exorcism to eject evil spirits but a ritual that builds a lasting bond with a figure or repairs a broken (or neglected) relationship between the seen and unseen worlds. Someone who is possessed by one of these spirits is "maskun," a term that helps to define this relationship. Maskun is an adjective that roughly means "occupied," like an apartment that has a tenant. Once a spirit overtakes a body for the first time, whether within a ritual or within everyday life, the person must attend to this lasting bond. The process necessitates attending or hosting ceremonies to allow the spirit to overtake the body, to dance, and to receive sacrifices, like the goats that opened the chapter.

Possession can be sudden or happen slowly over time. In her book on gnawa music, researcher Deborah Kapchan describes her growing relationship with Sidi Mimun, one of the spirits who began appearing in her dreams (Kapchan 2007). During one of the first events I attended, I was sitting next to a teenager who had fallen asleep in a metal folding chair. It was the middle of the night and the music had been playing for hours. Women and children were napping on couches along the walls, so his short break from wakefulness was hardly conspicuous. In one quick motion, his legs suddenly kicked out, sending both the chair that he was sitting in and the one that he was leaning on sliding across the room. He fell on his stomach and face, as if having a seizure. Men and women rushed over, grabbed him by the arms, and dragged his body over to the incense. They wafted the smoke into his face and the musicians' playing intensified. Soon, he was up and moving, dancing. This, I was later told, was the first time that a spirit had overtaken his body.

There are a number of spirits who are invited to join the gnawa ceremony. This fall into rough categories and the identity or division of these supernatural figures is hardly something that people agree about. For example, a gnawa elder named Mulay al-Tahir from outside of Marrakech described Sidi Hamu, one of the spirits, as a kind and generous butcher. He was a man who shared food with the poor and lived a saintly, virtuous life. During the gnawa ritual, there is a set of music from within the mluk segment devoted to Sidi Hamu. This version of history is present through symbolism, as those who have a relationship with the spirit wear red and drink a viscous red juice concoction that looks like blood. Sidi Mimun who, according to Mulay al-Tahir, was a physician who helped to heal his neighbors, now exists as a frightening spirit. His adepts wear black and frequently self-mutilate, cutting their arms and tongues with large carving knives, drinking boiling water, or pouring candle wax down their backs.

Part of this change in identity comes from the gnawa's history. Are these the spirits of local Moroccan saints as described by Mulay al-Tahir or other elders from the tradition, or are they vestiges of West African religious practices that slaves brought with them when they were captured and forced from their homeland? Or, are the gnawa charlatans, preying on ignorance, poverty, and mental illness? Different answers to this question place the gnawa within a local Islamic practice, make them demon-worshippers, or charge them with an evil fraud. These answers are unprovable; it is a matter of faith.

Regardless of the spirits's identity and the reality of what is happening in these evening ceremonies, there are three things that instigate and facilitate the transformations that occur on the rahba, the ritual space in front of the musicians: incense, colors, and music. Smoke rises up from the incense burner, literally feeding the spirits. When someone is in the process of falling into a trance—the Arabic verb tah or yitih actually means to "fall" into this other state—the incense helps the spirit to manifest, to take control of the moving body. The specific incense that is most effective in a given moment depends on the spirit: Sidi Brahim, who may be the Abraham of the Quran and Bible or may be a local saint, trances to frankincense, the same expensive aromatic given to Jesus at his birth and used in Catholic masses during holy days. Others prefer myrrh or a type of sandalwood from Mecca.

Each spirit also responds to a color. These relate to the spirit's personality. Sidi Musa—again, either the Moses who parted the Red Sea and delivered the Hebrews from slavery or a saint whose shrine rests on the Atlantic Ocean outside of Morocco's capital, Rabat—wears dark blue. The spirits of the sky, the unnamed samawiyyin, prefer light blue. Sidi Mimun, the frightening spirit who may have come from sub-Saharan Africa, wears black, while Sidi Hamu, the butcher, responds to red. Sidi Brahim, Abraham, trances to green, a symbol of Islam itself, while reciting prayers using prayer beads. Other spirits sit alongside these named ones, appearing during the same musical moments of the ritual. Lalla Mimuna arrives during the music for the "black" spirits, with Sidi Mimun and Ghumami. The evening plays out as a series of colors: the holy and noble Shurfa, those spirits who are said to be descendants of the Prophet Muhammad, show up while their adepts wear white. The order depends on where you are in the country, but in Fez, the music for the "white" spirits concedes to that of the "black" ones. They are followed by the "blue" spirits like Sidi Musa, and so on through the evening.

Colors manifest in the way people dress. They, like the incense, welcome spirits and strengthen their presence. The muqaddima also brings a bag of clothing or large cloths that she wraps around a trancing body to help solidify the possession. (She may also use the cloth to restrain a particularly intense trance in order to keep a person safe until things settle in). People who have an established relationship often come prepared. Those who carry a relationship with Sidi Hamu might wear red when going to a ceremony. One host in the city of Meknes left the room to change between each segment, returning with a beautiful new gown in the appropriate color, inviting each successive spirit to rise from within her. Historically, possessions were individual: a person had one spirit. This has changed over time, one among many shifts in the contemporary period. People may get up, dancing with a spirit, over and over again throughout the night.

There is a choreography to trancing, a dance of sorts that unfolds as a spirit emerges. Once a spirit begins to overtake someone's body and consciousness, she (most hosts are women, though men also fall into trance) will start to move in time with the music's rhythms, bending at the waist and throwing her hair from front to back or side to side. Eventually these movements synchronize with the sound of the quraqeb and hajhuj. As the intensity grows, the m'allem may sing more loudly, ask his ensemble to join in with the choral refrains, or stop singing completely. The dramatic change in the texture of the music from vocal to instrumental can excite a trance, driving it to a faster tempo until the person falls to the floor in catharsis. The muqaddima and others will then drag her over to the side, get some water, and nurse her back from this other state.

Rise to Popularity

Trancing, succumbing to a potentially violent possessing spirit, is well outside of the norms of ostensibly mainstream Islamic practice in Morocco. Yet, as we will see in Part III, it is hardly unique to the gnawa. Doubly problematic for this community is its history of slavery. Racism, both overt and subtle, continued through the country's independence and remain present today. Again, this is an outgrowth of past realities. Conquering Arabs defeated local populations, successive kingdoms built up a trans-Saharan slave trade, and European powers crystallized unequal realities for (and between) Moroccans of all regions and backgrounds. Gnawa music has not only proven to be transformative in a healing sense, though. It, along with shifting political realities since independence, has opened a space for the gnawa within a broader conception of Moroccan identity.

Gnawa music in the 1960s and 1970s was largely clandestine, though Moroccan and foreign tourists to places like Marrakech's Jamaa' al-Fana' heard its practitioners performing in the square. The Moroccan popular music industry was heavily regionalized, as well. Since the only way to hear or purchase cassettes of music from another area was to travel there and visit a shop, the sounds of groups like the gnawa stayed local, even within the neighborhood where you could hear them before lila ceremonies. In fact, there were few genres of music that spread past local audiences (Callen 2006). This began to change with Nass El Ghiwane and the similar bands who were borne of the era's protest movements, urbanization, and youth culture (see Chapter 3).

Nass El Ghiwane was particularly influential for the gnawa. After some early personnel changes, their long-standing lineup included Abd al-Rahim Kirouche, a gnawa m'allem who went by the name Paco. Paco was from Essaouira, a port city on the Atlantic that had previously gone by the Portuguese name Mogador. It, along with Marrakech and other inland towns, was one of the central cities of Morocco's slave trade, a primary center for slave ships that provided an alternative to caravans arriving from West Africa. Paco's hajhuj playing introduced large audiences across the country to the sound of the gnawa. The group went further, recording music from the tradition that appeared on the previously mentioned album called *Chants Gnawa du Maroc (Gnawa Chants of Morocco* [2014]*)*. This release includes the band's versions of songs from the gnawa repertoire, incorporating drums from other traditions, the banjo, and musical changes that put the music firmly within the style of Nass El Ghiwane's popular sound. Paco's long introductions reflect the potency of the ritual, while their stylistic fusion opened the doors for projects that followed. They built an audience for this sort of musical collaboration, one that dug the groovy music. They also connected the sound of the gnawa and other marginalized populations to their social efforts—their protest music—in a way that reflects what was going on in 1960s America through the Civil Rights Movement. Just as James Brown was singing "I'm Black and I'm Proud," Nass El Ghiwane was using a distinctly black music to sing "Mahmouma," decrying the oppressions in Moroccan social and political life.[3]

The popular spaces that Nass El Ghiwane opened for musical communities that were outside of the mainstream included major theaters, arenas, and the radio. This transferred to television in future decades and now includes the satellite signals that pervade homes across the country (see Chapter 2). Gnawa musicians have since toured nationally and internationally. They appear on major festival stages and serve as a representation of Morocco's diversity, a position that both includes and overcomes their community's history. Despite persistent questions of racism and heresy that still pepper discussions about their religious practices, the gnawa are an important national symbol. In a country that relies on tourism for much of its economy, the realities of global politics necessitate an outward-facing identity of tolerance. The shift is not a story of complete success where past inequalities have vanished, but it is one of potential opportunities that have been made available because of the sound of a musical ritual.

As with popular music across the world, some artists have better positioned themselves for a transition from ritual to marketplace. Two m'allems exemplify the various approaches that can prove successful: M'allem Mahmoud Ghania of Essaouira and M'allem Hamid al-Kasri from Rabat. Ghania is part of a family lineage of gnawa musicians. He was born to a master m'allem and a muqaddima in 1951 and passed away in 2015. Throughout his life, he navigated the thin line between representing his local city's style—standing as a beacon of authentic gnawa performance—and engaging in the types of fusions and experimental recording projects that often brought criticism on lesser m'allems. His many recordings are an eclectic mix; some are similar to field recordings of ritual ceremonies, providing insight into what a lila sounded like in Essaouira, while others are exploratory, engaging new technologies and approaches to popular music and recording. Gnawa scholar Timothy Abdullah Fuson features one such cassette on his *Moroccan Tape Stash* blog (Fuson 2012). He calls it "the most psychedelic gnawa tape ever" and describes Indian instruments like the tabla drum, gongs, Australian didgeridoo, and others coming and going through the musical texture. The site includes a link to an audio file of the cassette tape.[4]

Hamid al-Kasri trained under master musicians from northern Morocco, including Mʿallem Abd al-Wahab Stitu of Tangier, before moving to Rabat, Morocco's capital city. He appeared on early television shows featuring the music of regional traditions.[5] Since then, he has served the royal palace by performing ritual ceremonies there, but he is arguably most well-known for his recordings. By restringing his hajhuj with nylon strings instead of animal intestine and performing in studios, Kasri has been able to create a series of crisp sounding versions of gnawa music that sell well in neighborhood CD stalls. While statistics are difficult to come by in Morocco's largely informal music markets (much of which involves pirating recordings by copying cassettes and, later, downloading files to burned CDs), almost invariably, I was told about Kasri when asking a CD seller about his or her favorite gnawa artist (see Figure 4.4).

Fusion Projects

Changes in the sound and reception of gnawa music filtered through other projects as well. Hamid al-Kasri found a great deal of success working with jazz artists in a group called Saha Koyo, a phrase used to greet, congratulate, or show respect and appreciation for a powerful moment within a gnawa mʿallem's ritual performance. Jeffery Callen describes how Kasri and his ensemble perform repertoire from the ritual by adapting rhythmic patterns, adding piano comping and bass lines, and including a drum set to accentuate and compliment the quraqeb patterns (Callen 2006, 230). Hamid al-Kasri's television appearances, which are widely available on YouTube and similar video platforms,[6] show an artist who firmly combines the role of ritual practitioner and pop

Figure 4.4 Hamid al-Kasri performing in Essaouira with the American jazz group Snarky Puppy in 2018.

superstar. His drari are highly trained and acrobatic. They sing and dance alongside horn players behind Kasri, who plays standing up under the flashing stage lights.

Similarly successful on the international stage is Majid Bekkas, a multi-instrumentalist who plays the ʿud, hajhuj, and who is also trained as a jazz guitarist. His first album, 2001's *African Gnaoua Blues* (Majid Bekkas 2002), begins with a song titled "African Blues." It opens with a stereotypically familiar blues guitar lick accompanying the words (in English):

The gnawa music
I got it in my mind
These African blues
I, I got it in my soul

The sound of the hajhuj quickly enters, laying down a groove that could come straight out of a ritual if it were not for the added drum set and other instruments. His more recent album from 2013 is aptly titled *Al Qantara*, "The Bridge" (Majid Bekkas 2013). This collaboration includes Moroccan and Middle Eastern instruments like the ʿud alongside Indian percussion in the form of the tabla, a pair of drums common to Hindustani classical music, and the bansuri, a wooden flute. This album was featured on National Public Radio in the United States, demonstrating how his bridge to other musical traditions has taken his music to international audiences (Huizenga 2014).

Mʿallem Mahmoud Ghania and other respected gnawa practitioners recorded similar jazz fusions. In 1994, Ghania released the *Trance of Seven Colors* (1994), which included two songs that were written or co-written by the experimental American jazz saxophonist Pharaoh Sanders ("La Allah Dayim Moulenah" and "Peace in Essaouira"). He also included a piece called "Hamdouchi" where he collaborated with other Moroccan artists playing instruments that are not typical to the gnawa tradition in a similar way to what Nass El Ghiwane had done decades earlier.

Jimmy Page and Robert Plant exemplify the interest rock and roll musicians had in gnawa music. These two, who rose to prominence as leaders of the English band Led Zeppelin, traveled to Morocco among other places to record the album *No Quarter*, released in 1994. They worked with Brahim El Balkani, Hassan El Arfaoui, and others while recording "City Don't Cry" and "Wah Wah" in Marrakech. These tunes feature the sound and instrumentation of the gnawa ritual underneath Plant's singing and Page's guitar work. "Wah Wah" and a video of the recording session were released in 2004 when the album and an accompanying DVD titled *No Quarter: Jimmy Page and Robert Plant Unledded* celebrated the album's tenth anniversary.

Randy Weston, a jazz pianist, maintained what was likely the longest-running international collaboration with the gnawa tradition until his death in 2018. In 1967, Weston served as a cultural ambassador by touring the Middle East with his sextet. Visiting places like Cairo, Egypt, he and his ensemble would play "African Cookbook" and others of his African-influenced compositions. This was a period of time in the United States where battles over Civil Rights for African-Americans were increasingly tinged and influenced by a connection with the "motherland," continental Africa. Malcolm X had been assassinated in 1965 and Martin Luther King Jr was killed in 1968, marking an escalation and transformation in the movement. A sense of cultural nationalism brought artists to the musical styles of their ancestral homeland. Art Blakey, a jazz drummer and bandleader, had been traveling to Africa since the late 1940s and had incorporated elements of the patterns that he heard there into his own music. Other artists were incorporating the music and imagery of the continent within their own performances, making explicit what was becoming both a personal identity and a political ideology.

Weston returned to Morocco after his State Department tour and opened a club in Tangier called the African Rhythms Club in the summer of 1967. His ensemble played regularly and it quickly became a central social scene within the country, both for expatriate foreigners and Moroccans interested in these new styles of musical fusion. During and after his time living and working in Morocco, Weston noted the dramatic change in the gnawa community's social status. In his autobiography, he writes:

> when I first came to Morocco, the Gnawa were viewed as street beggars, undesirables. Some Moroccans initially tried to discourage me from having anything to do with the Gnawa. They'd ask me, 'What do you see in these people?' Everywhere you go the black folks are always on the bottom. But now the Moroccans are all touched by Gnawa; all the young, educated Moroccans are all influenced by Gnawa culture—black culture. They've now seen the importance of Gnawa traditions to overall Moroccan culture.
>
> (Weston 2010, 172)

After some early experiences visiting lila ceremonies, Weston had a conversion. He developed a relationship with Sidi Musa, Moses. This spirit wears blue and the pianist was especially taken by the story, in both the Bible and the Quran, of Moses freeing the Hebrews from slavery, delivering them from Egypt by parting the Red Sea. The resonance with an African-American activist's own efforts and experiences during the Civil Rights movement in the United States was powerful. It led to one of Weston's most well-known compositions: "Blue Moses." Shortly after witnessing his first ritual, Weston wrote the piece, which he loosely based on a song from the ceremony. But a local chief within Tangier's gnawa community forbade him from playing it:

> He said, 'Don't play that in public, that's sacred music.' So for one year I wouldn't play that piece. Finally I went back to him to ask his permission. His name was Fatah, so I said, 'Fatah, I think the world needs to hear this music and I'm not going to commercialize it or disrespect it in any way. I'm going to put all the proper spiritual power behind this music because I respect you and I respect the Gnawa people.' Finally Fatah relented and said OK, that I could finally perform 'Blue Moses.' But you can bet that if he didn't give me the OK, there was no way I was gonna play that piece, because I've seen some strange things happen in Africa when there's even a hint of crossing the spirits.
>
> (Weston 2010, 176)

In "Blue Moses," Weston incorporated musical elements from the gnawa into his music as well. There are no borrowed instruments, but the rhythms, timings, and textures that he heard in those first ceremonies percolated into his jazz combo's sound. The song is structured around a handful of repeating phrases, ostinatos. It builds by layering these ostinatos to increase both energy and sonic density. In his *Live in St. Lucia* recording, he begins the song on piano by playing this main melody. The saxophone enters, doubling that line, playing the same melody over and over. The percussion comes in with a figure that, while it is not a standard quraqeb pattern, has the same outline as many of the most energetic rhythms that animate trance. Example 4.1 shows some of these melodic ideas. The saxophone and piano lines are largely identical to start, the bass plays the same thing, and the trombone holds long notes, drones, to thicken the sound. Furthermore, the bass line evokes the hajhuj in both sound and melody. The running eighth notes would feel at home in the rahba's incense.

After introducing the band, Weston improvises, toying with this melody by changing up rhythms while the rest of the band continues in their repetitions. The figures themselves imply a common popular music harmony (I–IV–I–V–I), but there are not enough aural markers to solidify it as "functional" in the Western sense. Instead, Weston's composition enjoys a synergy between gnawa music and jazz in the 1960s; they are both modal, using melodies like these ones to propel the songs and build tension. Roughly halfway through the track (about two and a half minutes in), the ostinatos suddenly disappear as the song transitions to a new section. The bed of sound changes dramatically as the saxophone takes off in a solo of its own. Everything returns to the opening segment, but only long enough to regain its footing before the feel changes again, this time shifting to a funk beat (see Example 4.2). The new melody uses the same pitches and a similar contour. It's both a dramatic reversion to an African-American style and a consistent manipulation of this gnawa-infused modality. And the move from a "rolling" 6/8 meter to an "angular" 4/4 funk beat is almost physical. It's not easy to sit still while listening.

The fusion of musical styles comes through in more subtle ways as well. By shifting between duple and triple meters, Weston alludes to the two-against-three and polyrhythmic elements of the gnawa sound. His composition is pentatonic, using scales of

Example 4.1 Some ostinato patterns that appear in Randy Weston's "Blue Moses."

Example 4.2 Saxophone melody that appears during the "funk" section of Randy Weston's "Blue Moses".

only five notes instead of the more common seven. This leads to an openness that allows the soloists (whether Weston on piano or one of the other band members) to explore more complex scales without clashing with the rest of the group. While this piece was only one of many African-themed compositions from Weston's career, it holds up as an early and effective example of what the artist was doing. From this point on, he also made more explicit collaborative efforts, bringing gnawa artists into the mainstream music industry and the world of jazz.

One of Randy Weston's collaborations involved bringing together nine gnawa mʿallems and two percussionists on one recording session in Marrakech in 1992, some of whom were elders and who passed away shortly after. The session, released in 1994 as *The Splendid Master Gnawa Musicians of Morocco* and nominated for the Best World Music Album Grammy award in 1996, serves as an historical document, but it is also an innovation: mʿallems had never performed together in this way, not at least while in front of a microphone (McNeill 1993). Weston's efforts to bring the gnawa to an international audience continued. In 1999, his ensemble recorded with Mʿallem Abdellah el-Gourd and his group in a church in Brooklyn, NY. Weston brought the group to the United States as part of a tour. In 2015, they were back in New York City, performing in Manhattan at the New School.[7]

Collaborations, from Nass El Ghiwane's hits that featured Paco's hajhuj playing to Weston's international travels, bring gnawa music from the most localized and marginalized neighborhoods of Morocco's cities to stages around the world. The international pop marketplace increasingly has a space for gnawa music. Hassan Hakmoun, a gnawa musician based in New York who plays with a wide range of international artists, provides one example. After moving to the United States in 1987, he has incorporated elements of jazz, pop, and avant-garde classical music into an innovative and wide-ranging personal style. After working with jazz trumpeter Don Cherry, he started his own group called Zahar. This rock fusion group brought electric guitar, violin, drum set, and Latin percussion (among other things) together in some of New York's most prominent rock and jazz clubs, eventually making his way to the stage of the 1994 Woodstock festival, where Zahar was introduced by Peter Gabriel.[8] Moving beyond rock and jazz fusion, in 1992 he performed with the Kronos Quartet, one of the most well-known contemporary classical string quartets.

These efforts from Weston, Abdellah el-Gourd, Hassan Hakmoun, and others have influenced the social position of the gnawa back home. These black ritual musicians are still regularly criticized by conservatives and even audience members—at almost every ritual ceremony I attended, someone leaned over to me to say that the gnawa represent Moroccan culture, but not Islam—but their groovy sound underlines hip hop beats and funk fusions on festival stages and popular radio. Musicians and groups like Houcine Slaoui, Nass al-Ghiwane, and Fnair demonstrate that this entry into popular culture—and often, resistance movements—is not new to the history of the gnawa. The level of access afforded to gnawa musicians throughout the country now, however, represents a dramatic change from what they were able to do before. In Part III, these ideas will return as gnawa music influences the ritual practice of other groups in Fez.

Notes

1 In 2011, a terrorist bombing killed 15 people, many of whom were tourists, at Cafe Argana. The restaurant looks out over the Jamaa' al-Fana' and was a respite that I, personally, had enjoyed a few times before. I was there a few weeks after the bombing and a giant tarp over the restaurant's facade served as a stark reminder of political realities. Morocco has relatively few instances of terrorism, partially because the government consistently works to prevent violent extremism within its borders. See Chrisafis 2011 and CNN 2011 for coverage of the attack.
2 Halal is a term that refers to what is permissible (neither "beneficial" or "forbidden") within Islamic law. It includes a series of rules pertaining to food preparation, much like kosher law within Judaism.
3 For a discussion of the role of music within the Civil Rights movement, see Garofalo (1992).
4 Fuson's discussion of the music and a link to a digitized version of the cassette are available at Fuson 2012.
5 The history of Morocco's television representations of local and regional musical styles is an important one, but it has received little attention and is largely under researched. James Miller, the director of the Moroccan-American Commission for Educational and Cultural Exchange, described his memory of Kasri on television from decades ago to me during a casual conversation in Rabat.
6 One such performance is "Bania," available in the playlists referenced in the Resources section.
7 Coverage of this event is available at https://events.newschool.edu/event/the_ganawa_abdellah_el_gord_and_randy_weston_present_the_traditional_music_of_morocco#.WckY1ky-KRs.
8 See the playlists referenced in the Resources section for a link to Zahar's performance at Woodstock in 1994.

PART III

Focusing In: Faith and Fun in Fez

Morocco's cities have long and unique histories. Just as Part II explored a range of marginalized outsiders, distinguished for regional, political, racial, and social reasons, who found prominence in part through the attention that came to their musical and religious practices, Part III zooms in more closely on a single city to examine how its long sacred history intertwines with the contemporary lives of its inhabitants. While these three chapters focus on Fez, it is worth noting that the deep historical connections between musical practice and specifically local religious beliefs exist in many of the country's major urban areas.

Music and religion in Morocco can serve as local markers, just as they can identify the regional and national identities that comprised each of the previous chapters. This connects to traditions that appear within only one city or forms of religious music that people know of from a place and time. Music, especially sacred music, often has these local meanings because of important scenes or performers that existed in the past. With the rise of social media and migration around the country, the actual musical boundaries are no longer as firm—gnawa music that was primarily located in Marrakech and Essaouira now appears in every major city—but the links persist within conversations about authenticity and heritage. In many cases, the fount of a genre's essence still links back to where it came from.

Fez, the city that will receive the focus of the coming chapters, shows how music can reinforce a sense of identity, especially when that music shows up in major festivals or other large-scale projects. In this case the presented image is one that highlights a local history of sacred authenticity and reverence. Fez was also, for a long time, a seat of political power. It is home to a long-standing religious institution and university. It houses the pilgrimage sites revered by many of the country's religious brotherhoods. The Fez Festival of World Sacred Music, which began in 1994, includes an interesting mix of activities. Instead of exclusively including music that is affiliated with religious practices, the organizers have taken a wide view of what is meant by "sacred music." When I was last at the event, the American guitarist Ben Harper was one of the festival's headline acts. Indian musicians are regularly invited, as are popstars whose link to "sacred music" might be tenuous at best. The ticketed concerts—which are expensive and therefore exclusive to the elite and middle classes—often see the experience of music as sacred in and of itself. Alongside this series, two others broaden the scope further. The "Sufi Nights" free evening concerts feature the music of local and international Sufi grssoups, presenting the diversity of Islamic practice to audiences while the open-air free concerts at nearby Bab Boujloud give audiences the opportunity to see popular Moroccan acts that include rappers, gnawa musicians, and shʿabi singers.[1] Not only does music, therefore, represent a diverse understanding of Islam, it positions Fez as a sacred place to experience the transformative sacred power of diverse sounds.

Note

1 Shʿabi music is a common genre of popular music that has spread across the country. See Chapter 6 for a short discussion.

CHAPTER 5

Sufi Ritual

In early October 2012, Abderrahim Amrani invited a friend and me to attend a healing ceremony performed by his hamadsha group. He described how a prominent business man who was from Fez, and who still owned a large home in the city, had moved away to Casablanca or Rabat. He suffered, however, from an illness that he couldn't shake. His family had a history with the hamadsha, a Sufi brotherhood with adepts in cities like Fez and Meknes, who could help. He regularly travelled back to his palatial home in Fez's old city to host one of these ceremonies in an effort to renew his relationship with Lalla Aisha, a spirit who was causing the malady. The performers did not share many of his details with me, but most people afflicted by Lalla Aisha attend or host an animal sacrifice and accompanying ceremony annually. We missed the sacrifice, but if there was one on this particular evening, it likely played out in a similar fashion to the one described in Chapter 4 for the gnawa. When we arrived with the bulk of the group, about 15 men, it was time to speak more directly to Allah and Lalla Aisha.

As is so often the case in Fez, the tight alleyway led to a nondescript door that opened into a massive home. The courtyard was large, complete with a green tiled fountain in the center and pillars rising up to support an open roof. Ornate tile work lined the floor and made its way up about eight feet of the walls and pillars. Black, white, and yellow geometric patterns were bounded by white and blue borders all around us. Potted plants added life and color in the cold autumn weather.

Amrani had rented sound equipment, emphasizing how this was no casual affair. The ensemble settled in, sitting on long couches that were brought into the courtyard and set up in a U-shape between two of the pillars. A number of microphones amplified the primary singers, including Amrani, the group's leader, the muqaddim. They had a small charcoal fire in a terracotta pot that served two purposes: they could use it to burn incense and welcome spirits, but in a more immediate practical sense, it served as a heat source to tighten the skins that were stretched across the drums that currently lay at their feet. The cold weather loosened the heads of the guwwal, large hourglass-shaped clay drums that heightened the energy of the coming ritual segments. Amrani sat at the center of the group wearing yellow, while his group members fanned out to either side in a mix of matching jellabas (long hooden gowns) and other forms of traditional clothing—some white and some white with green trim—the "uniform" that they bring to their many staged concert performances.

The chants began with an invocation, prayers to Allah, and supplications to Sidi Ali bin Hamdush, the hamadsha's saintly namesake. Chanting long memorized texts, this segment transformed the courtyard into a sacred space, preparing it for what was to come. Amrani, picking up the charcoal burner and adding some incense, walked around the room to envelop the musicians, the host, and the family and friends who were present for the evening in the fragrant smoke (women and children were keeping warm under blankets in the various rooms that opened onto the courtyard). Our host was already falling under the ceremony's effects. The businessman paced the room, raising his arms in the air and shouting.

The group stood to reorganize as another set of performers, four ghayati, prepared their oboe-like wind instruments. The ghita is a wooden double reed instrument with holes drilled into the sides. It is loud, made for projecting through large outdoor spaces (or, in this case, over drums), chanting, and the cacophony of ritual possession. They climbed into a bench to project better, to be even louder in the courtyard. The rest of the men stood and picked up the large drums, holding them over their shoulders. The hadra was beginning, the intensity rose, and the host picked up his pace as he wandered the large room. Facing a wall, I remember my own surprise when I saw him bash his head into the hard tile. He was bleeding, giving Lalla Aisha what she wanted.

The hamadsha brotherhood are one of many groups within Morocco who practice a form of Islam that is marginal to the mainstream. Like the gnawa, they consider themselves to be Muslim. Unlike the gnawa, their history is not aligned with specific forms of racial discrimination. They do, however, come from a reality that includes widespread illiteracy and poverty. Islam is a highly intellectual religion, but it can also be something different: experiential and "popular." This chapter outlines the history, beliefs, and rituals of the hamadsha community and, in doing so, further explores the idea of "Moroccan Islam." The country's religious uniqueness comes into focus through a closer look at the hamadsha community in Fez, Meknes, and the surrounding areas. This opens the space for Chapter 6, which follows the hamadsha and a similar brotherhood known as the 'issawa. As these groups gained prominence, they entered into a popular music scene that highlights sacred entertainment. In doing so, they navigate the tastes of their audiences alongside the needs of their ritual activities. What begins in this chapter concludes in wedding reception performances and fusion projects with international DJs.

Popular Sufism

The idea of "popular Sufism" as something distinct from mainstream Islam primarily comes out of a distinction in class and education. Musical ritual practices play a substantial role in creating this difference and bear the brunt of much of the criticism against these historically maligned groups. But they are the symptom of a more significant departure, according to critics. As mentioned throughout these pages, conservative strains of ideology have gained traction over the past three or four decades. With support from foreign governments (like Saudi construction and education projects around the region) or, more recently, influence from supra-national fundamentalist movements, "Islamism" has shifted away from being a wide range of local political movements with various local concerns. Instead, the term is now thrown around to represent (and often vilify) political opponents as violently radical. While in some cases the concern is warranted (most terrorism in the name of Islam is, in fact, committed against fellow Muslims),[1] aligning conservatism with violence can also be a political strategy to disparage religiously oriented political opponents.

Despite this, Muslims often vote for and follow leaders who share their moral values, not unlike how conservative political and social movements have been consistently powerful within the West. One concern of these leaders is the "innovation" that they see within so much Islamic practice. The term "innovation" is a loaded one within Islam: it is discouraged as inappropriate. Movements that want to pull communities away from the distractions of the world (whether the "modern" world, or otherwise) are also not unique to this region. Many world religions have a directive to focus on what is important and to build the self-discipline required to avoid temptations or distractions, usually through a combination of prayer, meditation, faith, worship, and the study of scripture. The drive is toward purity. In reality, however, every world religion experiences a wide diversity, something that might be unavoidable, since, by definition, a "world religion" like Islam, Christianity, Judaism, or Buddhism exists simultaneously in very different places, practiced by very different communities.

The historical effort within Islam, therefore, has a paradox: the religion spread quickly in part because it encompassed and allowed for local practices to remain, to be folded into the faith, yet that same strategy led to a heterodox community in which Islam in Morocco might look quite distinct from Islam in Egypt or Saudi Arabia. It looks (and sounds) different between those who can read scripture and those who are uneducated, even if they live within the same neighborhood. Charismatic leaders can invoke and impress their perspectives on what faith is and should be on their followers, further dividing the "paths" available to believers. Yet again, these debates reflect those that happen in other religious communities. While the metaphor does not hold up completely, the concern is between a "Catholic" and "Protestant" reading of religious practice. Whereas the Catholic church allows for individual leaders, parishes, and worshippers to find a community that fits their tastes—many look for churches aligned with their ethnicity or whose music might closely match their own preferences—the Protestant reformation was borne out of a pushback against "innovations," against abuses of power. It was an effort to clean up what its leaders showed to be rogue (and corrupt) practices. More recently, the authority that comes with purity or a return to scripture defines many Protestant communities: Bible study holds a more central role than it does in so many Catholic communities, for example. Whereas Catholic practices invoke ornate ritual, certain Protestant ones can be (but are not always) austere. They are "fundamental." Within Catholicism, this debate also exists. It is almost fractal, as communities debate and claim their own authority through a sense of purity, fundamental respect for tradition, and authenticity, at every level.

Morocco's diverse forms of Islamic practice come from a long history of local Sufi thought. Fez's position as a spiritual center and a place of learning gave rise to both esoteric intellectualism and charismatic leadership. Sufism, often described as Islamic mysticism, continues to be an umbrella term: a tent containing innumerable individual practices. Many of these follow a lineage, looking back to specific holy figures, teachers, or sheikhs. In these chapters, the focus remains on the more "popular" variants of Sufism, but similarities do connect the musical rituals of poor neighborhoods and festival stages to the versions that hold sway in elite intellectual (and governmental) circles. Anthropologists long interested in Moroccan religious practice have focused on these overarching linkages, and it is worth outlining some major ones here.

First and foremost, Sufism in Morocco generally subscribes to the existence of baraka, a type of goodness or blessing that can be physically transferred from one person to another. The concept is not unlike those seen in other major religions: a holy person can bestow blessings by touch or prayer. Biblically, we see this as the sick yearn to touch the cloak of Jesus, the son of God. Within Catholicism, pilgrimages to holy shrines often involve touching an artifact, drinking or blessing oneself with holy water, or praying for a saint's intervention. In Morocco, shrines that dot the countryside serve this purpose. Holy men and women can grant baraka on supplicants. As we saw in Chapter 4 with the gnawa, and will see again here, music groups can invoke spirits who do the same.

This attention to holy blessings, to baraka, can also be controversial. Islam is intended to be a nonhierarchical religion (gender questions—which can also be political or social concerns couched in the language of religion—aside, of course). Any devout man can ascend a minaret, climbing to the top of a mosque, to recite the call to prayer. But some read more or have an ability to engage followers or are good teachers. They take on leadership roles, are celebrated, and might become a sheikh. The most notable have inspired followers to follow in their path, their tariqa. Their names live on in the name of their followers. The hamadsha are the followers of Sidi Ali bin Hamdush. How can these holy men rise above their peers? And how can any society where there are teachers and leaders remain devoid of a hierarchy?

As brotherhoods grow and saintly traditions embed themselves within each tariqa's unique ritual activities, the communities spread. Another element of many Moroccan Sufi groups is the development of a network of lodges that serve as resting places for travelers and meeting places for local adepts. The lodge is called a zawiya, literally a "corner." It can be a building or room, any place where the group might gather. In some cases, as with the tijaniyya in Fez, the zawiya is ornate, built-up, and beautiful. It serves as a major pilgrimage attraction for the world's travelers. In other cases, it might be a small side room in someone's home where a handful of followers come together every Thursday evening to recite poetry.

Many Sufi paths in Morocco are organized around these Thursday evening rituals that feature poetry. The poetry itself, in fact, is often a defining element of what makes the group unique from others. Walking around the streets of Fez's medina can be surreal at times; when you turn a corner, you may hear a brotherhood's chanting floating through the air, coming down from a distant window. At their most austere, these gatherings are reflective and meditative. Chanted poetry serves to help adepts remind themselves both intellectually and physically—through the pronunciation of the words and the synchronized breathing that goes into group chant—of their faith. As the evening goes on, the group may stand and recite shorter repetitive phrases: long texts give way to short sentences and, eventually, single words. "Allah, Allah, Allah, Allah" invokes God's name and forces the kind of rhythmic breath that can punctuate or heighten this communal experience. The members may sway back and forth, bringing their bodies into conversation with the words and their breath. A talented or inspired member may take off, raising his or her voice above the others in an ornate descant, adding to the texture of the sound.[2]

The provenance of Sufi poetry is wide-ranging. Many local brotherhoods feature texts written by their namesake or previous saints from Morocco. Most groups include an opening text, the hizb, which is a prayer written by a founder or prominent figure within the community's saintly lineage. Members memorize these words and recite them together at or near the beginning of an event. Other poetic texts come from the long international history of Sufi philosophy, scholarship, and writing. The poems of Jalal al-Din Muhammad Rumi, Ibn Arabi, or al-Ghazali, for example, are famous worldwide. They are printed in translations and read by Muslims and non-Muslims alike. Rumi and al-Ghazali were Persian, living in and around southwestern Asia, including present-day Afghanistan and Iran, during the 12th and 13th centuries, respectively. Ibn Arabi was active in present-day Spain, then part of the Andalusian empires during the 12th centuries described in Chapter 1. These writers and many others like them were philosophers. In some cases, they broke from orthodoxy in their writing to stress the experience of religious faith. The persistence of their works within religious practices across the Islamic world demonstrate their lasting relevance for believers.

While it is a gross over-generalization, this poetry tends to stress the mystical elements of faith. The term mysticism is often used without definition, but mystical practices in so many religions often engage a sense of "oneness" with the world. In Islam, this is known as tawhid, a word that shares a linguistic root with the word for the number one: wahid. This idea places the emphasis of religious practice on experiencing communion with one's community, surroundings, and God. There is a loss of the self as we experience a transcendence, something that can be familiar to lovers of the arts. In fact, the prevalence of the arts (especially poetry and music) within Sufi practice is what makes these religious paths interesting for adepts and ethnomusicologists alike. While that music may sound different across various groups—in many cases it is not music at all, but chant—communal practices that are musical (if not music) are relatively consistent. These activities carry an important role as members find their consciousness falling away, as they transcend and reach a "state" of being beyond the normalcy of everyday life called hal. The world disappears and the self is no longer distinct from the temporal or spiritual worlds. In Arabic, this is the experience of fna', the "extinction" of the self into God's grace. Poetry, chanting, and diverse forms of music can help bring it along. But, in Morocco as elsewhere, many brotherhoods have other aims—including healing and spirit possession—that fall further outside of the orthodoxy.

The specific esoteric and enclosed ceremonies of individual brotherhoods are not the only place where music plays an important role within these communities, however. Like the gnawa introduced in Chapter 4, many Sufi brotherhoods process through a neighborhood before settling into an indoor space for a ceremony.[3] The hamadsha and 'issawa (see Chapter 6) are two examples. Even more present within the larger urban landscape, however, are the major celebrations that overtake town squares on an annual basis. Many Sufi groups maintain a pilgrimage to a patron saint's tomb. For the hamadsha, this takes place in a small mountain town outside of Meknes called Sidi Ali (named after Sidi Ali bin Hamdush, the brotherhood's namesake: see Witulski 2016 for a description of this event).

For the ʻissawa, the pilgrimage happens in the main town square of Meknes itself, a market space similar to the one that serves as a major attraction in Marrakech. The street performers, women who draw henna designs, artisans, and herbalists who normally inhabit the square every day move aside as crowds gather around a long procession of ʻissawa groups. These men and women (groups are almost exclusively male, but many women are involved in the ceremonies in other ways) travel from across the country to join in this massive, and loud, show of reverence toward Muhammad al-Hadi bin ʻIssa, better known as Sheikh al-Kamil, "the perfect master." Dressed in heavy clothing and using a variety of instruments that include six-foot-long trumpets, the adepts make their way across the square and around a corner before winding their way down to the nearby shrine to the holy man. Many of the groups carry large banners with photos of their ensemble; some even include phone numbers for any present who might need to hire a troupe for a ceremony. Others, however, have large green tarps with Arabic embroidery of words from the Quran or other holy phrases. Alongside the marchers are ghita players on horseback, playing their loud woodwind instruments over the top of the chanting masses. The scene is not unlike a Mardi Gras procession (but without the alcohol); at once both a party and a reverent sacred act. The musical chants and accompanying loud instruments control the outdoors, making an entire city square, a marketplace, into a sacred space. Musical activities heighten and interrupt everyday rhythms, overtaking them to prioritize this one specific religious practice.

Hamadsha History and Beliefs

The massive spectacles that mark pilgrimages for groups like the ʻissawa and hamadsha are a highlight of the annual calendar. The smaller events in homes across the country, however, are the backbone of these traditions. The two examples that comprise this chapter and the next—the hamadsha and the ʻissawa—are related. They are generally seen as "popular" religion, a form of Islam practiced by the poor and uneducated. Many other forms of Sufism in Morocco are elite, well-read, and hew more closely to the religion's textual traditions. The butshishiyya are one example of a tradition whose ranks include the highest officials within the country's educational system and government. These two, however, make use of sounds, practices, and instruments in a way that is explicitly musical. Furthermore, as addressed in the following chapter, groups from within both of these brotherhoods have strategically taken advantage of the opportunities afforded by contemporary media, public concert performances, and other "gigging" opportunities. They have adapted their sacred practices into forms of religious entertainment, fusing fun and faith.[4] To better explore how this works, it is useful to dig further into the details of these groups, their beliefs, and their ritual practices. From there, the ways in which these religious men and women adapt become clearer. In this chapter, we turn to the hamadsha.

Abderrahim Amrani is the leader of a hamadsha troupe in Fez. He taught the men who chanted during the ceremony that opened this chapter. Some have been working with him for years, for most of their lives. They are experts with a deep understanding of the brotherhood and a close affinity for its approach to Islam. Others work as professional musicians as well. Their skills are not exclusively sacred in nature: they are talented percussionists or singers who perform with other brotherhoods, wedding bands, or in classical ensembles. Some of these men have a relationship with the brotherhood that goes beyond the norms of Islamic practice. They are possessed—owned, to be literal—by Lalla Aisha, a spirit who holds a primary role within the history of the hamadsha. She is also a spirit whose very presence brings condemnation on the group. To some, she is a "she-demon," to others, she is a wife. Amrani sees her position within the hamadsha worldview differently. He sees Aisha as a conflation of a number of different figures, each of whom was an important woman who once lived and died. Today's conception of her as a goat-hoofed beauty who tempts and ensnares men is a gross misunderstanding. Not unlike the situation with the gnawa, it is the discourse around the hamadsha and who this spirit is that can prove to be powerful in placing the group within or outside of social norms. And thanks in large part to Amrani's efforts, the brotherhood's position in the world is improving. His successes in staging and repackaging their musical traditions have been important to this end.

Amrani described the history of the tradition's three foundational personalities to me on a few occasions. He asked me to translate his words and share them after he had seen some of his music on a blog run by another ethnomusicologist. He wanted to clarify this history and to express his thoughts on his own brotherhood with the world. I shared these words with Timothy Fuson, that blog's author (Fuson 2013), and have reprinted them in other publications. But his wish to be clearly understood warrants repeating them here. His telling of the history, after all, is as straightforward as any interpretation on my part could be.

> The story of the hamadsha begins with Sidi Ali Bin Hamdush in the 17th century. Sidi Ali bin Hamdush, in that time, was studying at Qarawiyyin in Fez [a major religious university], where he lived. At one point during his religious studies, Sufi inspiration came to him and he fell into a trance. This state of Sufism was counter to his work in the madrasa [religious institution]. He stood at the door of scribes (near Qarawiyyin) and sat, spitting on the ground. He began to hate the life that he saw in his future, so he left Fez on foot and trekked across the nearby mountains until he reached Beni Rashd, the site of the current town that holds his namesake. He arrived at a place called the Large Spring ('Ain al-Kebir), where there was a tree near the water. Sidi Ali had a shaved head with a tuft of long hair coming from the back, called a gutaya. He tied his rope of hair to a string of reeds and connected it to a branch on the tree, pulling it tightly so as to hold his head upright and keep him from falling asleep. He pulled out his prayer beads and began repeating "Allah" 18,000 times. When sleep came over him [and his head began to sink down], the string tied between his hair and the branch above would pull him back up and awake, opening his eyes. He would continue to recite prayers and praise God.

> Here, the first people to come to him were the Amazigh who worked the nearby farms. They brought him a handira [a type of ragged and heavy cloak]. Then a man who lived nearby named Sidi Ahmed Dghughi came to him. He was a thief, stealing rams or roosters to feed himself due to his poverty. He was possessed and stole only to eat, like a wolf. He wandered the countryside until he found Sidi Ali sitting there, with his hair tied to a tree. He grew close to Sidi Ali and regularly brought wood so he could warm the Sufi master with fire. He became Sidi Ali's friend and would bring others to see him, providing food. He

no longer stole and became a servant. Day after day, Sidi Ahmed would return to see Sidi Ali. Sidi Ali then sent Sidi Ahmed to the Sudan [a region of West Africa, not the present-day country]. He left by foot and visited the king of that region, Abd al-Malik bil-Khir. Bil-Khir gave him a servant woman named Aisha to bring to his master. We do not know his intention, if she was for marriage or as a servant for Sidi Ali.

For six months, Sidi Ahmed traveled to return to Sidi Ali with Aisha. When he arrived to the place where Sidi Ali had been sitting, he found his master dead under the tree. Sidi Ahmed began to strike his head. In the poem "Al-Warshan" [The Carrier Pigeon] we hear the story. Then this Aisha, now without Sidi Ali there to marry or serve, began to do miracles of healing. She healed those who would come from afar: the desert, Algeria, Tunisia, and other cities across Morocco. In Tunisia, there is still an active hamadsha zawiya that celebrates the hamadsha mussem in the city of Um Al-'Arais with Moroccan clothing. She saw many people before suddenly disappearing. No one knew what happened to her or where she was. Her cave, however, remained and became a pilgrimage site just downhill from the zawiya of Sidi Ali Bin Hamdush. Despite the fact that she was no longer there, her cavern became a place where one could bring a sacrifice, light candles, and be healed. This practice entered the tradition, as people would continue to visit and live within the proximity of her past and continuing miracles. This is Aisha Sudaniyya. She was the one who came from the Sudan, from King Bil-Khir, to Sidi Ali Bin Hamdush.

After Aisha disappeared, Sidi Ahmed Dghurghi died near to where Sidi Ali was buried. Those students and pilgrims who lived in this area decided that they would not entomb Sidi Ahmed in the vicinity of his master. A woman arrived who owned a mule. She said to them, take this mule of mine and put his body on top of it. Let the animal go. Where he stops, bury the body. They put the body on the mule and let him go. He walked and walked until stopping next to a house on Jbal Bani Warad Dghugha, a nearby mountain. He sat and Sidi Ahmed fell from his back, into the house. This is where he is now buried.

Amrani goes on to describe a number of other figures and concepts named Aisha. The spirit looms large within Moroccan beliefs and culture. He bristles at the fear that many hold for Aisha, partially because he sees her as a holy figure who bestows blessings on hamadsha adepts and pilgrims. The cavern that sits within the small town of Sidi Ali hosts sellers of ritual and religious paraphernalia that includes goats, chickens, and cows used in sacrifices during the week of pilgrimage itself, when the town gets crowded. They also sell candles, milk, candy, fruit, and dates that pilgrims can bring to her cavern and leave there. The small creek that flows underneath the cavern is filled with these items, artifacts of the people's relationship with this mysterious spirit.

But Amrani attributes the dismissal or debasement that comes from outside of the hamadsha community, however, to misunderstanding. Not unlike the gnawa, this is a practice that many condemn as extraneous, or outside of proper Islamic piety. By reclaiming and redefining Aisha, Amrani works to pull away layers of what he sees as confusion. Instead of one figure with a host of frightening traits, he sees four distinct Aishas from Moroccan history and culture who have been fused into one ghoul by superstition. Alongside the devout follower of Sidi Ali, there was a second Aisha named Aisha Bahariyya (Aisha of the sea). She came to Morocco from Baghdad and fell in love with a local holy man who lived by the ocean. Perhaps inspired by, perhaps despite her love, she became a devout follower of his Sufi teachings, going so far as to sleep on the beach. The tide took her one day and she drowned. After her body washed up, she was buried on the shore and her shrine has become a minor pilgrimage site for those who experience unrequited love.

A third Aisha was Aisha Qadissa. The she-demon of Moroccan superstition is known as Aisha Qandisha, which Amrani argues is a mispronunciation of this woman's name. She was an attractive woman and, after the Portuguese colonizers killed her husband, she weaponized her beauty. As Amrani describes it, any man who saw her, wanted her. Using this advantage, she killed 500 Portuguese solders. Amrani's description invokes an implication of seduction, even prostitution. This characteristic certainly looms large on the way people think about the mysterious Aisha Qandisha, who seduces men before ensnaring them. Amrani told me that "She was like Zorro," referencing the fictional vigilante.

Amrani is clear in stating that these three Aishas were real people. They were not spirits like the jinns in the gnawa ceremony. The fourth Aisha, he goes on to say, is the life that we live. In Moroccan Arabic, ʿasha means to live or to reside in a city. Or, to live within this world. Related to the name Aisha, it is our lives that can possess us so powerfully and our lives that can bring us closer to God.

Performing a Ritual in Meknes

The pilgrimage and rituals that punctuate life within the hamadsha brotherhood smoothly move between a sense of restraint and exuberance. The changing energy within the chanting creates a sense of motion that organizes the long evening. Unlike some of the more esoteric Sufi brotherhoods, musical instruments take a primary role within the ceremony. These include a string instrument called the ginbri, a variety of hand drums, and the loud ghita described earlier. Aside from these, much of the chant and music is accompanied by clapping, ululations, stomping, and other sounds. Alongside the poetry, the changes in these sounds help to differentiate the many ritual segments that progress through the evening.

As is the case with so many ritual-based groups in Morocco, handheld drums are central. While the group processes, large hourglass-shaped drums help to pound out the rhythm of the group's motion through the streets. This kind of percussion instrument, called a guwwal, is similar in shape to the darbuka or dumbek that animates bellydance around the world. But instead of being made from aluminum and resting on a seated player's knee, the guwwal is slightly larger, made of clay, and is carried over the shoulder (see Figure 5.1). By resting the guwwal on his shoulder and against his head, a player can march with this drum for hours. An expert can balance it effectively enough to free up both hands for playing, or use one hand to hold the instrument while hitting the drum head with the other.

A smaller hourglass-shaped clay drum with a similar shape is called a t'arija. This is held in one hand and hit with the other. Instead of getting a number of sounds out of a single drum, t'arija players work together to create a complex texture between them, utilizing the slightly different pitches of each one. The bendir, a large frame drum with a

Figure 5.1 Members of Abderrahim Amrani's hamadsha ensemble playing the guwwal during a ritual in Fez.

snare (a string or wire stretched across the back of the drum head) that appears in much of the region's popular music, can be present, but is less common.

Unlike machined versions of these instruments that appear in world music marketplaces, many groups use handmade drums. They glue the drum head to the clay, which makes it impossible to loosen or tighten the drum itself. This can be a problem in Morocco's dramatically changing weather: the winter is humid, rainy, and cold while the summer is arid and hot. Being made of skin, the drum head is sensitive to these changes and gets flabby, lowers in pitch, and generally performs poorly in the cold or damp weather. To alleviate this problem, ensembles bring charcoal burners to rituals that serve double duty. Aside from burning the important ritual incense, musicians or their young apprentices spend much of the evening leaning over these fires and holding the drums just a few inches away, rotating them slowly. Once the heat tightens the drum head, they pass the instrument off to a performer and grab one that has loosened, ready to repeat the process. When the ensemble is large and the instruments are especially cold, I have seen large groups of men huddled over burners and open-flamed gas stoves, each trying to get his instrument ready to play.

The ginbri is the main string instrument within the hamadsha tradition (see Figure 5.2). The name is somewhat generic and represents a number of other plucked string instruments across the country. Many use the word to reference the gnawa hajhuj. Like the hajhuj, the ginbri's body is carved from wood and it is attached to a long

Figure 5.2 Abderrahim Amrani playing the ginbri during a ritual in Fez.

wooden stick. Unlike a guitar, the stick is cylindrical. Three strings stretch from leather loops on the end of the stick that operate like tuning pegs. The wooden box, which is pear-shaped, unlike the rectangular hajhuj, is covered in a skin membrane. The strings are thin, giving the instrument a sound closer to that of the ʿud than the low pitches of the hajhuj. The player, usually the ensemble's leader accompanies himself on the ginbri while singing. The instrument requires a pick, again like a guitar, but instead of using a triangular plastic pick that might be available in a music shop, performers opt for a long, thin shaving of gazelle horn. When this gets lost (as picks always do), cutting a strip lengthwise off of a credit card gets the job done.

The wind instrument that is most closely associated with the hamadsha—one that is also prominent in the ʿissawa tradition—is the ghita. The wooden double reed looks and works much like the Western oboe, but it has open holes drilled into its body instead of the keys and pads that mark the oboe, clarinet, or similar woodwinds. Two or more players play ghitas simultaneously and ornament their lines, dancing around each other as they repeat a melody. The sound projects well, especially outside, which makes this an identifiable part of hamadsha processions (see Figure 5.3).

The hamadsha ritual itself demonstrates both changes in taste, as older austere segments were replaced by more intense ones, and the importance of devotional chanting that celebrates both Sidi Ali and the members' relationship with Aisha. The brotherhood's history sits alongside the healing service that it can perform for its adepts and clients, emphasizing a dual role: these groups increasingly navigate their own religious

Figure 5.3 Ghita player performing during a procession in Sidi Ali.

needs and the spiritual needs of those who invite them into their homes (and pay them for the service). While there is some flexibility in how these events may play out, I will follow what Amrani's ensemble did during one particular evening in Meknes as a general structure. This allows for the description of the minor, but significant, interludes that break up the larger segments of the overnight ceremony.

Like so many other ritual ceremonies in Morocco, the hamadsha ritual begins outside with a short invocation followed by the ʿada or dakhla, an opening or procession. What was historically a short procession to the home with reverent chants has been replaced. The prayers, known as "Salatu al-Nabi" (prayers to the Prophet), gave way to music and drumming that incite a trance state in those who are possessed by Aisha. This segment, known as the hadra, closes the event as well, bringing Aisha's prominence to the foreground by bookending the ceremony. I will return to this segment later. The older prayers punctuated neighborhoods with large hamadsha communities as recently as the 1970s, when people could join in these processions to remember the passing of a member of the brotherhood. Amrani remembered these times fondly before telling me that the change came from the people and from their changing tastes: "They decide, not us." The groups had to follow the demands of their audiences and, in doing so, lost this older opening segment.

Once the group and those who are there to experience the ceremony are inside and situated, after younger members have lit the charcoal and heated the drum heads, older members have rested momentarily, and others have returned from a smoke break, they begin the hizb. This rhythmic chanted poetry repeats the words of the brotherhood's important past figures. The lines are prayers that begin with the central statement of Islamic faith: "There is no god but God … ." The rhythmic patterns and melodic turns create a sense of syncopation and energy, all within the natural phrases of the memorized Arabic texts. To give an idea of the scope of these poems and prayers, their recitation in my recording takes nearly 18 minutes, despite a quick pace. The texture changes as the group moves from chanting together to passing phrases back and forth to singing well-known religious songs, but always with the focus on the clarity of these words.

After a series of blessings that draw on the text that opens the Quran—known as the fatiha—the ensemble members disperse for a break. Some enjoy tea, others step outside for a cigarette, and everyone falls into conversation with old and new friends, mingling with their peers and the large crowd of attendees. When they come back together, the group begins the first of two segments focused on a different type of poetry. These poems are long and regular in their structure and, unlike the bulk of the earlier hizb, here the rhythms of the poetry are oriented around a pattern. No longer does the musical setting of the text bend to meet the words. This trait aligns with the fact that one of the members (in this case, the leader and singer, Amrani himself) picks up the ginbri to accompany the words with an instrumental melody.

After a warm up of short songs that are appropriate for this setting, the group dives into the long poems, called al-unasa al-saghira. The later return of this genre of poetry, al-unasa al-kabira, adds drums. The "saghira" and "kabira" in these terms mean "small" and "large," respectively. The poems are from the same repertoire and can be interchangeable, but the addition of drums and energy makes the two sections feel dramatically different. Within the poetry of this first segment, al-unasa al-saghira, the texts continue praising the God, the Prophet, and the history of the brotherhood. One poem, "Warshan," (The Carrier Pigeon), tells the story of Sidi Ali, Sidi Dghughi, and Aisha that Amrani recounted earlier. The main singer ornaments the words and melodies as he recites the verses and the group joins him on the refrains. The group and many others who are present clap a pattern of short and long notes: short, long, short, short, long (see Example 5.1).

In terms of musical notation, the long notes within this rhythmic pattern are not twice the length of the short ones. This clear 5 note figure highlights the limits of western notation: in those terms, this is a 12/8 meter, but the regularity of the claps and the ways in which the spaces between them get filled in make it clear that this is "in five," though it may be an uneven "five." In nearly all music that contains a pulse, a beat, the

S = short
L = long

S L S S L

Example 5.1 Skeletal rhythmic clapping pattern used during al-unasa al-kabira.

pulse is imagined to be regular. It moves forward with consistency. Here, instead, the pulse is uneven, though the figure as a whole is consistent throughout the poem. This becomes clearer when the group moves from the al-unasa al-saghira segment, through an interlude, and returns to this pattern using drums and more embellishment.

After roughly 20 minutes that included 2 or 3 poems, but before the ensemble moved into the tasliyya section, a guest joining the group for the day sang a beautiful solo. Muhammad Soussi is a malhun singer who returns in Chapter 7, but his presence here shows his interest in and mastery of this particular style of Sufi music. Beginning the tasliyya, the group pulled out drums that included the ones described earlier, but added a new one that is generally associated with the 'issawa brotherhood. In fact, a member of a local 'issawa brotherhood was also joining the group for the evening and played the new instrument, a pair of drums tied together called a tabla, demonstrating how the lines between these groups are far from strict. The fact that Amrani described this as a local Fez practice (even though this particular event was in the nearby city of Meknes) emphasizes the flexibility that performers and audiences can have within a ritual. The group proceeded to sing songs that I had heard on other occasions with other brotherhoods and in concerts that had nothing to do with the hamadsha. This was a moment of respite, a rest from the brotherhood's heavier poetry. It was a period of sacred entertainment. And, like many of the other segments, it extended for about 20 minutes. At the energetic conclusion, Amrani completed a fatiha. He blessed individuals, orienting his words to match their individual needs, not unlike a priest or minister praying for individual members of a congregation outside of a service. The blessings were punctuated, once again, by rhythmic recitations of short holy texts.

After another break, Amrani returned to the ginbri for the second iteration of the hamadsha's long-form poetry. The next segment, called al-unasa al-kabira, mirrors the sound of the sung texts that appeared in the al-unasa al-saghira segment. The poems are interchangeable between these two, though the intensity of the "large" (kabir) version is heightened in part because of the presence of drums to accompany the ginbri and voices. Amrani began by singing a free rhythm version of a few lines of poetry over his ginbri playing. With a nod, members of his group entered with the main drum rhythm on the guwwal, a pattern that outlines and fills in the spaces between the clapping heard before (see Example 5.2).

A technical note about these figures points toward the difficulty in understanding and representing these rhythmic patterns and the ways in which they differ from western musical assumptions. I have intentionally omitted the time signature from these figures. While the patterns fit within a 12/8 meter that is standard to Western notation, the way in which players perform and sing over this pattern implies that the internal

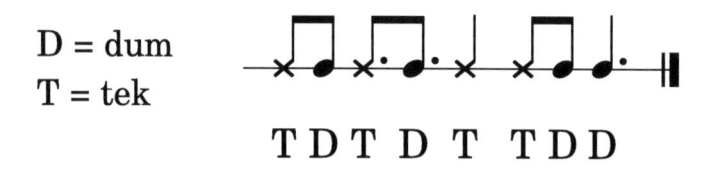

D = dum
T = tek

T D T D T T D D

Example 5.2 The guwwal pattern from the al-unasa al-kabira segment. The two types sounds, dum and tek, are made from striking different parts of the drum. The dum is a lower, more resonant pitch, while the tek is higher and often muted.

beats do not align with some assumptions that 12/8 implies. For example, there are not twelve eighth notes. Instead, I would argue, the five beats in Example 5.1 organize the time. That the beats are irregular, but the pattern repeats consistently is one of the features of these ritual segments and their poetry. To further complicate the matter, the final beat of each rhythmic cycle is often delayed. Examples 5.2 and 5.3 show that the short and long beats are important markers of time, not syncopations away from a regular pulse that would be expected within a standard western conception of meter. This, however, requires a dramatic reimagining of what beat, pulse, meter, and other foundational musical concepts might mean, evoking a larger discussion.

Example 5.3 better demonstrates how the melody and poetry work within this off-kilter rhythmic pattern. This is a short transcription from an interview where Amrani and Fredric Calmus demonstrated a commonly used segment of a poem. Amrani sang a line solo before Fredric, who was also playing guwwal, joined him for a choral segment. Likely because Amrani taught Fredric and the two have been working closely together for years, they ornamented the melodies similarly. I am adding a simpler version of the melody—a barebones version that would be close to what the ginbri would play if Amrani had taken his out during our interview—to show how much variance the performs have in the moment. The difference between the lines is telling, as is their close relationship to the guwwal pattern.

The event escalates as everyone stands and begins the hadra. In today's ceremony, this is a return to the sound of the opening. The guwwal players circle the room, holding their drums on their shoulders. As they beat out a new set of five-beat patterns (see Example 5.4), anyone who is possessed by Lalla Aisha might fall into a trance. The trancers, usually women, kneel on the floor, crawling and often making loud noises. It is similar to the trancing that happens in a gnawa ceremony, though here the group is mobile, and instead of the trancing bodies coming to the musicians, a circle of musicians encloses the trancer to build intensity. With the ghita players returning and the pace and density of the rhythmic patterns increasing, the trance gains a stronger hold until reaching a catharsis. Others on the room stand, dance, and sing along when there are words. The environment becomes a mixture: part ritual ceremony, part festive celebration.

Old photos of and writing about the hamadsha focus on these moments, which happen outdoors during major processions. There were a number of practices that have fallen out of favor, the most infamous of which was known as "head slashing." Vincent Crapanzano (1980 and 1981) describes this self-mutilation in detail, where Aisha's demands of blood caused her possessed bodies—in this case mostly men—to cut the top of their heads with knives. The drip of blood that would fall down their faces placated the spirit and reinforced the relationship between this world and the next. While the slashing is not particularly common in my experience, the importance of blood has not disappeared completely. In the ceremony that opened this chapter, the host spent a great deal of time pacing the room, stopping in front of walls or pillars, and slamming his head into the tile. He eventually had a similar dark streak of blood winding down his face, appeasing the spirit.

The final segment of the ceremony was a return from these heavy sounds and spirits. In the saf al-ginbri, Amrani pulled the ginbri back out and the group sang an hour's worth of songs. In a later interview, Amrani told me that there was a great deal of ʿaita in there, referencing another popular music genre. Interestingly, in his descriptions,

Example 5.3 A simplified version of the melody that Amrani and Calmus sang during a lesson (top line); an approximate transcription of what they sang that includes ornaments, syncopations, and other details (middle line); and the guwwal pattern that organizes the performance (bottom line).

Version 1

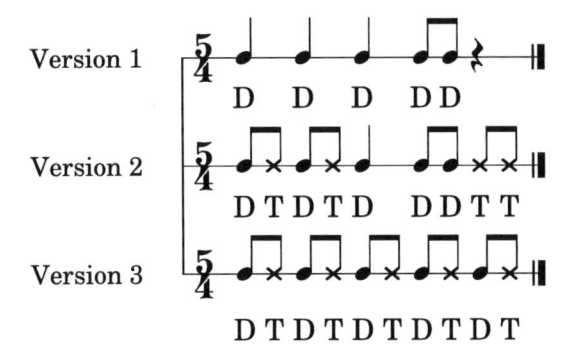

D D D DD

Version 2

D T D T D   D D T T

Version 3

D T D T D T D T

Example 5.4 Guwwal rhythms that are common during the hadra segment of the ceremony. Different players may add divisions that increase the overall density. Some "swing" their strokes while others do not, leading to a rhythmic tension that is similar to what gives funk grooves a distinct sense of forward motion (see Danielsen 2006).

this segment came before the hadra, while in performance, it closed the ritual evening that was, by this time, a ritual early morning. The 5-ness and metric play of this tradition's music continues here as the music follows a 5/8 meter, divided into 2 uneven beats. After an hour of these songs, which many sing along to, the event closes with a short invocation of "Amin" (Amen). The hosts pull out tables and a breakfast that they had been preparing, and everyone who stayed through the overnight ceremony sits, enjoying a meal together.

The hamadsha ceremony mirrors a number of similar Sufi practices that happen every week in neighborhoods—both rich and poor—across Morocco. It holds tradition highly, maintaining the musical ritual from the past. It also, however, shows how performers are willing to shift their work to meet the needs and tastes of their clients. By replacing the sounds that accompany the opening procession to provide an extra opportunity for those who are present to trance and reinforce their relationships with Lalla Aisha, they nod to what those clients want from the evening. It is also becoming more common for attendees who are possessed by other spirits like Sidi Hamu, those who are more commonly associated with the gnawa, to fall into a trance during these moments. As people's experiences of spiritual relationships change, and as they listen more widely to the music of different brotherhoods, practice changes too. This is especially the case as the hamadsha and groups like them step outside of the home or the ritual to find new venues and stages for sharing their sound with the wider world. What was a vocation is increasingly an occupation and, as such, the demands of a sacred-oriented music industry elbow their way into performance practice. This confluence of entertainment, taste, tradition, client demands, and ritual necessity play out in the music of the 'issawa, as seen in the next chapter.

Notes

1 Researchers at the National Consortium for the Study of Terrorism and Responses to Terrorism (START), for example, maintain a "Global Terrorism Database" (www.start.umd.edu/gtd/) that quantitatively demonstrates the victimization of Muslims by terrorists. This may appear

counterintuitive to Western consumers of the news, as described by Michael Edison Hayden in a short article for ABC News (2017).
2   Jonathan Shannon's *Among the Jasmine Trees* includes a chapter describing similar practices in Syria in great detail (2006).
3   It is worth noting that the gnawa do not generally self-identify as Sufi. Some, however, do. This can lead to confusion and very different representations within the popular press and outside of the community, as people consider whether this group is within, or sits outside of, appropriate Islamic practice (see Witulski 2018b).
4   Other groups within and outside of Morocco have made similar adaptations. Perhaps the best known worldwide are the "Whirling Dervishes," musicians and dancers affiliated with the mevlevi (or mawlawiyya) Sufi order based in Turkey.

CHAPTER **6**

Sufi Entertainments

In the summer of 2009, two ʿissawa groups invited me to join them for weddings. Muqaddim Abdellah Yâakoubi and Muqaddim Adil are both well-respected throughout Fez, though Yâakoubi has turned his success into a recording career and ascended the brightest stages across Morocco. His group was expensive to hire (not that anything relating to weddings is ever a bargain, one of the many ways in which Moroccan weddings mirror similar events elsewhere). In both cases, I followed musicians, recording or photographing their performances and sitting and waiting during the long periods of downtime that are familiar to any gigging musician. I was invited to attend multiple weddings later on as a guest, but this experience as a part of the entertainment was quite different.

One of Muqaddim Abdellah's wedding gigs was in a part of town that I had never been to. Instead of being nestled in the old city, where I lived and spent most of the time, we had to load into a handful of rented microbuses to drive out into the wealthier suburbs. Surrounded by new construction, beautifully manicured neighborhoods with leafy trees, and driveways with cars, we unloaded the drums and horns that would enliven the evening. The ensemble members unpacked bright orange jellabas, putting them over their dress shirts so that the collars came out over their draped hoods. The look is a common one, combining the traditional dress with more modern styles. It is a variant of dressy that bridged the Sufi brotherhood's norms and the elegance of the venue that we were entering.[1]

After much waiting, darkness came and the guests arrived. Abdellah's group performed two processions during the evening. The first felt preliminary, showing off what they could do for the assembled crowd. The second celebrated the couple, starting up the party. In the summer night's heat, the instrumentalists, all men, lined up in pairs. Two drummers with small marching drums slung over their shoulders led the way, followed by three more drummers, each with a large frame drum with large cymbals built into the rim (further description of these instruments follows). The thick rhythms from these percussionists formed a bed of sound for the two ghita players in the next row. As was the case with the hamadsha, the ghita players were forceful with their melodies; this was a loud processional music. Even if it was not necessarily meant for weddings, by maintaining the procession, today's performers effectively energize onlookers. The final row included two men holding six-foot-long trumpets out above the rest of the group, blasting rhythmic punctuations between them.

Once they made their way into the hall and out into a courtyard where guests were milling around tables and chairs (imagine a pre-reception cocktail hour, but without the alcohol), the ensemble lined up along a wall. The horns projected out toward the crowd and an older woman began dancing to the 'issawa's music in her green kaftan (a type of elegant gown) while others watched and clapped. The drummers were singing, but their words were inaudible over the sounds coming from the ghita, percussion, and nfar (six-foot long trumpets described later). Two little boys looked on. As the ghita melodies wound from one song to the next without a pause, the nfar players put away their instruments. The shouted lyrics from the drummers were slightly more present, and those in the audience who knew the songs were singing along. Abdellah stood off to the side, clapping along while watching his ensemble perform. Professional videographers and young men carrying their long cables passed by in front of the group, filming their performance for the later wedding video. As the ghita players worked their way upward to higher scale degrees, the percussionists increased their intensity and the nfar players rejoined to punctuate the increasing energy. Then, abruptly, they ended their performance, put down their instruments, and retreated back outside for a break before the second wedding procession began.

A short while later, the group and the guests came together back out in the garden in front of the venue. Young women dressed in kaftans, probably relatives of the couple, held large candles and led the procession back into the hall. Men dressed in traditional garments, servers from the staff, held up large trays with conical lids, carrying them in front of the 'issawa group. Under these lids were gifts to the bride and groom: foods, incense, and other traditional items. Then came a cluster of guests (many holding cameras to record the event) and the musicians, organized as they were before. The crowd moved slowly—I was at the end, so I can only imagine that the pauses came from delays in putting down the trays or figuring out which direction to go in. The horns blasted their way from the back of the line as we made our way through the doors. This time, instead of heading to the courtyard, the train of people took a left turn, entering the venue's main hall where the wedding was set up.

Again, Muqaddim Abdellah looked on from the side. This time he stood in front of the room's focal point, where the couple would later sit on a large throne. He had set up his own instrument of choice, a set of drum heads attached to a stand. These look and sound like the timbales that appear in so much music derived from Cuban or Puerto Rican styles (like salsa or Latin jazz), but unlike the hand drums that his group played, they were not easily picked up and carried in a procession. With the nfar, ghita, and drummers circled around him, and with the videographer's lights and cameras focused on him (he shines for a few moments in my own video), Abdellah begins playing along with his ensemble. Some guests look on, some clap along, and others greet each other, smiling in the excitement of the celebration. Again, when the group finishes, they pick up and leave quickly, getting out of the way of the next stages of the evening's agenda.

About a half hour later, Abdellah's musicians were called back into service. Introducing the bride and groom, the ensemble stood off to the side playing loudly, but this time the crowd's attention was focused to the center. The couple—having married earlier in the day—were sitting in two ornate thrones that were being held up by the crew of servers who had earlier carried in the wedding gifts. They were rocking back and forth, dancing to the music, while slowly turning to show the newlyweds to the wide circle of friends, family, and loved ones. When the ʿissawa group concluded, other music was already being pumped through the speaker system.

The evening went on like this, alternating between a bustle of activity and waiting, a normal state of affairs for a professional musician. There was a stage set up to one side of the room where at least two groups took turns performing through the evening (there may have been more; this was obviously an expensive wedding). Abdellah set aside his group's role in leading the ritual procession to stand and sing, and the boisterous sound of his ensemble transferred into a tight act. He is a charismatic performer with a smooth voice, one of the reasons that he has been able to parlay his ritual into a successful recording career. He invited me to join them, sitting me down with a small drum. In an effort to not make a fool out of myself (and to make it easier to stare at my neighbors and copy what they were doing), I stopped recording at this point. The evening as a whole was fun. That was the point: it was entertainment and celebration. This was not a time for spirit possessions, but weddings have a tendency to be sacred, though a different sort of sacred. They are periods of thanksgiving and praise, especially for religious families. It turns out that, as has been the case for me as a classical musician playing in string quartets back home, they are also an important part of making a living.

Weddings in Morocco, as in so many other places, are extravagant affairs. And they are expensive. Couples and families who have the means rent out elegant facilities in the new city or palatial homes in the medina. Even those who have a reception at home must account for the numerous kaftans (ornate dresses) that the bride wears throughout the evening and the copious food that the hosts provide for guests. And while I've been to events where the couple uses CDs instead of musicians, hiring an ensemble (or two or three) is the expectation. There is some leeway as to what kind of group a family may choose, but at the fanciest weddings I attended, there was a premium on having an alternation between shʿabi music and the ʿissawa brotherhood. One that I went to had another folk group standing outside, singing to guests as they left. The tastes differ across the country: I was told that Tangier often featured gnawa musicians during weddings. In all cases, though, the presence of the musicians served to heighten the experience for guests, to entertain.

If the point was entertainment, then, why invite a bunch of Sufis? The marriage itself happens before the celebration begins. As is the case in the United States, the legality of marriage is akin to a contract, signed before witnesses. The ʿissawa enter the picture later, when the guests have gathered. They lend an air of the sacred to a major life event. The songs that they sing are popular and it is often difficult to tell if they are singing to, or following, the crowd. But on another level, being an ʿissawa performer at a wedding is just like any other gig. When I joined Adil's group, we spent the vast majority of our time sitting, chatting, smoking, and drinking coffee in a row of chairs, outside, behind the coffee service. We waited. Every once in a while, the muqaddim would beckon us back and the musicians would get up to perform, I would get my camera and recorder ready, and they would play for a few minutes while the other group took their seats.

What role, I wondered, does gigging play in making the sacred lives of the ʿissawa public? With so many groups competing for these gigs, how does each navigate the pressures of the local music industry?

In preceding chapters, ritual performers have been adapting to the changing realities of their audiences and occupations. While membership in a brotherhood can still be a vocation—exclusively a duty or avenue for worship—it has also turned into an opportunity for economic gain. Importantly, there are few performers for whom the sacred elements of this practice are subsidiary to the economic ones (though it's impossible to know people's hearts, I have to trust their words and actions). For most, new opportunities give them a chance to share their music and their worship with a wider listenership. They are expanding their community, marketing their faith. They are also speaking out about their own relationships with Islam, each other, and the divine. I imagine that similar opportunities inspire many Christian rock and pop stars, not to mention churches themselves who utilize and advocate through new technologies, festivals, and social media.

The fact that so many groups have been successful demonstrates that there is a fertile body of listeners who enjoy and are inspired by these forms of religious music. To be clear, few of these artists achieve stardom or even find ways to make a living through music alone. While sacred music has some clear structural benefits (venues for performance at pilgrimage sites, for example), the competition is increasingly tough. Groups are generally supportive of each other, but they do vie for the same clients or stage time at major events. For most, these types of performance are a part of worship: they stay local and help out when someone needs healing, for example.

The groups that tour or regularly play wedding gigs, however, must contend with a difficulty that is specific to this context, where religious musical activities come out of the mosque (or church) and ascend to a stage: they have to entertain, too. Questions that these artists must constantly ask themselves are numerous. Is this appropriate for a stage, where people may or may not be paying attention, listening with an open heart, or may even be drinking and smoking? How far can I stray from the ritual to appease these audiences while remaining true to this worship? What is my goal here, to proselytize or make money for my group? Can I serve two masters at once?

Performing in these contexts force a religious musician to navigate a host of difficult pressures. Perhaps the most important is the audience, for without an audience, there is no gig. In other chapters, clients have demanded new styles or songs from religious performers. The same is true for weddings and festivals, no matter the brotherhood. What the audience says, goes … unless it's too far. But where is the line? For these professional settings, the power rests with the crowd or the paying host. Describing music at a wedding in 2011, Muqaddim Adil noted that popular (shʿabi) and spiritual (ruhiyya) styles are both common: "When people want shʿabi, we play shʿabi. When they want ruhiyya, we play that."

Shʿabi is a broad term for popular music. The word also references youth, making explicit the connection between this music and a younger generation's tastes. That those tastes also align with questions of loose morality fits within common discussions about "kids these days," to use a familiar phrase. The variety of styles that fit within the shʿabi category come from cities and regions across the country. They often feature a number of percussionists beating out an energetic rhythm under (or over) a singer and one or two instrumentalists. The instruments here are also usually strings and can include guitar, violin, banjo, or others. More frequently now, the groups include a keyboard player using synthesized string sounds to gain a degree of flexibility. Pitch-corrected vocals—electronically modified singers using software like "Auto-Tune"—figure prominently, making the sound of the electronic enhancement a part of the aesthetic.

The music is for dancing and many groups maintain two or more women who dance in front of the ensemble.[2] The dance itself draws on a long history of singers and dancers known as the shikhat (see Ciucci 2010), who were—and in many cases still are—stereotyped as prostitutes living on the outside of acceptability within Moroccan society. This gendered dynamic of popular music where men sing in styles derivative of women's practices is an important one. There are significant counter-examples of women who have gained a great deal of fame in the popular music industry, but in many cases they still carry a stigma. It was not uncommon for men to lean over to me and wonder aloud about a woman's sexuality or promiscuity. As if to prove the importance of continued research in to the gendered dynamics of popular music in Morocco, it was also common for these same men to question a male singer's sexual orientation if he sang popular songs "like a woman." Perceptions of sexual transgression are central, and only sometimes unspoken, in how adaptation plays with audiences. This is especially the case when the group doing the innovating is coming from a place of sacred reverence, which is how these Sufi groups build and maintain their own authenticity and legitimacy.

The 'Issawa and Their Ritual

The 'issawa were founded in the 16th century as a part of another long-standing Sufi tariqa called the idrissiyya. Like Morocco's monarchy at that time and since, the founders claimed to have sharifian descent: they were within the Prophet Muhammad's bloodline through the new group's namesake, Muhammad bin 'Issa. Bin 'Issa lived from 1465 to 1526 and is remembered as a complete or perfect teacher, as reflected in the name that he's most known by: "Sheikh al-Kamil" (The Complete Sheikh). His tomb is in Meknes and is the destination for the procession described in Chapter 5. The group has spread widely since the 1500s, with membership throughout Morocco, across North Africa, and elsewhere around the Mediterranean. Other country's 'issawa brotherhoods have close affiliations with music, economics, and politics in the same ways as the ones in Morocco. The successes and concerns described here are hardly unique. In fact, the 'issawa population in Tunisia has long been a focus of ethnomusicological scholarship (see Davis 1997 and Jones 1977). Most research on Morocco's 'issawa population has come from Moroccan or French scholars, much of which informs the background to my own experiences described in this chapter (see Nabti 2006, Nabti 2007, Langlois 1999, Saghir Janjar 1984).

Unlike the gnawa, the brotherhood has a strict organizational hierarchy thanks, in part, to the status of its leaders as sharifian, as descendants of the Prophet. While the central zawiya is in Meknes, many cities have more local leadership. Each of these figures, called a muqaddim, organizes a wide array of smaller groups. Each group's leader is also a muqaddim. Thus, the city heads are the muqaddims of the muqaddims (in Arabic, muqaddim al-muqaddimin). While Muqaddim Abdellah runs his ensemble, he answers to a higher figure who, in turn, answers to the heads of the brotherhood in Meknes. The administrative leaders also hold another role that affiliates them with the government: they control which groups lead the major processions each year in Meknes and Fez (the Fez event leads to the tomb of Moulay Idriss, the city's founder who is the namesake for the idrissi brotherhood that the 'issawa branched off from). They also determine who represents the 'issawa in other events during the year, at Ramadan celebrations, and on television. The range of public events that feature the 'issawa can be staggering, especially during wedding and festival season when these groups appear in all sorts of public spaces. But the central mission of the administrators and "workers" (khadam, ensemble members) alike, according to Nabti, is to spread the brotherhood's baraka. This involves austere ritual ceremonies focused on both devotional poetry and demonic exorcism, the second of which puts the brotherhood into the same conflicted gray areas as the gnawa and hamadsha, described in earlier chapters. So how is it that these public and private facets of 'issawa practice coincide?

Part of this contention comes from these myriad contexts in which groups like the 'issawa perform. Notably, however, the lines of conflict and debates are hardly clean; they are not as straightforward as a revivalist perspective of Islam that pushes back against the innovations made by certain brotherhoods. Instead, they carve out distinctions between communities while also splitting those same communities and pitting themselves against each other. These debates challenge the authority of the very people who stand in positions of authority. They force musicians and listeners to consider their own intentions toward this music. As if this were not enough, these questions all unravel within a larger set of pressures around the idea of a Moroccan national identity itself, as described throughout Parts I and II. Kamal Feriali describes how the state itself contributes to confusion over these Sufi organizations and their place within wider society. While the palace theologians regularly denounce trance activities like those of the 'issawa, hamadsha, and gnawa, he explains, the monarchy send financial support to major events including the mawlid processions in Meknes that celebrate the lives of "model" saints like Bin 'Issa, the namesake of the 'issawa brotherhood (Feriali 2009, 49).

The efforts undertaken by the musical and religious groups described throughout these chapters emerge from this complex of creative ideas and complex ideologies. The very concept of innovation is questioned within Islam; the Arabic word, bida', carries a connotation of departure. It is a willful move away from the right path. But, as is the case with music, the use and intent of changes matters. How and how much each innovation (or each musical activity) pulls you toward or away from God is the open question. This chapter and Chapter 7 show religious brotherhoods navigating the pressures of the contemporary world. Famous ensemble leaders like Abdellah Yâakoubi (see Figure 6.1) have leveraged their opportunities well to create an occupation out of a vocation. This opens them up to concerns from outsiders and insiders alike that question their intent. Are they in this for the right reasons? As will become clear, these criticisms can emanate from the highest offices of the 'issawa brotherhood itself. They are not only the recourse of reformists. But these groups have fans, too. They bring people into the brotherhood and help religious practices and Moroccan traditions to percolate through everyday life.

The 'issawa use a number of instruments to engage these large crowds and, by swapping different instruments in and out of various ritual segments, they build a wide range of textures to do the same for spirits. Like the hamadsha, the 'issawa are mostly a percussion ensemble. Two melodic instruments come into play, but both are mostly reserved for the processions and highest intensity moments of an evening ceremony.

Figure 6.1 Abdellah Yâakoubi, a prominent ʿissawa muqaddim, performing at the Fez Festival of World Sacred Music.

The first is the ghita, an instrument that has appeared with other traditions described in previous chapters (see Figure 5.3). Ghita players, in fact, are professionals who regularly move from one tradition to the next. They are hired and paid. Unlike the members of the ensembles themselves, they may be outsiders in this sense and, in my experience, many ghita players step away from an all-night ceremony—whether for a cigarette or a walk to a nearby café—during the majority of the event.

One of the instruments that most directly announces the presence of the ʿissawa is the nfar, a long trumpet. At roughly six feet, the nfar has to be assembled and disassembled before and after each use. Players separate the pieces of metal tubing and stash them away in a bag. But when they get them out, the nfar creates a formidable sound. Because it has no valves, it only uses one pitch (though others are possible because of the overtone series). Because it is a wind instrument related to a trumpet, I include it here alongside the ghita, but it is not melodic. Instead, two or more players each use different nfars to create a rhythmic sheet of sound. Adding to the drums, the nfar is as much a percussion instrument as anything. Furthermore, it contributes to the spectacle of an ʿissawa procession as the nfar players join or cross their instruments out in front of them and above the heads of the rest of the group (see Figure 6.2).

To thicken the rhythmic texture of their music, the ʿissawa use a range of drums. These include large bendir-like frame drums with cymbals built into the rim that look like oversize tambourines (see Figure 6.3) and the small marching drums that Muqaddim Abdellah's ensembles carried during the wedding described above. Notably, the marching drums are not played only with drumsticks on the top head, as is the case

Figure 6.2 Nfar players and other members of Muqaddim Adil's ensemble parading into a wedding ceremony in Fez.

with a western marching drum. The player uses one hand to play the top head with a stick and the other to beat a counter-rhythm on the bottom head. Within the ritual, I have seen groups use old fire bells like those that used to hang in schools, the quraqib from the gnawa tradition, small hourglass-shaped drums like those used in malhun (see Chapter 7), and the tabla, a pair of drums tied together (not to be confused with the Indian tabla, this tabla is a pair of clay drums played with sticks).

While many of the ʿissawa muqaddims that I have seen perform are primarily singers, some, like Abdallah, lead the ensemble while playing the tabla. Other ensembles have incorporated instruments like the electric keyboard or borrowed elements of shʿabi groups. This adaptation can serve a pragmatic role, as it allows the groups to perform popular tunes alongside their religious repertoire. Instrumentation, therefore, is an important marker of ʿissawa identity (the sound of the nfar travels widely) and the brotherhood's willingness to meet the needs of their clients and adepts where they are by outfitting themselves to perform a wide range of borrowed material.

As was the case with other religious traditions, these instruments create distinct textures throughout a structured ritual event. The opening segments of the all-night ʿissawa ritual are devoid of other instruments. These invocations and recitations follow an outdoor procession that sounds and operates like the wedding reception processions that opened the chapter. After entering a space, usually the home of a client, the ceremony—called a lila, the same name used in gnawa and hamadsha traditions—departs

Figure 6.3 A member of Muqaddim Adil's ensemble during a demonstration in Fez.

from the structure that animates a wedding. The ensemble gathers and sits, readying themselves to bless the space and audibly mark the evening as sacred. The ʿissawa move through a series of texts, rhythmically reciting words written by past Sufi masters, including the brotherhood's namesake, Sheikh al-Kamil (Muhammad bin ʿIssa). The first moments, which prepare the minds and spirits of practitioners and clients alike, is the dhikr, a set of repeated phrases that remind everyone of God's presence. These phrases can include the ninety-nine names of God used in the Quran or the statement of faith, the shahada ("There is no god but Allah and Muhammad is his Prophet").

The texts that follow begin with the rabbaniyya. Mehdi Nabti translates this as "the divine office," reflecting a Catholic set of prayers and scripture readings used by both clergy and lay people. Like the Catholic Divine Office, the rabbaniyya includes prayers collected by past figures within the brotherhood's history (and leaders of Sufi brotherhoods that preceded the ʿissawa) alongside readings from the Quran and other common forms of prayer, such as a return to segments from the dhikr. Long memorized devotional poems can also appear here, such as one called "Al-Burda," a 13th century metaphoric text about the Prophet's cloak (Al-Sayid Ibrahim and Bin Zuhair 1985). The wird, the next segment of these opening invocations, has the ʿissawa members professing their adherence to the brotherhood. This relationship goes above and beyond the standard of Islam and, in fact, members are required to recite the wird texts that Sheikh al-Kamil wrote after each of their five daily prayers (Nabti 2006). This opening concludes with a similar text, the hizb. Some of these terms and concepts mirror those seen in the hamadsha ceremony from Chapter 5, and they appear in most, if not all, Sufi organizations throughout the country and region. Yet, as a whole, they demonstrate the uniqueness of each group. Leadership and tradition dictate different texts, though some (like "Al-Burda") appear in many contexts. In this way, these devotional recitations simultaneously connect and distinguish various sects of Sufism.

The poetic texts continue as the evening shifts into the qasida segment. As was the case in sections of the hamadsha ritual, the music begins to be dominated by long poems within a classical style called qasidas. Unlike the preceding sections, these poems can come from a variety of sources. Nabti (2006) describes how, in the 17th century, malhun composers who were adepts of the brotherhood used their artistry to create new poetry for inclusion within the ritual. The sung poetry that appears here is devotional, and the style of singing and accompanimental percussion is unique to the 'issawa brotherhood. Their ways of singing poems that can be shared with other groups is one of the things that identifies the group and differentiates them. For example, the moments from the Meknes hamadsha layla described in Chapter 5 that used an 'issawa tabla (a pair of drums) were easily distinguishable from the hamadsha's own way of performing the qasidas during the al-unasa al-saghir and al-unasa al-kabir segments of their ritual (see Example 5.3 in Chapter 5).

As demonstrated throughout previous chapters, brotherhoods commonly adapt their ritual and public performances for a variety of reasons. The 'issawa, however, have a tendency to go further by devoting entire segments of their lila to the music of other groups. In responding to the demands of their clients, they change the overall dramatic arc and feel of the evening ceremony. Further, they have a history of marginalization that is shown in stories of eating scorpions, drinking boiling water, and other extreme demonstrations of faith and possession. By discarding these practices and replacing them with borrowed music and spirits, they show how adeptly they can navigate the changing landscape of religion, entertainment, and the business of being a professional troupe in the 21st century. It is not uncommon to hear repertoire from the darqawiyya, jilala, and sadqiyya brotherhoods in an 'issawa setting. These other groups each maintain their own groups and zawiyas across the country. They specialize in their own songs and musical styles, though, like so much of the poetry, many texts appear in across brotherhoods. By learning and performing other songs, the 'issawa can provide an extra service for clients. For example, there are few active jilala groups in Fez. Whenever I sought one out, I came across the same two organizations, one male and one female (see Figure 6.4). But their music and its unique rhythms regularly appear in 'issawa music. The small flutes and frame drums that animate them are replaced by the percussion and ghita players who adapt the songs to their own instrumentation. The 'issawa are hardly the only group that does this—the gnawa also incorporate jilala rhythms into some of their songs—but, at least in my experience, they do so more regularly than any others.

Mehdi Nabti further describes the incorporation of the ahl twat tradition, from the country's south-east, into their ceremonies. This group's popular music involves an intricately choreographed dance in which a group of men use large sticks as

Figure 6.4 Members of the two main jilala-focused groups collaborating to demonstrate their rituals in Meknes. The men seated on the floor are using bendirs, and the two behind them are each playing a qasba. Note the use of the gnawa quraqib. Women seated on the other side of the room are also playing guwwal drums.

props (Nabti 2006). While I have not seen a group enact this particular drama, reading about it struck me because of a visit that a friend and I made to Abderrahim Amrani in 2013. Expecting to sit and talk about Moroccan music, a common occurrence, Phil Murphy and I made our way out to his home on the far side of Fez's old city. When we arrived, however, we were surprised to see a flurry of activity. Amrani was in the middle of a class. He was teaching a group of boys to dance, sing, and play the music of the ahl twat. I went upstairs and took some photos of the "students" (who were quite good), while Phil, with his better camera, stayed closer to the action (see Figure 6.5). That this group with roots distant from Fez and Meknes, would be in demand elsewhere in the country is significant enough. That ʿissawa groups are incorporating their sound into their rituals and a hamadsha muqaddim is training his own ahl twat ensemble demonstrates the competitive need for these religious leaders to meet the demands of their audiences, to offer something fresh and different while respecting their own traditions, and to support and maintain a sense of Moroccan heritage.

As the evening continues, the ʿissawa extend their borrowings further. To open "doors" into the spirit world, they make use of music and ritual practices that are associated with the gnawa. Other groups do the same, showing the potency of a tradition that has been historically marginalized. While gnawa music and ritual is far from normal or acceptable in many Moroccan communities (see Chapter 4), its inclusion in these Sufi rituals demonstrates the respect that many clients have for their efficacy. While ʿissawa, hamadsha, and other groups are also marginal for reasons of social class, poverty, and the questionable "innovations" featured in their practice, they are just as often held up as pillars of Moroccan cultural identity. By including gnawa music (if not the gnawa themselves), they show the growing centrality of these forms of religious practice (or cultural performance, or entertainment) within a national identity. Even

Figure 6.5 Neighborhood youth from Amrani's ahl twat class practicing a stick dance. Photo courtesy of Philip Murphy.

so, the ʿissawa recognize their own limits. They recognize the gnawa, themselves, as the masters of these trance segments (Feriali 2009, 66). While they will work to cure or facilitate certain illnesses that grow from injured relationships between a client and a possessing spirit (a mluk), they are just as apt to refer someone who needs more intensive ritual care to a gnawa mʿallem from the neighborhood or city. While mysterious in so many ways, this therapeutic work done in ritual still operates through the organizational logic of an informal healthcare system, one that lives alongside the "Western" system of medical clinics, doctors, and hospitals.

It is also noteworthy that these borrowings invite criticisms from within the ʿissawa community. In an interview in Rabat in 2011, a prominent ʿissawa muqaddim flatly told me that "there is no gnawa in ʿissawa." Nabti cites a similarly strong perspective from Mulay Idriss ʿIssawi, the spiritual director of Meknes's central ʿissawa zawiya:

> Those things that the muqaddims you know do with the mluk, they're not right. If people have problems with demons, there are real Sufi techniques to get rid of them. But singing 'Lalla Malika,' 'Lalla Aisha' [borrowed songs used to incite trance], what does that mean? It's just psychological, nothing more.

> The mluk ritual has no basis in a mystical tradition. Our tariqa [brotherhood] does not condone it.[3]
>
> (quoted in Nabti 2006)

It may be that the choices that ritual music performers are making—and the criticisms leveled against them—are beginning to sound repetitive. Throughout my time in Morocco, I consistently found myself surprised at the commonalities that extended across and between religious groups. This went beyond the realm of religion (whether formal or informal): moral questions extended into popular culture in clear ways. The connections between personal values and national identity, global community, or diasporic identity were parts of earlier chapters, but these ritual experiences confirmed the constant negotiations that these artists were balancing. Where is the proper line between fidelity to the practices as they have been handed down over the decades or centuries and the demands of today's client-audiences? How much change is too much? At what point is the customer wrong?

The fact that so many groups are simultaneously active within any given city alludes to the close association between these questions and the economic realities of contemporary religious life. A client or audience looking for a certain type of 'issawa ritual can probably find it. If the best groups are unwilling, there is likely to be a younger musician who is looking to make it onto the scene who will adapt. While it is not an 'issawa example, the gnawa birthday party that I describe below shows the commonality of these negotiations. And if the adaptation is questionable, it can always be strategically redefined as a performance. In this way, the overlap between ceremony and performance can be an important tool for these artists as they work to make it within the local "sacred music industry."

Navigating Pop Careers

Fez's old city has two main types of record stores. Most are tiny, little alcoves with some posters and CDs on shelves like one described in an earlier chapter. The CDs never really come down from the shelves anymore. It is MP3 files that are bought and sold. The proprietor will burn a disc of ripped audio files or, as a service, compile a "mix" CD of some hits, a complete ceremony recording, or whatever else the customer needs. Other stores, however, are more firmly linked to record labels like Fessiphone. These larger shops have CDs in cases with simple inserts. The glossy photos can have track information or even a local artist's cellphone number. VCDs (lower quality video CDs that are cheaper to make and play than DVDs) are also common. Instead of a ripped knock-off, a customer can get the original. With the pirated versions selling for around five dirhams (about 60 cents in US currency) and the originals going for closer to 15–20 dirhams (around $2), it is unsurprising that the nicer shops are rarely packed. There is one that sits in Bab Boujloud, a main tourist entrance to the old city, that is always playing music loudly from its speakers. These spaces can sell the newest music, but the novelty fades quickly when the "pirate" shops catch up. Their apparent legitimacy and the cost of their central locations in areas like Boujloud, however, appeared (from my unscientific observation) to keep a steady line of tourist clients coming.

These shops, unlike those that would sell whatever a neighborhood needed, prioritized the local artists who recorded on their affiliated labels. Before I met Abdellah

Yâakoubi, I had seen his face on posters in Bab Boujloud and Rcif, a major market closer to where I had been living. Even when the posters were swapped out for newer releases, his CDs and VCDs, pressed with professional-looking labels, remained ever-present on the store shelves (see Figure 6.6). Yâakoubi's success in professional side of Fez's sacred scene led him to the stages of the Fez Festival of World Sacred Music, where he performed as a featured artist alongside an elite group of renown 'issawa muqaddims (as pictured in Figure 6.1). This creates a feedback loop: his group performs for the most extravagant weddings, demands a large fee, and grows its influential audience.

Abderrahim Amrani, the hamadsha muqaddim from Chapter 5, similarly has many facets to his career. Where the 'issawa were notorious for eating scorpions, and the gnawa were questionable for eating glass and drinking boiling water, each group has been able to largely move away from their marginal status to become symbolic of a local and national heritage. Amrani's role is central to the same move within the hamadsha. He has long considered himself a religious musician, someone capable of operating in a wide variety of settings. In one conversation, he described hanging out with Paco, the gnawa musician who was a prominent member of the famed band Nass El Ghiwane (see Figure 6.7). In another instance, he explained God's grace as the water that nourishes so many types of flowers. Morocco's wealth of Sufi groups and musical styles, he explains, are those flowers. He loves all of their colors.

Alongside his well-trained ensemble, which regularly appears in major festivals and on television, he is quick to take on new innovative projects. I remember my first time listening to *Baba Bahri*, an early release of his that is full of synthesizers and heavily produced dance tracks. It blended religious songs into a pop aesthetic, something he has continued to do. More recently, he created a music video full of scenes from around Rcif, right in the center of the city. His ensemble members performed with malhun groups (as seen in Chapter 7) and on stages with pop acts who came to town.

He went so far as to collaborate with a DJ based in France named DJ Click. The group performed a set that brought their ritual music into a performance where DJ Click could explore and augment the off-kilter rhythmic hamadsha beats. He added to the standard hamadsha instruments by introducing the mouth harp, theremin, and, of course, a wealth of electronically produced beats of his own (see Figure 6.8).

Figure 6.6 One of Abdellah Yâakoubi's VCD recordings.

Figure 6.7 Screenshot from an undated video of Amrani casually singing with a group of other ritual musicians. Amrani is on the left in the foreground and Paco of Nass El Ghiwane is lying down to the right, singing along. See the resources section for a link to the video.

Figure 6.8 A member of Amrani's ensemble playing ghita along with DJ Click, who is playing the theremin.

The lines between sacred ritual, public performance, and educational demonstration are rarely clean. 'Issawa, hamadsha, and gnawa groups are regulars on festival stages and, depending on the region, at weddings and other major events. Their pilgrimages are simultaneously heavy, sacred events and times of entertainment, celebration, and fun. Abderrahim Amrani is not the only one to collaborate with foreign artists: gnawa musicians have been working with jazz players like Randy Weston or rockers like Jimmy Page and Robert Plant for decades. Even within clearly defined boundaries, the experiences of audiences can be flexible. I was invited by a gnawa group in Fez to a gig that they were playing one summer evening in the renovated old city house of a British expatriate. The family had hired the gnawa ensemble to provide entertainment for their son's birthday party. He was college age, and a number of his friends had flown down to Morocco from England (an inexpensive prospect thanks to the accumulation of low-cost airlines between Fez and Europe). I had met the gnawa performer at a previous event at a Fez-based Arabic language school where he played a sampling of the lila repertoire for American and British students.

I had not known what the event was when I arrived, but I was surprised to find Rashida, a woman who I had known for a while who cooked and cleaned for a number of the foreign homeowners across the city. Despite her knowledge of my work, she had never mentioned her interest in gnawa music to me. Though she was there as part of the hired help, I was a guest of the ensemble. Neither of us really knew any of the hosts, a group of white college students, who were drinking and dancing to music from an MP3 player in the courtyard. The ensemble began, playing a similar "set" to what I had heard at the language school. The young musicians used the ritual repertoire as an "act," it was their entertainment for the party. When it became clear that the hosts and guests were enjoying it (they resumed dancing), the group picked up on cues to further engage their audience, as any good professional entertainment should. The music was groovy; it did the job.

But for the Moroccans in the room, including Rashida, this music was something else entirely. Some might have been offended to hear ritual sounds used in this way. She, however, was profoundly affected by the music. She eventually became unable to do her work, she did not fall fully into a trance (perhaps the distractions of the dancing students or her duties in cooking and cleaning up kept the spirits at bay), but she did have to sit and then lie down for periods of time. The sacred power of the music overcame her, even though the intention of these musicians was to entertain. The music has a certain power distinct from the goals of the rest of the people who were at the party.

A similar event with an ʿissawa group solidified the fluid nature of experience, ritual, performance, and entertainment. I was studying Arabic and working on my early research in Morocco when a faculty member from my university reached out to ask if I was interested in helping out with a study abroad program that she was running. Her group was going to be in southern Spain to learn about the arts in medicine. They decided to take a ferry to Morocco and come down to Fez to experience how music could elicit and influence healing. I gave a handful of lectures and organized two demonstrations of ritual ceremonies. One was with the gnawa (led by Abd al-Razaq, from Chapter 4). The other was an ʿissawa lila directed by Muqaddim Adil. One of the hardest parts of arranging the event was finding a space. Because, unlike so many other brotherhoods, the ʿissawa, hamadsha, gnawa, and groups like them perform their ceremonies in clients' homes and we were split between some apartments, I had limited resources for finding a spot for the ceremony-demonstration to happen. Adil reached out to friends and colleagues and eventually located a home for us out in the suburbs of Fez. The family hosted us and, to be honest, likely took in a little bit of the ensemble's money as a fee. Or, perhaps, they did it for the baraka, the graces bestowed by the ensemble during the event. Small questions like this, many of which remained unanswered because of the opaque nature of negotiations in Morocco (or anywhere, for that matter), illuminate the economic activity that underpins so much religious practice.

On the day of the event, we piled into three rented vans and made our way out to the suburban home. After the ensemble members who were with us unpacked, we waited for the rest to arrive. They lit incense in a coal-burner and used the heat to warm the skin drumheads on their instruments. We were all milling about in the street and many of the students were taking pictures when the group began making some progress toward starting their procession. They surprised us by inviting volunteers to wear the gandiras, robes made from dense cloth that feel almost like carpets draped over your shoulder. Once three of us were properly dressed (they made me participate, along with a student and one of the study abroad chaperones), they wrapped our foreheads with a wide scarf. We had no idea what we were doing, but we looked the part. Other students were enlisted to carry the flags and candles (see Figure 6.9).

Within a few short moments, Muqaddim Adil and his ensemble had effectively changed the tenor of the event. Instead of a demonstration, students were watching their peers and teachers try and learn chants and movements to participate alongside expert drummers and ghita players. We were embarrassed, laughing, trying not to look goofy, and the entire thing shifted from being a classroom to being fun. I was later told that the 'issawa ritual was one of the highlights of the students' month-long trip to Spain and Morocco. But this was just the opening; we had not even entered the home yet.

This collaborative demonstration continued through the evening. Members of the ensemble encouraged students to stand and chant along with them as they lit and passed incenses. At one point, the class was circled around the room, everyone holding hands with a few of the 'issawa members, chanting "Allah" and swaying forward and backward. While not identical to the actions that play out during a ceremony, these invitations gave the students a close approximation of the excitement that comes along with

Figure 6.9 Members of Muqaddim Adil's ensemble showing me (left, in sandals) and others from the study abroad group what to do during the 'issawa procession.

embodying an experience rather than observing it. The very idea that this collection of American college students could be included within the ʿissawa ritual tradition is novel. Most Moroccans have not had this type of proximity, though events like the free performances during the Fez Festival of Sacred Music are similarly open to the public. On one hand, this speaks to the uneven privileges afforded to tourists, study abroad students, expatriates, and others. On another, it demonstrates how ʿissawa groups are, themselves, taking control of the narratives surrounding their own practice, whether it be debates about the adopted ritual segments or the economic opportunities available to those who can find and engage new audiences.

One moment from that evening stuck out to me on a personal note. The ritual leaders blessed candles and gave them to some of those who were present. The gracious hosts took one, as did the course's directors. The group insisted that I take one, as well. The intersection between demonstration and ritual felt as if it were shifting: I had seen so many who were ill or elderly request similar blessings in ceremonies and what was being enacted here certainly seemed to be heartfelt. An ensemble member rhythmically improvised a number of prayers, each punctuated by the rest of the ensemble. They prayed for my research, my health, and for my future family. As I sit and write this first draft almost ten years later, my wife and I have two beautiful children and are awaiting our third, who is coming any day now. That candle is broken in half now—it has moved to and from Morocco and across three states during that time—but it still sits on my office shelf, within arm's reach.

Notes

1 See the resources section for information on how to find my videos of the moments that I describe here.
2 For one of many possible examples, see the video of Najib (ft. Manzid Nsawal Fik) singing "Gari Gari" using the playlists in the Resources section.
3 "Ce que font tous les muqaddem-s que tu connais avec les mluk, ce n'est pas correct. Si les gens ont des problèmes avec des démons, il existe de vraies techniques soufies pour les éloigner. Mais chanter Lalla Malika, Lalla Aïcha, ça veut dire quoi? C'est juste psychologique, rien de plus. Le rituel des mlouk n'est pas relié à une tradition mystique, notre tarîqa ne cautionne pas cela."

CHAPTER 7

Malhun As Pop, Piety, and Local Pride

In October 2014, Muhammad Soussi asked if I wanted to join his group for a gig in Mulay Yaqub. I had been to the small town once before, but only to visit the well-known sulfur springs. It's a common day trip for residents of Fez and Meknes, a chance to get out of the big city and enjoy the rejuvenation and commonly described health benefits of these natural mineral waters. When I had made my first trip out there, I had expected outdoor pools and was surprised to find that the springs—at least the cheaper "public" ones—were housed within what felt like a busy YMCA. I was told that there were much nicer places to enjoy the sulfur springs, for a price. The small hilly town and its idiosyncratic market left a mark on me. It felt like a local excursion, in the way that visiting a boardwalk can. Stores focused on soaps and bath supplies as if the entire town were a giant hammam (public bath house).[1] When I heard that we were making our way in a van to Mulay Yaqub, it was this small town that I had in mind.

Instead, as we got close our van took a turn up and away from the town. As we rounded a few small mountains, we arrived at a large flat patch of land where a group of workers were setting up a huge tent (see Figure 7.1). We had a great deal of time to sit, wait, and chat before the gig began. I was increasingly less clear on what we were up to. As musicians arrived, I recognized and knew some from my time spent with Soussi's group, but it became obvious that we were not the only ones scheduled to perform. As more and more instruments were unpacked—things like large frame drums and nfar trumpets (see Chapter 6)—I noticed that we were being joined by an 'issawa group, one that I had not met before. The workers lined the tent's floor with ornate carpets, its interior walls and ceiling were covered in ornate patterns, and they even brought benches that were upholstered to feel like the "couches" that line most Moroccan living rooms (see Figure 7.2).

116 • Focusing In: Faith and Fun in Fez

Figure 7.1 The venue where we were to perform outside of Mulay Yaqub.

The far side of the tent had delicious food laid out as the busload of guests arrived. I never had the chance to speak with them, in part because this was a well-oiled tour. This mountainside concert was part of a guided experience in which—so I was told by the artists—well-off individuals from Casablanca and Rabat were able to experience their own families' cultural heritage by visiting Fez and Meknes. Mulay Yaqub was a respite, a stop on the way to the many tourist sites in the big cities.

Once the concert began, Soussi and the ʿissawa leader took turns singing the long poems that comprise the malhun repertoire. As each progressed, the beats gained intensity. The ensemble shifted from a malhun group to a sort of malhun-ʿissawa fusion. All of the instruments that signify this local Sufi ritual came into conversation with the austere sounds of malhun's ʿuds and violins. At times, they felt as if they were in conflict, but for the most part this combination led to joyous dancing. The small crowd clustered around the corner of the tent where the ensembles were set up, dancing as if they were teens again. The fresh air flowing through the tent, the beautiful views of the countryside, and this energetic music kept everyone moving. The ʿissawa group's percussionists often stood as the songs came close to their ends and danced with the guests (see Figure 7.3). This was a high-class party. It was a celebration of a region and its heritage and culture. It was a chance for the visitors to experience—in a visceral way, through loud music, dance, and good food—their own histories, even if they, themselves, live their lives in the businesses and government offices of far-off Rabat and Casablanca.

Figure 7.2 Part of the ensemble preparing for the performance, including Muhammad Soussi (in gray, next to the violinist) and the author (in the foreground, facing away from the camera). Unknown photographer.

Celebrating an Urban Identity

During one of my visits to Fez, I saw banners everywhere. Major citywide events are not uncommon, but these ones featured a number that gave me pause. Fez was celebrating its 1,200th anniversary. Each of the main gates to the old city, the medina, was draped in these signs that celebrated the city's longevity and historical importance. It was founded in 789, though did not develop for another 20 years, in 809. I did not take any pictures of these signs, so I cannot remember with certainty, but I assume that these signs were pointing to this latter date (this visit was probably in 2009).

Twelve hundred years. A quick Wikipedia search of the world's oldest continuously inhabited cities[2] (Wikipedia is good at these kinds of things) shows a number of earlier cities in North Africa. Places like Luxor, founded in around 3200 BCE, highlight ancient African civilizations in Egypt. A handful of cities on the Mediterranean, like Carthage, Tunisia (c. 814 BCE) and Tripoli, Libya (c. 700 BCE), point to the sea's importance for early trade routes and its utility for the expanding Roman Empire so many centuries later. The same is true for Western Asia, with places like Damascus, Syria (date unknown, perhaps the oldest); Beirut, Lebanon (3000 BCE); and Jerusalem, in Israel/Palestine (2800 BCE). Perhaps 1,200 years is not so long after all. But for someone who grew up in the United States, where few places remain that have been continuously populated for more than 300 years, this age gives a place a sense of aura, of heft.

Figure 7.3 Members of the 'issawa ensemble dancing with guests during the concert outside of Mulay Yaqub.

I learned about the Iroquois who had lived in my native Western New York when I was in middle school. But their towns, their settlements, are gone. Even if the names remain (my middle school was called Iroquois), the world around me was, relatively speaking, new. My new home, Bowling Green, Ohio, and nearby Toledo are from the 1830s, not yet 200 years old. A lot can happen to a city in those other 1,000 years.

Perhaps more astounding is the city's university, al-Qarawiyyin. Founded within a few generations of the city itself, the mosque, library, and university have been operating continuously since 859 BCE, about 1,160 years. According to UNESCO, this is the oldest university in the world.[3] After Idris II began building up the city that his father had founded, new arrivals came from al-Andalus (see Chapter 1) and a city in Tunisia called al-Qarawiyyin. These two groups began two large mosques, both of which are still open today. They settled on opposite sides of the river that runs through the city and gave the names of their native regions to the medina: the area around the university, popular with tourists, is known as al-Qarawiyyin; turning another direction and crossing a bridge brings you into al-Andalus.

This history of incoming knowledge and piety weaves through Fez's geography. Idris and his family were descendants of the Prophet Muhammad. Mulay Idris's tomb is a popular site of supplication and veneration, especially for the city's Sufis. His is one of the many saintly tombs that orient the city's religious life. Another, not far from the leather tanneries that make for a different stop on guided tours, is the tomb of Sidi Ahmed Tijani, a holy man from southern Algeria who came up to Fez both early and late in his life. Members of the popular Sufi brotherhood that follows him, the tijaniyya, are pilgrims to Fez, coming to the city to visit his resting place. Religious groups and their zawiyas can be extraordinary or hidden away, but they are all over. The sound of chanting frequently spills into the winding alleyways in the evening. Men stand in the doorways of neighborhood mosques, small ones that have no towering minarets or electronic speakers, loudly giving the call to prayer into the road. But the city is also a regular city, business goes on. Donkeys carrying bags of concrete make their way up the jagged inclines toward construction projects, kids play games in rare open spaces, the homeless find rest on garden benches, and teenagers duck into corners to smoke or hang out with their dates in a moment of privacy.

Under the colonial period and during the country's early independence, Fez became more than a site for a major university and an economic center. The intellectual life of the communities surrounding al-Qarawiyyin and the power of the city's merchants helped to build a powerful political force pushing back against French occupation. The Istaqlal Party, a group of activists who published a manifesto for an independent Morocco in 1944, were based in Fez, which had been the country's capital up until the French moved it to Rabat in 1925. Their commitment to a new country continued after the French left, as they became strong supporters of the renewed monarchy. Since then, it has splintered into other groups, but continues to be a religiously conservative oppositional party within the country's politics.

Morocco was once home to a large and influential Jewish community. This is borne out through the geography of its cities, and Fez is no exception. In describing Fez as "actually a series of cities, strung together from east to west," Susan Gilson Miller, Attilio Petruccioli, and Mauro Bertagnin (2001, 310) explore the geography of Fez's Jewish quarter, which is called the mellah. The old city, the medina or Fes al-Bali, sits at the bottom of a valley between mountains, al-Qarawiyyin at its center. Adjacent and up high on the hill is Fez Jdid, "New Fez." Built in the 1800s, Fez Jdid houses the Royal Palace. It still stands, symbolizing the city's past political strength. Fez Jdid also features the ornate Jnan Sbil, gardens that stretch alongside the palace. Most of the activities for the Fez Festival of World Sacred Music happen here and the "blue gate," Bab Boujloud, is one of the main entry points to the older medina for tourists and Moroccans alike. Running alongside Fez Jdid is the next in this "string" of cities, the mellah. This Jewish quarter looks and feels architecturally different. Instead of neighborhood mosques, it is lined with synagogues. Miller and her co-authors note that the proximity to the palace may signify the important relationship between this past community and the political authority of the state. They write that "it was at moments when authority broke down and rebellion erupted over the question of succession [in the monarchy] that the inhabitants of the Jewish quarter suffered most" (Miller et al. 2001, 311).

Jewish communities had been making their home in Fez since the city's founding, in part because of their wide family networks and artisanal skills. Thanks to the form of Islamic law being practiced in Morocco, they experienced similar peaceful relationships with the Muslim communities as those who were in Spain. After paying a tax, they enjoyed a degree of autonomy. The community found success in trade and became an important part of Fez's early rise as an economic center in the region. Many Jewish scholars, both native to the city and coming from elsewhere, added to the local Jewish community's international prestige.

This status was not consistent, however, as various dynasties throughout Moroccan history had differing opinions about the legality of the relationship between Jews and the Muslim majority. Some required all to convert at the threat of exile, though many Jews stayed and resisted by continuing to practice their faith in covert ways. After these periods passed, with one of the most notable happening in the 12th century, more open rulers took hold. Another struggle came in the 1400s, when the tomb of the city's founding saint, Idriss II, was rediscovered in the old medina. The entirety of the old city was deemed sacred and non-Muslims were pushed out, forced to abandon their homes and shops. At this point, the community converged on the nearby mellah, where they remained until the middle of the 20th century. The concentration of the Jewish community within this neighborhood was so strong that other cities used the same term when constructing Jewish neighborhoods in later centuries. Instead of its literal meaning (a place of salt), the word mellah basically translates to "Jewish Quarter."

As the Jewish community grew and codified into a single geographic part of the city, it did not avoid internal struggles of its own. Immigration from Spain and elsewhere added stress to the population, especially since the practice of Judaism can differ linguistically, culturally, and in other ways. Sephardic Jews from Spain spoke Spanish and carried out their rituals using methods that were quite unfamiliar to the native Jewish population. It took about 300 years (from the 1400s to the 1700s) for these two Jewish populations to coalesce in Morocco, where they kept Arabic, while incorporating many Sephardic practices. In today's Jewish communities around the world, this can lead to a similar cultural distance between those who trace their lineage back to Morocco and others who look to Eastern Europe or elsewhere for their family histories.

The relationship between the Moroccan government and the country's Jewish population, one that was never steady, took a turn for the worse after the establishment of Israel in 1948. Governmental protections failed to stop riots against Jews within the country, while the new Jewish state encouraged their immigration. By 1967, the Arab–Israeli Six Day War that, while it did not involve Morocco directly, certainly increased the antagonism between Muslims and Jews across the Middle East and few Jews remained in the country. Many were now leaving for other parts of Europe as they saw their relationships with the Muslim majority and the government deteriorate. When I speak to musicians in Morocco, they lament this 20th century exodus. The most famous composers and performers, and much of the professional class of musicians across the country, were Jewish. They left their mark on the performance styles and songs that remain in the country, but they are now gone. Even while hearing dramatic criticisms of Jews that replicate what appears in media discussions of the Israel/Palestine conflict, the personal connections that once existed between Muslim and Jewish performers continues to be heartfelt.

Powerfully influential migrations were not limited to religious communities. Before the arrival of the French, empires came and went, bringing new ideas and people into different regions of the country. Under colonialism, local power structures and economic relationships altered the population's structures, not to mention the physical and geographic structures of the cities, towns, and rural areas themselves. During this time and since, many families with the means to do so moved from the older medina sections of cities and took up residence in the newly-minted villes nouvelles. These French "new cities," adjacent to the old ones, housed most modern businesses and civil administrations. The wide roads allowed for cars and trucks to drive alongside the now ubiquitous mopeds. With this change in urban geography, housing prices in the old cities and outskirts dropped, in part because landowners divided homes—many of which were once palatial—into smaller apartments. What once housed a single wealthy family and, perhaps, some domestic help or slaves could now "accommodate" a number of families, one or more in each room.

As rural populations moved to the cities for work, a sense of decline came over the medinas. While not so dire as the shantytowns that fill empty spaces within and outside of the city, the tight roads and maze-like alleys have come to be seen as ghettos. Many who I talked to spoke with a frustrated pride when talking about their changing neighborhoods (see Hachimi 2012). They saw old men and teenagers drinking or smoking, urinating in dark corners. They noted the homeless living in squalor on the edges of marketplaces. In many cases, they spoke of this recent influx of rural poor, who they referred to as ʿarubi, a word that carries connotations similar to "hick" or "bumpkin." This change has been happening for decades; it was the confluence of diverse backgrounds that gave rise to Nass El Ghiwane, as described in Chapter 3. But class and education can be a powerful markers of difference and, of course, one way in which this difference is enacted week in and week out is through religion. It is no coincidence that the variants of Sufism described in earlier chapters are widely criticized as being superstitious or uneducated. They live and thrive in the medinas and other neighborhoods where poverty is rampant. And yet, in no small part because of this connection to "the regular people," they have found recent attention as markers of a national heritage, of a Moroccan authenticity. It is an authenticity that gives Moroccans, especially those who trace their lineage back to Fez, a sense of pride. By conflating local music, local history, and local pride, musicians can be a powerful force in defining who we are and who we strive to be. I return to this idea in the conclusion that follows this chapter, which explores how Muhammad Soussi takes an ostensibly secular music and makes it both local and sacred, much to the delight of his audience.

Malhun's History and Structure

Malhun, a genre of accompanied sung poetry popular across Morocco, operates on a number of levels for a wide range of audiences. It bears a close resemblance to classical poetic forms, maintaining a heightened place within the country's arts, yet many love it irrespective of their educational background or economic stature. The poorest Moroccans memorize long segments of their favorite texts, ready to sing upon request, while the wealthiest gather in hotel ballrooms to celebrate malhun as a national cultural heritage.

Most scholarship on malhun focuses, and rightly so, on the texts' form and content, with their unique register of Moroccan Arabic and themes that range from devout to satirical. These poems, however, are meant to be sung. Unlike the poetry, the music is repetitive and derided by listeners and performers alike as unremarkable (especially when compared to Morocco's Andalusian tradition, al-ala), but I argue here that the sound of performances holds keys to understanding the genre's prominent place in the country's cultural sphere. Changes in contemporary performance practice clearly demonstrate performers' successes in engaging new audiences, both locally and nationally. Furthermore, malhun in Fez demonstrates the influence and use of religious piety in two distinct ways. First, common musical innovations incorporate the music from the heavily contested and often-marginalized spirit possession rituals of local Sufi brotherhoods like the hamadsha and ʿissawa into malhun performances. Going beyond borrowing musical elements, artists clearly link music with religious ideologies by freely crossing any perceived boundary between ritual singer and malhun soloist. Local forms of the music inform conceptions of right behavior by including these semi-marginal Sufi practices on elite stages. Second, the use of musical ritual content from a different group, one not generally assumed to be local to Fez, nor one that the performers participate within, shows a certain economic pragmatism. By creating "the first gnawa malhun" on the Fez Festival of Sacred Music stage, Muhammad Soussi recognized the powerful commodity that this sacred music was, and the opportunity that it presented for expanding his own audience. Performers are working within the tradition to find new modes of innovation, incorporating local sounds, instruments, and styles that are popular with mass audiences. The fact that many of these importations come from popular religious brotherhoods shows how powerful a site of negotiation the genre's stages can be, especially regarding local conceptions of religious piety and community (see Figure 7.4).

Malhun has long roots as an artistic tradition. It shares its origins in the Tifilalt region near the desert cities of Errachidia, Erfoud, and Risani with the current ruling family, the 'Alaouite dynasty. Some early monarchs from the family were poets, writing within the tradition (Schuyler 2002). With the genre's expansion across the country, other regions contributed their own master poets, lending a diversity of approaches that continues today. Contemporary ensembles carry badges of their geography through the use of specific instrumentations and nuanced performance practice decisions, some of which I describe in detail later. The poems generally follow a handful of forms that have been described elsewhere (see Magidow 2013, also Shannon 2003a and Reynolds 1995 for descriptions of similar poetic forms). While they are in Moroccan Arabic, it is a unique register of the dialect. Many terms are specific to the malhun repertoire and even the biggest fans rarely understand all of the language in a text. The genre prioritizes the poems and poets and the text is prized over the music, leading to a vast lacuna of scholarship on the musical practice.[4]

Figure 7.4 Muhammad Soussi (left) preparing for a malhun performance in Fez.

Malhun is a largely conservative musical genre. Most listeners prefer the previous generation's great singers—Toulali and Bouzoubaa, for example—to today's live performances. The nostalgia surrounding these performers' scratchy recordings, now available almost exclusively as MP3, CDs, or YouTube videos, certainly bleeds into popular opinion regarding their stature and authenticity. Contemporary performances remain consistent with these older styles, as the most widely performed poems in today's concert settings are compositions from generations ago. Musical material is recycled, with melodies from old and famous performances reappearing in new contexts, so much so that Muhammad Soussi explained to me that, while there are many hundreds of options, roughly 30 melodies animate the vast majority of the musical output. While my interest began as an examination of this musical conservatism, during my time researching malhun, it was the innovations occurring within the genre's standard musical systems that struck me. Performance contexts are changing, musicians are importing new musical ideas, and—perhaps most interestingly—performers reorient old musical ideas under the guise of new labels for explicitly commercial reasons.

Morocco has seen a resurgence in this music and poetry since the 1970s. Nass El Ghiwane and Jil Jilala, two ensembles coming from the post-independence moment described in Chapter 3, sang malhun-influenced pieces. Nass El Ghiwane, arguably the more famous of the two, had a lasting hit with "Allah ya Moulana," but Jil Jilala essentially "covered" a wide variety of poems from the malhun tradition (more recent Ghiwane albums have moved closer to malhun, perhaps because of the music's rising popularity). Jilala's "al-Shma'a" (The Candle) tracks closely with the original malhun poem of the same name, albeit with a very different aesthetic, one devoid of the complex texture that results from the genre's instrumentation. With minimal accompaniment including a solo string instrument (likely an 'ud), prominent rhythmic clapping, and very light drums, the arrangement brings the poetry itself to the fore. Furthermore, the melodic difference between this version and another famous one from the celebrated Houcine Toulali illuminates the musical flexibility that malhun artists enjoy while performing identical poems.

The current generation of malhun singers continue to innovate dramatically. They do so, however, within the genre's conservative structures. Singers redefine melodies while incorporating novel elements from throughout Morocco's rich musical landscape to orient their sound toward increasingly large mass audiences. They are aware of trends and tastes, just as many of the poets are. Moulay Ismail Salsouli composed poems infused with technology—such as "Khsam l-portable", framed as a debate between a cellphone and a landline—that were full of humor (Magidow 2013, 123–4). Singers demonstrating their genre's contemporary viability provided me with this example on more than one occasion. Yet the musical innovations from importing rhythms and instruments from prominent local ritual practices to adding jazz or rock instruments like the saxophone and electric bass equally change the aesthetic through intentional efforts to expand audiences.

The conservatism remains powerful, however, as malhun lives within the same postcolonial national pressures that guided the performance practice of Andalusian music seen in Chapter 1. Andalusian music, in its many forms across North Africa, has been heavily influenced by state projects. These top-down attempts to promote the music as a piece of national cultural heritage has affected performance practice through the development of new ensembles with specific goals related to the economics of the heritage industries in each location. State influence, however, is not the only pressure upon the practices of Andalusian musicians. There are also close ties between Andalusian music and forms of Sufism, links that malhun artists carry into their performances, as I describe later. The practice of the tradition in Morocco often blends Sufi and al-ala aesthetic ideals. As such, much of the performance practice dominant today plays specific roles within both Morocco's popular culture and heritage industries. Its linkages to state authority and to regional Sufi practice are important social and political elements, while its musical connections with (and differences from) the Andalusian tradition often define the ways in which listeners and musicians view the genre. These trends underline the careers of malhun musicians, both ensemble leaders and hired instrumentalists. Many operate in both scenes and recognize the economic opportunities available to those who can operationalize adeptness with navigating state priorities, popular tastes, and public religious pieties.

During my time in Fez, Muhammad Soussi and his group welcomed me into their ensemble, first on violin and then on banjo. Soussi attempted to teach me the melodies ahead of time by rote, but he made my primary task finding and purchasing the white long shirt and baggy pants, red hat, and yellow pointed shoes that would look just right for concerts. I followed the ensemble's melodies in performance, taking advantage of the repetitive nature of the musical content to "fake" my way through gigs. While it was a mentally exhausting task, as I had no idea where the next melodic turn would go, it taught me to hear patterns within the lines and ornamentations. In fact, the rest of the ensemble was doing something similar as they worked to follow the soloists' improvised twists and turns through specific passages (though they had the luxury of knowing the melody ahead of time!). I performed with the ensemble in unexpected settings, ranging from the stage of the Fez Festival of World Sacred Music to a suburban fashion show. In each instance, I learned a bit more about how the music worked and what it meant to the listeners.

While flexibility proves important for malhun's renewal and recent expansion, it is enabled by the genre's musical consistency. Musical structures are highly segmented and provide clear sections and easy-to-sing repetitive phrases, elements that facilitate memorization and my playing with these groups on stage. Each refrain is called a harba. It is a short phrase, usually 2 lines, that serves as a guidepost through a poem that may be 25 minutes long. The poem itself is a qasida, the same term used for both ancient Arabic poetry and the contemporary Sufi forms seen in the previous chapters. The qasida is divided into different verses, each of which is a qism.

The general model for a performance begins with one or more improvised solos. Common instruments include the violin or viola, held upright on the knee in the same way that they are used for Andalusian music; the ʻud, which also mirrors Andalusian instrumentation; and the swissen, a small plucked instrument that with three strings stretched across a skin like a banjo. The swissen closely resembles a miniature hamadsha ginbri (see Figure 5.2). There is no conductor, so the group relies on members' impressive listening skills to hear and follow lead players and soloists. Percussion often includes a tar—a small riqq-like frame drum with jangles—and a number of small hourglass drums, each called a tʻarija. Singers play two interlocking patterns on the tʻarijas to build malhun's core rhythm (see Example 7.1). Historically, ensembles were smaller and could include only a violin or ʻud, percussionist, and vocalist. Now they are often quite large with three or more violins, two ʻud players, two percussionists, multiple soloists, a

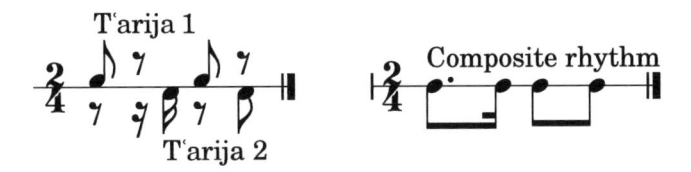

Example 7.1 Interlocking t'arija patterns combine to create the most common rhythm used in malhun music.

chorus of singers, and a swissen. Festival ensembles frequently include an electric piano (known as al-orq, a term derived from organ), bass, cellos, saxophone, and a variety of additional percussion and wind instruments from other local musical traditions. The vocalist may perform a short prelude based on one of a number of fixed texts unrelated to the main qasida. After these opening solos, the ensemble moves into an iteration of the harba, the refrain, or the initial qism, a verse. The vocalist sings the harba, the ensemble repeats it back, and the ensemble plays a heavily ornamented instrumental variation. A dedicated chorus is not required, as instrumentalists sing the refrains while playing. The closing verse of a malhun poem, called the insiraf, incorporates a dramatic change in rhythm, melody, texture, and overall energy. The ensemble moves into a new meter—or at least a quicker tempo—and typically shifts into a call-and-response iteration of the poem's harba. Audience members often stand and begin clapping and singing along, sometimes going so far as to climb onto the stage with the ensemble.

A Wide Popularity

While playing or listening to this music, I felt a constant sense of familiarity that doubtlessly came from the repeating melodies. Yet, it seemed to extend across poems: I kept thinking that I had already heard these melodies or motives before. In fact, many of the musicians that I worked with disregarded malhun's music as simple. The repetition that helped me to play along with these groups also seemed to diminish the respect that the music could earn from its players, even though they had no qualms about taking malhun gigs. Much of my malhun-related fieldwork was casual. In enjoying the experience of being a colleague and musician, on many occasions I chose to put my notebook away. This was not my central ethnographic project at the time, but a way to enjoy playing within a community. Even so, I was struck by many offhand comments from professional malhun performers that put the music down. The harshest came from those who worked both with al-ala ensembles and malhun groups.

The lack of respect surrounding malhun's musical accompaniment correlates with a perceived simplicity in melodic and formal structure. There is little research on how malhun operates at a technical level as a genre. The scholarly focus on texts (see Jirari 1969, Gessous 2008, Magidow 2013, Magidow 2016) shows how powerful these feelings are, even outside of malhun's performers and listeners (it is worth noting, however, that what I am referring to here is mostly about the instrumental portions of this music. Singers are often celebrated for their nuance, virtuosity, and creativity). This reasonable bias toward the poetry and singing risks limiting an understanding of how musical innovations come about in malhun performances. Those moments of creativity, in turn, operate to construct and reinforce religious identities within a genre of music that is not necessarily sacred. It speaks to how artists and audiences build communities that are informed by religious ideologies and moral or pious forms of entertainment.

These communities, however, spread beyond explicitly religious contexts. Even more than Sufi music appearing in new social spaces, malhun artists can adapt to their environment. The simplicity of the music helps anyone to feel able to participate, singing along during the refrains, during the most exciting moments. Particularly intimate gatherings in households can similarly turn into evenings of laughter and storytelling alongside the singing. Also, like so many of the genres of musical practice that appear throughout these chapters, malhun has earned a certain cachet due to its uniqueness. It is widely viewed as distinctively Moroccan and, therefore, as intrinsic to a sense of national identity. Malhun appears on national stages and television broadcasts, celebrating local poetry, religious holidays, and musical taste.

This renewed celebration comes despite the continuing opinion that malhun is musically simplistic when compared to the "high art" of al-ala. As a more "popular" art form, malhun now occupies a symbolic space that can be more flexible and more fun than al-ala. Its social and cultural meanings are a bit more fluid, the religious connections are more tenuous. Innovative artists have more wiggle room, more opportunity for change and creativity. This situation where a genre can be what its artists and audiences need allows for some interesting gigs, like that performance in a tent outside of Mulay Yaqub. Malhun was Fez, it was heritage, it was fun, and it was Moroccan Islam.

On one evening in 2012, Soussi invited me to perform once again, in the new city of Fez. As was often the case, I had no idea where I was going or what was going to happen when I got there. When I did arrive, I was surprised to find that a huge white tent was set up alongside a beautiful pool. The setting felt like an outdoor wedding with tables crowded together under the bright lights. A stage was set up on one side with a large runway protruding through the tent. We were playing for a fashion show (see Figure 7.5). The models came up from the side of the stage in beautiful kaftans, ornate dresses that

Figure 7.5 The runway and crowd during Muhammad Soussi's fashion show performance in Fez.

women wear to weddings and similar events. While I am no expert on Moroccan women's fashion, the designers were obviously playing on "traditions." Makeup, hairstyles, and the cuts of the gowns themselves incorporated a mixture of influences. Some were like those that I saw for sale (or rent) in shops in conservative areas of town. Others looked more like the covers of women's magazines that I saw on newsstands (see Figure 7.6). A radio host was the emcee for the evening and we were the background entertainment (see Figure 7.7). We played while each model came up to the stage and made her way down the catwalk. The emcee introduced the designers and the event moved forward as expected. The audience, too, was dressed in their finest. This was a high-society entertainment on a beautiful evening in one of the nicest parts of town.

The flexibility that allows this music to reach such wide audiences is exemplified by an example mentioned above: "al-Shmaʿa" (The Candle). Aside from the Jil Jilala "cover version," which has a dramatically different structure and sound, there is a general consistency in how artists perform the song. This is often the case with most well-known songs across the world. Malhun, however, allows for artists to bring dramatically different approaches to a common poem, making this one an interesting case. Links to the recordings that I will discuss here are available in the resources section and they are worth listening to while reading.

Figure 7.6 A model preparing for her trip down the catwalk.

Figure 7.7 Soussi's ensemble and the models as they returned to the stage at the end of the show.

While conversations about a "music theory" of malhun were hard to come by, my questions about the musical structure circled around the concept of qiyas. This term, which refers to "form" or "shape," alludes to something like a musical contour, the outline of a melody's peaks and valleys. In performance, a singer has a great deal of leeway, especially during the long verses of each poem. But when the refrain comes back and the ensemble joins in, that flexibility can turn into a productive restriction: the song's melody must be recognizable, though the singer can still venture away from it in virtuosic flourishes. What caught my attention was the rôle that the qiyas played throughout a song, even as so much other musical content shifted. For example, many malhun performances move from one mode to another, either as key areas change or scales modulate (to loosely borrow a Western classical term). Despite the dramatic, and often quite striking, changes, the qiyas—the shape of the melody—holds things together.

Haj Houcine Toulali is one of the most famous malhun singers. He is revered as an example, someone whose style has influenced the generations that followed. His version of "al-Shma'a" can provide a small example of how this works. A recording of one of his performances begins with a pair of long instrumental solos. After about three minutes, he arrives at the first iteration of the harba, the refrain. By the time Toulali arrives at the

Malhun As Pop, Piety, and Local Pride • 129

fourth repetition of the harba, about eight and a half minutes into his performance, he has changed the mode (the pitches that he is using to sing the song), but the qiyas—the melodic contour—is still very similar, at least until the end (see Example 7.2).

The modes keep changing throughout the performance and different singers can take them in different directions. "Al-Shmaʿa" happens to be a relatively consistent example, but even with a qiyas that holds within and across performances, there is a substantial degree of variation in how that qiyas appears in each instance. To better visualize this relationship, one that helps to make both the nuance and the consistency of malhun clearer, Example 7.3 graphs the melodic contours of Toulali's harba performances alongside those of another important figure named Thami Haroushi. Because the final harba in Toulali's performance, the insiraf, changes dramatically for reasons described later in the chapter, I am leaving that one off of this graph. Even though they begin and end in different places, the general outline, the qiyas, of these melodies remains similar. They all start with a series of notes at the same pitch before descending and ascending. As each melody nears the end, the artist takes some time liberty to push the refrain to its conclusion, growing the energy and introducing the ensemble's instrumental version of it. While these relationships may seem unimportant or obvious, they create a sense of unity across a long vocal performance in which the text reigns supreme. The music here, as was the case with al-ala, supports the poetry. The poetry, in turn, can lead the listener toward a rumination of the beauty of nature, a meditation on the joys of love, or a worshipful engagement with the grace of God.

Example 7.2 The first and fourth iterations of the harba in Houcine Toulali's performance of "al-Shmaʿa," 3:10 and 8:30 in the example cited in the resources section, respectively. The backward flat in the second line's key signature denotes a half-flat, a microtone common in a number of Arab music traditions.

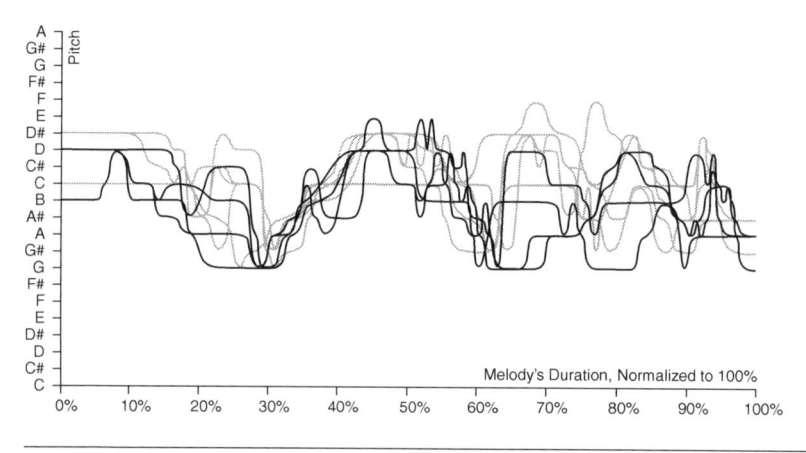

Example 7.3 Melodic contours from Toulali's and Haroushi's performances of "al-Shma'a," excepting Toulali's final harba.

All of these influences came together during a concert in Casablanca. Abderrahim Amrani, the hamadsha muqaddim, invited a friend and me to join him for the event during Ramadan. Philip Murphy, a fellow researcher whom I had worked closely with for a number of projects during my time in Fez and who had attended the hamadsha ritual from Chapter 5, and Sandy McCutcheon, a photographer living in Fez, Amrani's ensemble members, and I piled into a small yellow van one morning. Being Ramadan, the group members were fasting and, since it was going to be a long night, the easiest way to fast was to try and use the piles of instruments and bags of clothes as cushions and sleep through the three-hour drive from Fez to Casablanca (see Figure 7.8).

After we arrived and settled in to the large apartment that was rented out for visiting musicians, we made our way to a rehearsal and sound check. The venue was the

Figure 7.8 Members of Amrani's ensemble sleeping in the van on the road to Casablanca.

courtyard of a beautiful building with chairs lined up in rows that were interrupted by large trees and a stone fountain. As was so often the case, I had no clear idea of what we were going to be doing later in the evening, but I was starting to get a taste for the scope of the event. The rehearsal was quick, since most of the musicians knew the songs well. I distinctly remember taking a moment to try and figure out how to play my violin upright on my knee so that I could visually fit in a little better with the other string players. I failed in that task completely, abandoned it, and held my instrument back up under my chin (a few years later, for a different gig back in the United States, I spent a few months working on playing "the Andalusi way"; it changes the sound and feel of the violin, almost turning it into a completely different instrument). I was embarrassed with my floundering and hoped that the evening's concert would go better. It was getting late, the sun was setting, and the time was coming to break the day's fast. Friends and fellow musicians used the celebratory opportunity and the fact that so many had gathered from around the region to catch up, tell stories, and laugh.

When we returned to the venue, I was surprised to learn that our performance was a part of a much larger concert. Television cameras from Morocco's major stations were there as Amrani gathered his ensemble and handed out drums. It turned out I was going to be playing guwwal in a procession through the city streets. The bright lights from the cameras lit the way as our crowd grew to include the well-dressed concert audience. As was the case with the fashion show in Fez, this felt like something of a transformation, an instance of a ritual music transcending its social station. Amrani's efforts (described in Chapter 5) have been instrumental in changing the perception of the hamadsha, and this gig—where he was more of an impresario–demonstrated the fruits of these labors (see Figure 7.9).

After winding our way around the castle-like venue, we ascended the stage for the malhun concert. I took up my violin and, as I had done so often before, worked hard to follow the music inconspicuously. The performance featured a number of star vocalists who took turns leading the ensemble through much-loved poems. The hamadsha opening had framed the event, emphasizing a sense of ritual within this concert and highlighting the sacred nature of this beautiful Ramadan evening. But not all of the music

Figure 7.9 Amrani leading his hamadsha group through the Casablanca streets. Photo courtesy of Sandy McCutcheon.

was religious. One of the performers led us in a famous song called "Ya Riyah," (Oh Traveler). The high-energy tune is from further East and is known, at least in Morocco, as part of a repertoire called gharnati. There are a number of older famous recordings, though one of the more notable ones is a recent punk-influenced version from an Algerian singer named Rachid Taha.[5] The performance moved the crowd, who joined in the singing. The joys of this special event and the celebration of Ramadan were palpable.

After we finished our malhun performance, the concert continued. As if to clearly demonstrate this close link between reverence and fun afforded to sacred practices, and the ease with which malhun sits within that category of pious entertainment, the final set featured Hamid al-Kasri, the famous gnawa artist from Rabat who has been transforming the sound of his own tradition (see Chapter 4). As his group danced and sang music from the gnawa ceremony, the crowd remained deeply engaged. Many sang along, some stood and danced, and almost everyone seemed to have a cellphone out to record this superstar. The crowd went wild when Amrani returned to the stage to join Kasri in singing "Aisha Hamdushiyya," the powerful song from the gnawa ritual that was borrowed decades ago from the hamadsha. Amrani expanded the normal gnawa performance of it by adding more of the hamadsha text than gnawa mʿallems usually know (see Figure 7.10). The collaborations and fluidity between religious and ostensibly secular genres (like malhun) were clearly on display through this Ramadan evening. The results of mass media's role in bringing practices like the hamadsha and gnawa, and, to a lesser extent, malhun, into mainstream upper-class acceptability were also made obvious by these concert organizers. It is notable that Amrani, a hamadsha muqaddim, was one of them. He was a significant part of a collaboration that was featured on national television news, one that brought his own tradition's music into the center of a major Ramadan celebration, a celebration of Morocco's Islamic faith.

A Local (Sacred) Aesthetic

While performers and recordings circulate nationally, localized musical practices give artists further opportunity to both revere their native regions and introduce inspired

Figure 7.10 Abderrahim Amrani (center) performing "Aisha Hamdushiyya" with Hamid al-Kasri (right). Photo courtesy of Sandy McCutcheon.

novelty. In Fez, uniqueness came from the dramatic blending of malhun tradition with the local Sufi sounds that conclude most poems. The idea of importing elements of various Sufi ritual practices into musical performances is certainly not specific to malhun, nor to Fez. Al-ala (Andalusian music) often blurs the line between religious devotion and entertainment, as did Nass El Ghiwane and Jil Jilala. Lura JeFran Jones (1977) describes the intersection of Tunisia's ʿissawa brotherhood and maʿluf, a local variant of Andalusian music. Jonathan Shannon does the same in Syria (2006) and Morocco (2015). This blurry line provides an opportunity for artists to build a sense of individuality and innovation into their performances. Moving from the previous discussions of how this music works within wide contexts, the pages that follow incorporate examples that show how these ensemble leaders can innovate musically within the expectations set by the genre's strict norms.

For many malhun singers in Fez, participation in a variety of local Sufi practices remains a prominent part of their religious and musical identities. They do more than sing religious texts: they participate in and intimately know the rituals introduced in the previous chapters. Being a Sufi, even when not "confined" to a single brotherhood, can be central to who these singers are, whether personally or professionally. One singer I worked with named Driss, for example, shows his Sufi bona fides through his social media presence. Since he friended me on Facebook in 2012 or 2013, I have watched as Driss continues to post his performances not only as a malhun singer, but within various ritual settings with different brotherhoods throughout Meknes, where he lives. At one point, I had to change my own Facebook settings because his tags and shares overwhelmed my news feed and profile. In some rituals, he was an onlooker, observing and participating alongside so many others. In most, however, he was featured. He went from being a malhun singer to a munshid, a reciter whose technical mastery and beautiful voice made his contribution central to the ritual experience for those around him (and for those who were watching through his Facebook posts). The interactivity between Sufi ritual, public performance, and social media has only become more enmeshed since Facebook introduced their "Facebook Live" feature. Now the feedback loop between audience, worshipper, and at-home viewer is more complete. Driss's rituals are performances and his audiences can be there with him, albeit virtually, participating in a form of ritual entertainment.

Muhammad Soussi, the performer with whom I worked most closely, consistently put on long videos of Sufi rituals that he was a part of after we concluded a lesson or interview. These included examples of hamadsha, ʿissawa, and other rituals, demonstrating his love of and familiarity with a variety of traditions. When I attended the hamadsha ritual in Meknes described in Chapter 5, I was surprised to find that Soussi was an invited featured singer. His voice added a great deal of beauty to the proceedings as he sang a number of solo passages throughout the ceremony. This heterogeneous attitude toward ritual inclusion informs these musicians' malhun performances as well, as they often now feature ʿissawa, hamadsha, and gnawa percussion sections in their ensembles to engage larger audiences and localize their sound.

In practice, artists use the closing segment of each poem, the insiraf, to feature innovative fusions of local ritual sounds into Fez's malhun. To borrow Jonathan Shannon's term, it is "Suficized" (2011). This localizes the music while differentiating it for national audiences; it makes Muhammad Soussi's performances on satellite television unique, even sacred. It makes them fassi, audibly linked to Fez. My work with Muhammad Soussi's ensemble, especially during the performances like the Fez Festival of World Sacred Music in 2011, provide plenty of examples of this type of adaptation. He often includes members from local troupes within his group. In that particular concert, he took it further than any other malhun singers that I had seen by incorporating gnawa music, something normally well outside of malhun, to further widen his ensemble's appeal.

These borrowed sounds add to a climactic energy that already exists within the insiraf. Responding to a quickening pace and call-and-response structure, connoisseurs listening to these long poems jump to their feet and take to the front of the stage to gather, clap, and dance when the poem nears its conclusion. The audience involvement turns a thoughtful performance into a participatory experience (see Turino 2008). To get this sound and atmosphere, the insiraf moves away from the standard rhythmic pattern that organizes most malhun. One influential inspiration heard in Fez's insiraf segments is the 5/8 trance feel that closes the hamadsha Sufi ritual (see Chapter 5). Another is the flali pattern that appears in both 'issawa music and popular genres. Example 7.4 shows the closing passage of Soussi's "Hakim al-Dhati" where this subtle shift dramatically increases the energy of the closing passages. This is a subtle change: the shift from the standard pattern to the two-against-three flali rhythm looks minimal out of context. The relationships between the durations of each stroke are nearly identical, yet the addition of the hemiola is a powerful force in energizing a crowd. I recommend listening to the audio example in the resources section to better hear (and feel) the dramatic nature of this subtle change.

Alongside these metric and melodic changes that exemplify the shift into the insiraf section of each poem, Soussi went so far as to invite entire troupes of Sufi musicians on stage, featuring their iconic movements and chanting during the final cataclysmic minutes. Otherwise, musicians might use instruments identified with these different traditions. In Fez, this takes on a localized aesthetic as the embodied movements of listeners and additional percussion during this segment carry aural elements of prominent local Sufi brotherhoods. 'Issawa and hamadsha drums (including the tabla, a pair of drums played with short sticks, the bendir, a frame drum, and the guwwal, an hourglass shaped drum that balances on the players shoulder), ghita (an oboe-like instrument), and nfar (long trumpets) animate the end of the poem, bringing it to a close as if it were a Sufi trance-based hadra.

Soussi's goal in his 2011 festival performance, however, was even greater: he aimed to infuse an entire poem with the sound of gnawa music, something never done before within malhun tradition. Because of the gnawa population's association with ritual possession and a history of marginalization because of slavery, this musical fusion with

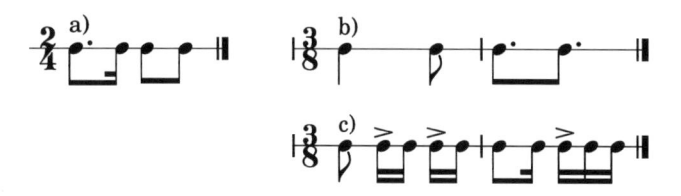

Example 7.4 The rhythmic transition from the majority of "Hakim al-Dhati" (a) to the insiraf segment (b), which is influenced by the flali pattern (c).

a genre that includes a great deal of religious poetry could very well have been problematic. Since independence, however, the gnawa ritual music's tremendous growth in popularity—despite its connotations of questionable spiritual power and the grave concerns from many regarding the ritual's appropriateness (see Chapter 4)—turned the commercial possibilities for such a fusion into a substantial potential opportunity for Soussi. To create a new setting for an old poem, Soussi invited gnawa percussionists to perform with the ensemble.[6] An elder member enacted some movements featured in the opening portions of the tradition's possession healing ritual.

Like many malhun melodies, the song features the repetition of a melodic phrase performed simultaneously by the entire group, but ornamented differently. While this sounds more like malhun than gnawa music, the melodic shape did follow a pentatonic structure similar to that of the other tradition. Perhaps most telling, when I asked him why he wanted to play a gnawa style malhun piece for this particular large, open air crowd, his response was strikingly simple: "Because the people will like it." But what was Soussi providing for his audience? What did they like so much during his rousing festival performance? The concert was part of a series that included Moroccan rappers, a famous gnawa musician, and a shʿabi popular music singer of the type heard at weddings across the country. Each night drew a very different crowd, but many were there for every concert, eager to get out, hear some music, and enjoy the social scene around the square.[7] Soussi wanted to appeal to this wider audience of Moroccans of all ages, and, in doing so, hoped to expand his own fan base. He alluded to the gnawa, using the percussionists, timbre, and dance, but the poetry remained purely within the malhun tradition. And it worked: the crowd was energized, screaming when they heard the qaraqib, iron castanets that are a distinctive sound associated with the gnawa ritual, opening the song.

In that tent on the mountainside near Mulay Yaqub, sulfur springs outside of Fez, I played a gig that was for well-off Casablanca residents who were visiting their ancestral home city. They spent the weekend bussed around enjoying those arts and excursions deemed traditional. Malhun was a remnant of a city left behind, this Suficized malhun especially so. For these groups and others, malhun remains a proud cultural artifact, yet it is one that has both kept up with the times and maintained its local nostalgia. Its proponents regularly cite a conservative celebration of the old while recognizing and enjoying innovation and change. The incorporation of Sufi musical aesthetics that so effectively mark malhun in Fez contributes to an interesting dual usage of sacred music, one that clearly symbolizes some of the larger pressures on Sufi and non-Sufi performers alike right now. On one hand, the comfort with which these artists bring their sacred and secular lives together, if malhun can indeed be called secular entertainment at all, demonstrates an eagerness to perform ideologies of piety within these communities. By putting hamadsha and ʿissawa groups on stages and accepting invitations to act as munshids, singers within local rituals, Soussi, Driss, and others blur, or altogether erase, aesthetic lines between sacred and secular entertainment. Yet the project of incorporating gnawa music for expressly commercial purposes insinuates a certain playfulness embedded within economic opportunism. Music, even sacred music, is a commodity within these circuits, and a career depends on sales or other lucrative activities. The joining of piety and pragmatism makes this poetry an important part of Morocco's sacred music industry.

Malhun performers locate geographic and religious identities within music. The addition of musical instruments that bear explicit connotations to local religious practices, like the tabla, bender, guwwal, and others coincides with their ability to gauge audience reactions and control the pacing of long insiraf passages. This begs similar questions to those that informed previous chapters. Primarily, how does performance fit into a set of expectations for musical manifestations of religious faith in Morocco? Have these expectations remained consistent over the history of malhun, or are they shifting based on new influences from popular styles, religious practices, or mass media's globalizing tendencies? The musicality of malhun is an essential tool for performers as they connect themselves to the genre's history or reach out to their audiences. Through outright borrowing and more nuanced changes, artists can create moments of musical—and even moral—intensity. Audiences jump up, swarm, even climb the stage as they lose themselves before sitting back down to enjoy the esoteric instrumental opening for the next poem.

Notes

1. Hammams in Morocco serve as neighborhood bath houses. For a minimal fee, men and women can enter (either in different spaces or at different scheduled times) to make use of the hot and cold water. Some are picturesque and remain tourist spots, while others are a simpler series of tile rooms, each hotter than the last.
2. See https://en.wikipedia.org/wiki/List_of_oldest_continuously_inhabited_cities.
3. See http://whc.unesco.org/en/list/170.
4. See Schuyler 1984 for a rare example that includes musical analysis.
5. Examples of "Ya Riyah" are available on the playlists found in the Resources section.
6. This performance appeared on one of Morocco's popular satellite television stations. A number of versions appear on YouTube; one example is available in the playlists referenced in the Resources section. In the opening, the emcee announces the poem, which begins at 16:25, as being in a "gnawa rhythm" (iqa' gnawiyya).
7. This event occurred at the Fez Festival of World Sacred Music's Boujloud Stage, which features music aimed at local audiences. The paid events tend toward featuring international artists and attract the crowds of European and American tourists as well as wealthy Moroccans.

Conclusion
Who We Are and Where We're Going

Despite their focus on Morocco, these chapters have explored how music and religion play intersecting roles in helping us define ourselves wherever we might be or come from. Like history, piety, and difference—or geography, migration, race, and nostalgia—the diverse performative styles that run through these pages become aesthetic elements of individual and social identities. Taken as a whole, musical identities inform a vast complex of personal and social awareness: not only do they tell us who we are, they can give us insights into where we come from and where we are going. As a way to conclude this book, I would like to bring some of these previous issues into a more intentional look at this idea: who we are and who we want to be. I say "we" because these musical and religious identities are rarely (if ever) generated solely by and for individuals: they help us to put ourselves within a larger community. More accurately, how we live our lives both musically (as listeners, performers, or otherwise) and religiously (as believers, skeptics, or however else we might engage with spirituality) situates us within a number of different communities. Some overlap while others might be difficult to reconcile. What does it mean to be an atheist who loves sacred music styles? What about a devout Christian who connects with death metal despite its overt Satanic symbolism? In some cases, these are aesthetic choices. In others, the distance is not so far as it may seem at first glance, as artists are constantly innovating to reach changing audiences. In any of these cases, however, the choices do not live within a strict sense of individuality. They reference and react to social expectations.

Also pressing, and perhaps even more so, is the stress on a community that arises when the "who we are" part changes in a very real way: when demographics or generational shifts make tradition or continuity unsustainable. What happens when the very people who make up the "we" are no longer the "we" that we had previously identified with? Ideologies and practices, whether musical, religious, or both, play an outsized role here as defenders of identity or as arenas for the development of a new sense of "we." For example, as generations pass and demographics change, persistent racial insecurities are often situated at the intersection of musical and religious practices. Just as the 1950s and 1960s saw a conservative white backlash against how African-American singing and dance styles were influencing popular culture, the 1980s and 1990s struggled with the advent and growth of hip hop. As these new genres and the communities that were attracted to them matured, they became vehicles for outspoken forms of social and political protest. In the earlier example, especially, religion played a substantial role: artists like Ray Charles were both revered and demonized for drawing on black gospel traditions and spirituals in creating a form of music that animated drinking and dancing at bars and clubs.[1] These pressures on artists and wider social discourse have found new voices in today's popular culture as artists like Beyoncé, D'Angelo, Childish Gambino, and Chance the Rapper draw on this history of incorporating gospel and spirituals into politically engaged musical activism. Chapter 2 featured hip hop artists in Morocco going to similar lengths as they spoke out for and against government actions toward social injustice. Other chapters witnessed the conjunction of race, religion, and nationalism in a different way, as racially, economically, and religiously marginalized groups struggled for the opportunity to represent their homeland.

Dramatic generational and demographic shifts can have cataclysmic effects on social and political life that extend to religion and the arts. As immigration, migration, and the incorporation of marginalized ethnic groups change the overall makeup of a society—or at least give voice to those who were previously voiceless—conservative pushback is inevitable. Europe and America show today's resistance to changing values as electoral politics responds to concerns over national identity thanks to persistent immigration, and movements like #BlackLivesMatter instigate responses like #BlueLivesMatter and #AllLivesMatter that can obscure or diminish efforts toward inclusion and social justice.

In various ways, the distancing and distinctions that pervade Anglo-American society, Moroccan communities, and other contexts around the world come about because of a strong sense of nostalgia. Efforts to hinder or prevent change have a strong tendency to reflect an interest in maintaining the past. These can take on various guises, but they often view the past as a time when morals and values were stronger, when people's actions more closely aligned with their beliefs and faith, when music and entertainment were wholesome representations of a more pious and respectful society. This logic is often true: youth cultures have a tendency to rebel and each successive generation's rebellion against the past necessitates a more extreme break from what came before. Yet we also have a tendency to forget the problems of times gone by at the same time, as we struggle to view the present in a way that forgives the daily drip of terrible news that comprises Twitter and Facebook feeds. Whether accurate or not, nostalgia for a disappeared past colors the protectionism and identity politics of today.

Representing Ourselves

To make the geographic connection more explicit, and at the same time, argue in the opposite direction (that "who we are and where we are going" informs our musical identities), I turn toward sounds coming from a very different time and place. Migration and generational change have always had a profound effect on music, religion, and identity. In the United States, for example, rural blues styles from Texas, Mississippi, and elsewhere in the south took hold in cities during periods of massive migration. As

African-Americans moved north and west for work opportunities, musicians came too. Drawing upon new experiences—the urbanization of rural communities—they tried new ideas, electrifying sounds and incorporating other genres. The Chicago blues of Howlin' Wolf, Buddy Guy, and Muddy Waters combined older styles with new instruments and styles for hard-driving nights in dark clubs. Perhaps more dramatically, blues and similarly rural country styles combined in cities like Chicago and Memphis to generate the newest fad in the 1950s: rock and roll. Elvis Presley was famously identified as a white singer who could sing like he was black, providing a huge economic windfall during a period of massive inequality of access where black musicians struggled to reach richer white audiences. The ways in which these divides are drawn and crossed are not identical in Morocco, but the larger narratives of migration, loss, and innovation woven through these chapters may have sounded familiar.

More concrete efforts reinforce these links today. The most obvious and intentional of these is Morocco's substantial and growing music festival circuit. Events around the country bring artists and audiences to a different major city every weekend throughout the summer. Major festivals serve as tourist attractions, drawing foreigners and domestic tourists alike. They aim for different audiences—some target the wealthy, while others are more "popular" in nature—but most have a free and public component. Buses fill up as young people undertake sacred music "pilgrimages" to Essaouira, Fez, Marrakech, Tangier, or go as far south as Agadir to dance to Europe's latest EDM (electronic dance music) trends. For artists, as well, an invitation to a festival like Fez's Festival of World Sacred Music can be a religious experience—a pilgrimage—in itself. Moreover, these events give local and national government administrators an opportunity to define, reinforce, and redefine their cities' identities to their constituents and tourists alike. Fez, always seen as a seat of sacred authority, continues to serve in that role. Marrakech and Tangier reach outward through jazz and film festivals, committing to their cosmopolitanism. Essaouira owns its history as a slave trade post by celebrating the sub-Saharan gnawa population that made its home within its walls.

So many of the country's cities carry some type of religious and musical identity that outlining them all would be the subject of a chapter of its own. It is worth it, however, to explore some major ones because they contribute substantially to Morocco's strong tourism market and the ways in which foreigners view the country. Furthermore, much of the country's history is bound up not in national and regional movements, but in local ones.

Two cities whose identities became clear in Chapter 4 are Essaouira and Marrakech. These two were both important trading posts during the pre-colonial period when Morocco controlled and traded with various regions of West Africa. The land route, via caravan through the desert, came to Marrakech after stopping at some more wayward posts further afield within Morocco. Marrakech was also home to the capitol of different Moroccan empires throughout the country's history. During the 1990s, however, its cosmopolitanism grew even more, as low-cost international flights made it a major tourist destination from across Europe. Vacationers coming for "exotic" walks through marketplaces and the sights and smells of Jamaaʻ al-Fnaʼ quickly bought up real estate and changed the economy of the city. With this influx of tourism and Marrakech's status as a celebrity hotspot (majestic villas just outside of the city boundaries regularly grace magazines and TV shows), festivals quickly arose to capitalize. The city's National Festival of Popular Arts, which King Hassan II started in the 1960s, gained in notoriety and is now firmly established as one of the major folklore festivals in the world.

Its International Film Festival began in 2001 and regularly attracts the world's biggest movie stars in shows of tradition and contemporary glamor.

Situated on the Atlantic Ocean, Essaouira was a major sea port that served as an alternative to the land routes running through Marrakech. While under Portuguese control, the town was known as Mogador and was a hive of trading activity. This included the sub-Saharan slave trade, making Essaouira a prominent space for today's gnawa community, also like Marrakech. More recently, as seen in Chapter 4, the city has embraced this history by celebrating that diversity through the world-renowned Essaouira Gnaoua World Music Festival.[2] This event, which recently celebrated its 20th edition, brings international jazz and world music stars to Morocco to play in collaboration with the country's gnawa musicians. It emphasizes the ideal of collaboration and is a demonstration of Morocco's tolerance. The city's identity, as performed on stage, reflects on a national ideology for both international tourists and domestic youth: this is a place for working together, not revolutionary or ideological violence. It is a place where difference is celebrated. The Essaouira festival is cultural nationalism; it shows the state supporting a specific version of Moroccanness, and it does so through music.

Tangier's history as an international zone, one that was politically separated from Morocco before and during the colonial period, also comes to the fore in music festivals. The city's history includes a period where it was loosely governed by a consortium of between two and eight different European powers. Its position at the mouth of the Mediterranean ensured its strategic importance, but governance was never much of a priority. European visitors and settlers enjoyed a great deal of legal freedom, and many came to Tangier to escape. More recently, the city's European focus comes through musically with major events like TANJAzz, the Tangier jazz festival. Rabat, the country's capital, has what might be the largest music festival in the country with Mawazine (Rhythms), an event that brings in the world's biggest popstars—people like Shakira and Kanye West—for massive, open, free concerts. In each of these cases, musical activities celebrate specific versions of city identities that, in turn, represent urban residents. The chapters of Part III demonstrated how this process works in Fez, a city whose sacred history gives its residents an extraordinary local pride.

Representing Changing Communities

As is the case in so many places across the world, one of the primary distinctions within the Moroccan population aligns with these urban areas. Morocco's landscape includes a long coastline attracting tourists; swaths of flat farmland; lush foothills rolling up to rocky, snow-topped mountains; and deserts peppered with communities that had settled around an oasis. The infrastructure winding within and among these disparate regions is capable when compared to other African ex-colonies, but it is by no means outstanding. Roads and railways that were built up during the protectorate are deteriorating, and driving through the winding mountain roads that dodge sharp cliffs at every blind turn can be scary. All this is to say that, as is common across the world, real and stark divides separate the nation's regions and its rural and urban populations. Even with economic activity and increased mobility, the lifestyles, languages, and cultures of small towns are disappearing—or at least that is what so many fear.

Morocco's urban landscape is centered around a historical focus on the "imperial cities," including Fez and nearby Meknes. These major areas served as centers of power for much of the country's past. More recently, and especially since the period during and just before the protectorate, ports have become more important. Access to the Atlantic Ocean and the Mediterranean Sea gave traders routes to Europe and elsewhere. Tangier's history as an "international zone" governed (at least in name) by eight countries demonstrates the significance of this strategic access. Casablanca has risen to become the country's commercial center, its largest city. Rabat, only an hour away by train, has been the political capital since the French took hold. Both are major ports and, as such, both provide substantial economic opportunities for out-of-work farmers. But just as festivals hold up and represent identities, changes in the population can problematize those same ideas of who we are. Urban migration and political strife bring these demographic shifts to the foreground in powerful ways and reflect the similar questions of identity that are playing out in today's politics across Europe, in the United States, and elsewhere.

The mass migration from farm to city predated the protectorate, but the policies of the French toward their settlers hastened the process. By selling off large plots of land, which then fell into the monarchy's hands only to be turned over to wealthy supporters after independence, government changed the agricultural sector. It modernized and improved output in many ways, but removed livelihoods in many others. Youth flocked to the growing cities where, after independence, wealthy Moroccans themselves left their traditional family homes to inhabit the newer, more modern, French-built city centers, called villes nouvelles. The demographics of the medina, each city's traditional quarters, shifted dramatically. Landlords divided palaces into tiny apartments and neglected upkeep or built low-quality shantytowns as the rural poor, the impoverished, searched for urban dwellings. Nass El Ghiwane's music was born from this process, as the young founders from Casablanca brought their parents' and grandparents' music together in a poor neighborhood's community center. For so many other youths, however, the music of the countryside was a thing of the past. Migration was changing the sound of generations. Religious traditions, in some cases, proved more durable, but more frequently the urban poor attached themselves to new communities, distinct from those of their families' pasts.

In some cases, it is ideas or identities that migrate as much as people themselves. Layered into Morocco's specific form of Arab identity is a history that predates the arrival of Muslim traders and armies. The Amazigh population remains important within a sense of place. How that role continues to exist in today's political and social world is contentious, however. There are lines drawn around a sense of race within the country that include or exclude according to different fissures. Language may be the most politically salient as of late, with wide-ranging struggles to determine the place of Tamazight, the umbrella term for languages spoken by Amazigh communities. Following consistent pressure, and finally the Arab Spring revolutions of 2011, the national government acceded to adding Tamazight as an official language and, in some communities, teaching it in school. This has not been a universally celebrated change; these communities, which are often rural, worry that by teaching the language spoken at home, their children will miss the important linguistic training in Arabic and French that can support upward social and economic mobility.

The linguistic debates are one example of a larger question over national identity, something that pervades these chapters. Powerful urban elites and rural struggles for recognition fuel these debates, which draw on far more complexity than the (markedly complex) linguistic concerns imply (see Ennaji 2010). It is not only a conversation about cities and rural towns: those who look to non-Arab sources for their own sense of identity draw more widely than an Amazigh cultural history alone. In various parts of the country, Moroccans speak Moroccan Arabic (a dialect of Arabic that serves as the "lingua franca" of urban life), fusha (standard or classical Arabic used in educated religious circles), French, Spanish, and other dialects of Arabic and Tamazight including Hassaniyya, Tashelhiyt (also known as Shilha), Tarifit, and so forth. These languages serve to demonstrate the variety of cultural identities, as each grows out of a local history and serves a purpose in building cohesion alongside foods, stories, musical practices, religious variants, dress, and other elements of everyday life.

These elements are (unfairly, I must admit) outside of the scope of this book. My own experiences centered on urban areas, especially in the north. The book's chapters reflect this, to the exclusion of much of the country's diversity. This has been the case for a while, as most scholarship on the region focuses on urban Arab identities. Perhaps this is likely, given the centrality of cities in creating and maintaining religious authority and political power. Many anthropologists, however, have spent a great deal of time in rural areas and smaller towns. In the process, they have made arguments that are core to anthropological theory itself. Music has rarely featured prominently in these discussions, even though rural sounds and Amazigh artists regularly play from radios, cassette tapes, and CDs. In fact, one of the reasons that I often chose to take a grand taxi (a large car whose seats are sold individually and whose riders are packed too tightly) when traveling between cities instead of a bus is the chance to sit back (or squish up against the window) and listen to whatever music the driver happens to be playing. More often than not, it was an old cassette from an artist like Muhammad Ruicha.

These older songs, and the newer ones that sound like them, have an identifiably unique acoustic quality and participatory energy. The main string instrument is Ruicha's lotar, though groups around the country make use of guitars, violins, and other things, not to mention programmed electronics and all of the other expected trappings of a globally-informed popular music. The backing group includes a number of drums, most of which are bendirs. For Ruicha's groups, a small group of women are backup singers, though the gender dynamics are flexible. This music highlights a distinctive vocal sound—especially for the women who are singing backup—that can come across as surprising for someone who has little experience with this music. Other groups like Oudaden, Izanzaren, or similar bands take after the stylistic innovations made by Nass El Ghiwane described in Chapter 3. In Oudaden, a group from the late 1970s, electric guitar and banjo join together to create a sound that approximates the "desert rock" of more recent Sahelian bands like Tinariwen, though with clear underlying Moroccan beats.[3] Within these approaches to popular music, Amazigh groups in Morocco and across North Africa are clearly attuned to global trends, whether musical, professional, or political (Goodman 2005, Schuyler 1984).

Blurring Sacred and Secular

In her book on Quranic recitation and religious popular music in Indonesia, Anne Rasmussen describes how

> Islamic music is performed and experienced, produced and purchased in a rather messy Venn diagram of overlapping categories, interdependent

> processes, and reciprocal influence that eschews tidy boundaries or unidirectional cause and effect.
>
> (Rasmussen 2010, 167)

In trying to discern the circles for a Venn diagram of this sort, I can't help but to imagine oddly shaped amoebic figures reaching from one artist to the next. But even this type of "messy" diagram would fail, as artists shift their focus between—and even within—performances. The edges on the circles that comprise this diagram would not only have to be jagged like a heavily gerrymandered political district, they would need to be moving in real time. And yet, this would fail to account for differences between a singer's intention and an audience member's opinion on what is happening. Is a particularly powerful vocal melisma helping me to connect to the devotional poetry in the case of Andalusian music? Or is it distracting me from the esoteric texts? The diagram's lines would have to slide one way or the other to properly account for my opinion of the boundary. What about the person sitting next to me? Is her perception the same? Are there two boundaries? Is this diagram edge losing its definition? Perhaps it is blurry, with the depth of color representing the probability of a performance being distinctly within or outside of a category.

Or maybe a diagram is a tool and, as Rasmussen states, it is simply a messy attempt to represent reality. More likely, ideas of sacred and secular are not so easily pulled apart. Sacred experiences weave through everyday life before coming to the forefront during major experiences or events: pilgrimages, worship, prayer. It would be difficult to defend the idea that time spent with family or friends, moments of joy, or even pain and grief are not sacred in some way, regardless of religious affiliation. The Merriam-Webster dictionary allows for a definition of sacred that is broad in this way: something sacred is "entitled to reverence and respect." Just below, however, a clear boundary is set up: "of or relating to religion; not secular or profane." Within the music discussed in these chapters, both versions of the definition can apply, sometimes at the same time about the same thing.

One of the aims of this book has been the consideration of the relationship between people and their everyday religious lives. Sufi rituals and possession healing ceremonies are central sacred experiences that heighten the experience of a world beyond our own. They may bring spirits from another realm of existence into engagement with our own. Worship and prayer in this Islamic context in Morocco focus awareness on morality, our decision-making, our blessings and failures, our life and death. Weddings celebrate the joys that come with major life events by reflecting on and connecting with religious faith. Funerals similarly bring remembered moments back to the present, as family and friends gather and share stories through the grief that can test or strengthen that faith. These feelings, however, can come and go in powerful ways; they are not relegated to periods of intensity, but can arise from nothing more than a fleeting thought, an old photograph, or a song.

Throughout a book on music and religion, I have not gone so far as to define religion (or music, for that matter). Instead, I hope to have shown how these parts of life can exist in broadly diverse ways within our experience. Even within a homogeneously Muslim population like Morocco, the variants of what that Islamic faith looks like can be dramatic. Furthermore, there are reasons to debate it or, as was the case in Chapter 3's political history, enforce a version of Islam that aligns with a powerful structure like the state.

To that end, the previous paragraph lists things like weddings and families that, for many, are far from everyday experiences. The "normal" life that features work, love, and faith is quite abnormal for those who are in poverty or prison; for discriminated-against individuals, including LGBTQ communities and minorities; or others like the mentally ill or disabled. That some in Morocco are atheists (often "closet atheists") or do not practice the tenets of their religion does not necessarily remove the importance of sacred experiences from their lives. Even when actively disavowing Islam, the realm of the sacred flows through everyday interactions and informs how we move through the day. How this plays into a communal self-identity that centralizes and nationalizes religious piety shows how difficult it is to draw circles around "who we are" or how we claim to know where we go next.

Many scholars have written about religion at length and it is not my goal to reiterate or expand on their words here. Instead, these reflections consider how music and fun intertwine within a wider context that is both specifically religious and, for lack of a better term, inadvertently so. Andalusian music ties faith and devotion into an experience of national heritage, one with an embedded sense of nostalgia that reinforces a link between today's Morocco and the country's history. Popular music, which I have seen criticized around the world as counter to a pious life because of associations with sex and commercialism, coincides here with global movements of ideas, bringing musical tastes and religious perspectives from abroad through the mass media, often in the same household depending on who controls the remote.

State control over so many aspects of life—including the structures of religion—connect outward political protests to internal attempts at bettering oneself. This reminds us that jihad, a term that appears often in the news today, is not intrinsically linked to a "holy war" on the battlefield, but is arguably better suited for the holy war that happens within us as we work to live righteously. It also reminds us that righteousness is not a simple concept that is widely agreed upon. Nor is Moroccan identity itself: beyond the ethical politics of Chapter 3, Chapter 4 considers one part of the country's racial diversity as West Africans brought to Morocco as slaves adopt ways of being Muslim that sit well outside of the norms described above. Even as these marginalized and underrepresented communities experience discrimination, their music can be immensely popular and can contribute to a widening—and economically useful—understanding of nationhood, nationalism, and identity. But they are still under-represented, as are other groups within the popular music industry and religious practice. This book struggles with the same difficulty: in a male-dominated hierarchical society, women making music appear far too rarely in public, let alone in scholarship. My own limits as a researcher (and as a young man working in generally conservatives communities) have prevented me from being able to sufficiently recognize these voices. Similarly, in a racially diverse country, music-fueled debates about "who we are" do not come across often enough in these pages. I have tried to foreground the music made and listened to by youth, but these creative forms of refashioning identity and religion certainly deserve more of a focus.

The final three chapters, based on different groups in and around Fez, show the complexities facing professional musicians as they attempt to navigate the pressures of making money and remaining true to their faith and practice. Not only do they concern themselves with what they believe is appropriate or right, they need to account for the perspectives and tastes of their perspectives and experiences. The observation that those tastes are changing shows them, and us, how the ways of practicing Islam in Morocco speak to new audiences. As the audience grows, however, so does the need to effectively approach and connect with a wider group of listeners. Large groups can fracture, creating opportunities for other ensembles who better fit the needs and wants of segments of the audience or better represent a changing audience. However, exclusively focusing on the logic of economics and capitalism—prioritizing strategic marketing of oneself, for example—can open a singer up to criticism. The balance of spiritual vocation and professional occupation is a difficult one to strike, and if it moves too far one way or another, a career can come to an end. Even so, the power of reaching an audience member by speaking to both a sense of piety and fun can be transformative. For these artists and their listeners, it is a valued project and a risky struggle that is worth undertaking.

Notes

1. For more on hip hop's maturation, see Jeff Chang's *Can't Stop Won't Stop* (2005). For background on rock and roll's position within the Civil Rights movement, see Garofalo (1992).
2. Gnaoua is another way to spell gnawa, one based on the French system of transliterating Arabic script.
3. See Muhammad Rouicha's "Inas Inas" and clips from a festival in Merzouga using the playlists in the Resources section.

Resources

Links to Spotify, YouTube, and Soundcloud playlists of music examples referenced in the text can be accessed on the eResource site from the Routledge catalog page: www.routledge.com/9781138094581.

Part 1 Introduction

For further reading on topics related to Morocco's contemporary history see:
    Miller, Susan Gilson. 2013. *A History of Modern Morocco*. Cambridge, UK and New York: Cambridge University Press.

Chapter 1

There is a great deal of recent writing on Andalusian communities and musical styles. See:
    Menocal, María Rosa. 2002. *The Ornament of the World: How Muslims, Jews, and Christians Created a Culture of Tolerance in Medieval Spain*. Boston, MA: Back Bay Books.
    Davila, Carl. 2013. *Al-Ala: History, Society, Text*. Wiesbaden, Germany: Reichert Verlag.
    Shannon, Jonathan. 2015. *Performing Al-Andalus: Music and Nostalgia across the Mediterranean*. Bloomington and Indianapolis, IN: Indiana University Press.

Andalusian music is also widely available commercially, including through services like Spotify. An anthology of one nuba, rama al-maya, is available on the Music and Religion of Morocco playlists.

Chapter 2

For more on the place of Morocco within American and European popular culture, see:

Edwards, Brian T. 2005. *Morocco Bound: Disorienting America's Maghreb, from Casablanca to the Marrakech Express*. Durham, NC: Duke University Press.

The history of some of the styles discussed in this chapter, including Egyptian music and rai, are well documented. See:

Danielson, Virginia. 1997. *The Voice of Egypt: Umm Kulthūm, Arabic Song, and Egyptian Society in the Twentieth Century*. Chicago, IL: University of Chicago Press.

Langlois, Tony. 1996. "The Local and Global in North African Popular Music". *Popular Music* 15 (3): 259–73.

Schade-Poulsen, Marc. 1999. *Men and Popular Music in Algeria: The Social Significance of Raï*. Austin, TX: University of Texas Press.

Music from this chapter and others is available at the Music and Religion of Morocco playlists.

Chapter 3

Albums of music discussed in this chapter by Houcine Slaoui, Nass El Ghiwane, and Fnaïre are available on the Music and Religion of Morocco playlists.

Chapter 4

TRT World produced a short documentary on gnawa music in Essaouira during the recent 2018 Essaouira festival, which is available in the Music and Religion of Morocco YouTube playlist.

My previous book discusses the issues presented in this chapter in more detail. For more about these issues, see:

Witulski, Christopher. 2018b. *The Gnawa Lions: Authenticity and Opportunity in Moroccan Ritual Music*. Bloomington, IN: Indiana University Press.

The album *Oulad Bambara: Portraits of Gnawa* is an excellent recent set of recordings of gnawa musicians. It is available on the Music and Religion of Morocco playlists.

Chapter 5

Short recordings of some hamadsha segments and a video of Abderrahim Amrani performing on television are available on the Music and Religion of Morocco playlists.

Chapter 6

Video from Abdullah's wedding procession, other clips of him and his ensemble performing, and video from the hamadsha collaboration with DJ Click are available in the Music and Religion of Morocco playlists.

Chapter 7

Versions of "al-Shma'a" by Houcine Toulali and Jil Jilala described in the chapter are available on the Music and Religion of Morocco playlists, as are recordings of "Ya Riyah" by Dahmane Elharrachi and Rachid Taha.

Conclusion

Muhammad Ruicha's "Inas Inas" and songs from Amazigh artist Oudaden are available in the Music and Religion of Morocco playlists.

Glossary

ʿ**ada:** see *dakhla*
ʿ**aita:** a form of Moroccan popular music
al-maghreb al-aqsa: the Arabic name for the country of Morocco
al-ughniya al-sharqiya: see *al-ughniya al-ʿasriya*
al-ughniya al-ʿasriya: modern song; this mid-20th century genre in Morocco showed the powerful influence of Egyptian tastes during the early post-colonial era
al-unasa al-kabira: a segment of the hamadsha ritual based on sung poetry with a percussion accompaniment
al-unasa al-saghira: a segment of the hamadsha ritual based on sung poetry
al-ala: a musical tradition historically associated with the Iberian peninsula that is still common in Morocco and related to similar traditions in Tunisia, Algeria, Syria, and Spain
Amazigh: the ethnic term for Morocco's indigenous population
Andalusian music: see *al-ala*
ʿ**arubi:** a pejorative term referring to people from rural areas
ʿ**ashiyya:** evening, also a name for a ritual ceremony that begins and ends earlier than a lila (night)
balgha: a traditional style of handmade shoes common in Morocco
banlieu: (French) the term used for suburbs in France that are often understood to be neglected, and inhabited by impoverished immigrant communities
baraka: divine blessing or goodness that can be passed through holy figures or objects
bendir: a large frame drum with a snare that creates a distinctive buzzing sound
Berber: see *Amazigh*
bidaʾ: innovation; a term used to describe a departure from proper religious practice, usually with a negative connotation
bughiyya: a piece of music in free rhythm from the Andalusian tradition that introduces a new section
butshishiyya: a prominent Sufi sect within Morocco

dakhla: entrance; the term used for the opening procession within some ritual ceremonies
daraja: degree; also the name of the Moroccan dialect of Arabic
darbuka: an hourglass-shaped drum used in many musical traditions across the Middle East
dhikr: remembrance; a term used to describe the repetitive chants that are central to many Sufi practices
drari: dependents; the term used for ensemble members within many sacred musical traditions
fassi: the adjective used for someone who lives in or comes from Fez
fatiha: a text from the Quran that is often used within ritual contexts to provide baraka
flali: a rhythmic pattern that appears in popular music
fna': extinction; the loss of self that comes with hal within Sufi usage
gandira: a heavy robe used by the hamadsha
ghita: a double reed oboe-like instrument used in a number of Moroccan traditions
ghiyati: a musician who plays the ghita
ginbri: a string instrument used in the music of the hamadsha, also a common name for the gnawa hajhuj
gnawa: a West African-derived community and religious practice that features a spirit possession-based healing ceremony
guwwal: an hourglass-shaped clay drum held on a shoulder and used during processions and other segments of ritual ceremonies in hamadsha and related traditions
hadra: the trance segment within hamadsha rituals and similar ceremonies
hajhuj: the string instrument used in gnawa ceremonies, also known as a ginbri or sintir
hajj: pilgrimage to Mecca, one of the pillars of Islam; also (along with the feminine form hajja) an honorific title for those who have undertaken the pilgrimage
hal: condition; the condition of losing oneself into Allah within Sufi usage
halqa: circle; refers to the circle of listeners surrounding musicians and other entertainers who perform in market squares
hamadsha: a Sufi sect prominent in Fez and Meknes that follows the teachings of Sidi Ali bin Hamdush
hammam: public bath
harba: a refrain within a malhun qasida
heterophony: a musical texture featuring many voices performing the same melody, but ornamenting it in different ways
hizb: a recited set of poetry unique to individual Sufi sects that opens many ceremonies
Islam: the most common religion in Morocco and across the Middle East. It focuses on submission to Allah, the Prophet Muhammed's life and leadership, and the texts of the Quran
'issawa: a Sufi sect prominent in Fez and Meknes
'issawi: a member of the 'issawa or the adjective used to describe something related to the 'issawa
jellaba: a hooded cloak that is a common traditional form of dress in Morocco
jihad: struggle; used to define external struggle against the enemies of the Islamic community or an internal one against personal sin
khadam: workers; a term used for ensemble members within some musical traditions like the 'issawa
lila: night; one name for a ritual ceremony carried out by the gnawa, 'issawa, hamadsha, or similar group

lotar: a string instrument used in Amazigh musical traditions
malhun: a tradition of sung poetry with musical accompaniment
maqam: a modal and melodic system used in many, but not all, Arabic musical traditions
maskun: the state of being possessed by a spirit within some ritual contexts
medina: an older district of many Moroccan cities that is often enclosed by large walls
mellah: the historically Jewish quarter of many Moroccan cities
mizan: a rhythmic pattern; could also be translated as "groove"
mluk: owners; the possessing spirits in some ritual ceremonies
mudawana: Moroccan family law, which was revised shortly after the Muhammad VI ascended to the throne
munshid: someone who chants or leads a chant of religious texts in sacred settings
muqaddim: the leader of musicians within Sufi groups like the hamadsha and ʿissawa
muqaddima: the organizer and leader of a ritual ceremony; in the case of the gnawa, this is usually a woman
mussem: pilgrimage; in some cases, a mussem coincides with a festival
mʿallem: the leader of the musical ensemble that animates the gnawa lila ceremony
nay: a flute-like instrument made from a reed that is common across the Middle East
nfar: long metal trumpet-like wind instruments with no valves that are able to play only a few notes and are used in outdoor processions for groups like the ʿissawa
nuba: turn; a structural term within the al-ala tradition that includes a connected set or repertoire that is often played together
qanun: a trapezoidal string instrument with courses of strings stretched across it. It is played with finger picks
qasida: a poem that, in some musical and religious traditions, can be sung with accompaniment
qism: section; a formal section within a qasida, or a verse when the qasida is sung as is the case in malhun
qiyas: shape, form; melodic structure of a melody
Quran: the holy text within Islam that was revealed to the Prophet Muhammad
quraqeb: iron castanets used in gnawa ceremonies and some other contexts
rabab: a bowed string instrument that is held upright and is central to the al-ala tradition
rabbaniyya: a set of prayers within some types of ritual ceremonies
rahba: the ritual space where possession trance happens during ceremonies
rai: a style of popular music in Morocco and Algeria
Ramadan: the holy month of fasting within the Muslim calendar
riqq: a tambourine-like frame drum
ruhiyya: sacred or spiritual, as in "sacred music" (musiqa ruhiyya)
saf al-ginbri: a segment of the hamadsha ritual featuring sung poetry accompanied by the ginbri
Sahel: a region of Africa that stretches across the Sahara and covers parts of Mauritania and Mali to Chad and the Sudan
salat: prayers
samaʿa: listening; can refer to musical listening or a spiritual openness to Allah
sanaʿi: an individual song or poem within the Andalusian music tradition
sawm: fasting
shahada: witnessing; the statement of faith within Islam
sheikh: a leader and/or teacher; often associated with Sufi practices
shikhat: women who sing and dance to certain styles of popular music
Shiʿa: a sect of Islam common in Iran, Iraq, and other regions, but rare in Morocco

sh'abi: youth; a broad category of popular music genres
Sufi: a term used to gloss a variety of forms of Islamic practice that generally includes mystical, musical, or trance elements
Sunni: a sect of Islam most common in Morocco
swissen: a string instrument used in malhun that is similar to, but smaller than, the hamadsha ginbri or Amazigh lotar
takht: a small ensemble that is generally associated with Arabic classical music styles
tarab: enchantment; a genre of music associated with Egypt, Syria, and other musical histories; also the state of a listener when listening to this music
tarbush: a red hat commonly called a "fez" outside of Morocco
tariqa: path, a term used to describe the various types of Sufi teaching and practice within Morocco
tasliyya: a segment of the hamadsha ritual that uses percussion accompaniment
tawhid: the oneness and unity of Allah and, in some Sufi senses, all of creation
tbal: large drums used in ritual processions
tijaniyya: a Sufi sect prominent in Morocco and West Africa that follows the teachings of Ahmed Tijani
tubu': natures; a melodic and modal system used in Andalusian and related traditions
tushiyya: an instrumental prelude or interlude within the Andalusian music tradition
t'arija: a small hourglass-shaped drum held in one hand and played with the other
'ud: a pear-shaped fretless string instrument that is held and played like a guitar
'ud al-ramal: a precursor to the modern 'ud used in some al-ala settings
ville nouvelle: (French) new city, usually built next to the medina of many Moroccan cities during the colonial period
wird: a profession of adherence to a Sufi brotherhood that is chanted during a ceremony
zawiya: corner; a Sufi lodge or space of prayer and refuge that is commonly affiliated with a specific Sufi organization
zikat: charity or almsgiving

References

Abouzeid, Rania. 2011. "Bouazizi: The Man Who Set Himself and Tunisia on Fire". *Time.com*. January 21, 2011. Available at: http://content.time.com/time/magazine/article/0,9171,2044723,00.html.

Al-Sayid Ibrahim, Muhammad and Ka'ib Bin Zuhair. 1985. "The Impact of the Ode 'Al-Burda' on the Sufi Tradition". *Alif: Journal of Comparative Poetics*, 5: 49–72.

Amine, Khalid and Marvin Carlson. 2012. *The Theatres of Morocco, Algeria and Tunisia: Performance Traditions of the Maghreb*. Basingstoke, UK: Palgrave Macmillan UK.

Apostolos-Cappadona, Diane 2005. "Discerning the Hand-of-Fatima: An Iconological Investigation of the Role of Gender in Religious Art". In *Beyond the Exotic: Women's Histories in Islamic Societies*, edited by Amira El-Azhary Sonbol, 347–64. Syracuse, NY: Syracuse University Press.

Bargach, Jamila. 1999. "Liberatory, Nationalizing and Moralizing by Ellipsis: Reading and Listening to Lhussein Slaoui's Song Lmirikan". *The Journal of North African Studies*, 4 (4): 61–88.

Bekkas, Majid. 2002. *African Gnaoua Blues*. Igloo Records 163. Audio CD.

Bekkas, Majid. 2013. *Al Qantara*. Igloo Records 250. Audio CD.

Boum, Aomar 2012. "Youth, Political Activism and the Festivalization of Hip-Hop Music in Morocco". In *Contemporary Morocco: State, Politics and Society under Muhammad VI*, edited by Bruce Maddy-Weitzman and Daniel Zisenwine, 161–77. London and New York: Routledge

Bowles, Paul. 1982. *The Spider's House*. Santa Barbara, CA: Black Sparrow.

Bowles, Paul. 2016. *Music of Morocco: Recorded by Paul Bowles, 1959*. Dust to Digital. 4 CD set.

Bozdag, Engin and Jeroen van den Hoven. 2015. "Breaking the Filter Bubble: Democracy and Design". *Ethics and Information Technology*, 17 (4): 249–65.

Burroughs, William S. 1990. *Naked Lunch: The Restored Text*. Edited by James Grauerholz and Barry Miles. New York: Grove Press.

Callen, Jeffrey. 2006. "French Fries in the Tagine: Re-Imagining Moroccan Popular Music". PhD dissertation, Los Angeles, CA, University of California.

Central Intelligence Agency. 2019. *Africa: Morocco — The World Factbook*. Accessed March 5, 2019. www.cia.gov/library/publications/the-world-factbook/geos/mo.html.

Chang, Jeff. 2005. *Can't Stop Won't Stop: A History of the Hip-Hop Generation*. New York: St. Martin's Press.

Chrisafis, Angelique. 2011. "Moroccan Tourist Cafe Terrorist Attack Leaves at Least 15 Dead". *The Guardian*. April 28, 2011. Available at: www.theguardian.com/world/2011/apr/28/marrakech-tourist-cafe-terrorist-attack.

Ciucci, Alessandra. 2010. "De-Orientalizing the Aita and Re-Orienting the Shikhat". In *French Orientalism: Culture, Politics, and the Imagined Other*, edited by Desmond Hosford and Chong J. Wojtkowski, 71–96. Newcastle-upon-Tyne, UK: Cambridge Scholars Press.

CNN. 2011. "Moroccan Cafe Bombing Deemed 'Act of Terrorism.'" April 28, 2011. Available at: www.cnn.com/2011/WORLD/africa/04/28/morocco.blast/index.html.

Crapanzano, Vincent. 1980. *Tuhami: Portrait of a Moroccan*. Chicago, IL: University of Chicago Press.

Crapanzano, Vincent. 1981. *The Ḥamadsha: A Study in Moroccan Ethnopsychiatry*. Berkeley, CA and London: University of California Press.

Danielsen, Anne. 2006. *Presence and Pleasure: The Funk Grooves of James Brown and Parliament*. Middletown, CT: Wesleyan University Press.

Danielson, Virginia. 1997. *The Voice of Egypt: Umm Kulthūm, Arabic Song, and Egyptian Society in the Twentieth Century*. Chicago, IL: University of Chicago Press.

Danielson, Virginia. 1998. "Performance, Political Identity, and Memory: Umm Kulthum and Gamal 'Abd Al-Nasir". In *Images of Enchantment: Visual and Performing Arts of the Middle East*, edited by Sherifa Zuhur. Cairo: The American University in Cairo Press.

Davila, Carl. 2013. *Al-Ala: History, Society, Text*. Wiesbaden, Germany: Reichert Verlag.

Davila, Carl. 2015. "The Andalusi Turn: The Nūba in Mediterranean History". *Mediterranean Studies*, 23 (2): 149–69.

Davila, Carl. 2016. *Nūbat Ramal Al-Māya in Cultural Context: The Pen, the Voice, the Text*. Leiden, The Netherlands, Boston, MA: Brill.

Davis, Ruth. 1997. "Cultural Policy and the Tunisian Ma'lūf: Redefining a Tradition". *Ethnomusicology*, 41 (1): 1–21.

DeAngelis, Angelica Maria. 2003. "Moi Aussi, Je Suis Musulman: Rai, Islam, and Masculinity in Maghrebi Transnational Identity". *Alif: Journal of Comparative Poetics*, 23: 276–308.

Dernouny, Mohamed and Boujemâa Zoulef. 1980. "Naissance d'un Chant Protestataire: Le Groupe Marocaine Nass El Ghiwane". *Peuples Méditerranéens*, 12 (July–September): 3–31.

Edwards, Brian T. 2005. *Morocco Bound: Disorienting America's Maghreb, from Casablanca to the Marrakech Express*. Durham, NC: Duke University Press.

Eickelman, Dale F. 1976. *Moroccan Islam: Tradition and Society in a Pilgrimage Center*. Austin, TX and London: University of Texas Press.

Ennaji, Moha. 2010. *Multilingualism, Cultural Identity, and Education in Morocco*. New York: Springer.

Epstein, Dena J. 2003 [1977]. *Sinful Tunes and Spirituals: Black Folk Music to the Civil War*. Music in American Life series. Urbana, IL: University of Illinois Press.

Erlmann, Veit. 1996. "The Aesthetics of the Global Imagination: Reflections on World Music in the 1990s". *Public Culture*, 8 (3): 467–87.

Farmer, Henry George. 1929. *A History of Arabian Music to the XIIIth Century*. London: Luzac.

Feriali, Kamal. 2009. "Music-Induced Spirit Possession Trance in Morocco: Implications for Anthropology and Allied Disciplines". PhD dissertation, Gainesville, FL, University of Florida.

Frishkopf, Michael. 2001. "Tarab in the Mystic Sufi Chant of Egypt". In *Colors of Enchantment: Visual and Performing Arts of the Middle East*, edited by Sherifa Zuhur, 233–69. Cairo and New York: American University in Cairo Press.

Frishkopf, Michael (ed). 2010. *Music and Media in the Arab World*. Cairo and New York: The American University in Cairo Press.

Fuson, Timothy Dale. 2012. "Most Psychedelic Gnawa Tape Ever". *Moroccan Tape Stash*. July 8, 2012. Available at: http://moroccantapestash.blogspot.com/2012/07/most-psychedelic-gnawa-tape-ever.html.

References • 155

Fuson, Timothy Dale. 2013. "Hamadsha Information and Jilala Tunes". *Moroccan Tape Stash*. January 14, 2013. Available at: http://moroccantapestash.blogspot.com/2013/01/hamadsha-information-and-jilala-tunes.html.

Fuson, Timothy Dale. n.d. "Slaoui, Houcine". *Grove Music Online*. Oxford, UK: Oxford University Press. Available at: www.oxfordmusiconline.com/subscriber/article/grove/music/48495.

Garofalo, Reebee. 1992. "Popular Music and the Civil Rights Movement". In *Rockin' the Boat: Mass Music and Mass Movements*, edited by Reebee Garofalo, 231–41. Boston, MA: South End Press.

Geertz, Clifford. 1971. *Islam Observed: Religious Development in Morocco and Indonesia*. Chicago, IL: University of Chicago Press.

Gilson Miller, Susan. 2013. *A History of Modern Morocco*. Cambridge, UK and New York: Cambridge University Press.

Glasser, Jonathan 2016. *The Lost Paradise: Andalusi Music in Urban North Africa*. Chicago, IL and London: The University of Chicago Press.

Greene, Andy. 2008. "Track by Track: Crosby, Stills & Nash on Their Self-Titled Debut". *Rolling Stone*. August 18, 2008. www.rollingstone.com/music/news/track-by-track-crosby-stills-nash-on-their-self-titled-debut-20080818.

Goodman, Jane. 2005. *Berber Culture on the World Stage: From Village to Video*. Bloomington, IN: Indiana University Press.

Grame, Theodore C. 1970. "Music in the Jma Al-Fna of Marrakesh". *The Musical Quarterly*, 56: 74–87.

Gross, Joan, David McMurray, and Ted Swedenburg. 1992. "Rai, Rap, and Ramadan Nights: Franco-Maghribi Cultural Identities". *Middle East Report*, 178 (October): 11–24.

Guessous, Fouad. 2008. *Anthologie de La Poésie Du Melhoun Morocain*. Casablanca, Morocco: Publiday-Multidia.

Guilbault, Jocelyne. 1993. "On Redefining the 'Local' Through World Music". *The World of Music*, 35 (2): 33–47.

Hachimi, Atiqa. 2012. "The Urban and the Urbane: Identities, Language Ideologies, and Arabic Dialects in Morocco". *Language in Society*, 41 (3): 321–41.

Hagedorn, Katherine J. 2001. *Divine Utterances: The Performance of Afro-Cuban Santería*. Washington, D.C.: Smithsonian Institution Press.

Hammoudi, Abdellah 1997. *Master and Disciple: The Cultural Foundations of Moroccan Authoritarianism*. Chicago, IL: University of Chicago Press.

Hayden, Michael Edison. 2017. "Muslims 'Absolutely' the Group Most Victimized by Global Terrorism, Researchers Say". *ABC News*. June 20, 2017. Available at: https://abcnews.go.com/Politics/muslims-absolutely-group-victimized-global-terrorism-researchers/story?id=48131273.

Hendrickson, Jocelyn 2009. "Andalusia". In *The Oxford Encyclopedia of the Islamic World*, edited by John L. Esposito, Oxford, UK: Oxford University Press.

Huizenga, Tom. 2014. "NPR Music's 25 Favorite Albums Of 2014 (So Far)". *NPR Music*. June 30, 2014. Available at: www.npr.org/2014/06/30/326541189/npr-musics-25-favorite-albums-of-2014-so-far.

Jirari, Abbes ben Abdallah. 1969. *Al-Qasida: Al-Zajal Fi Al-Maghrib (The Qasida: Zajal in Morocco)*. Rabat, Morocco: Maktaba al-Talib.

Jones, Lura. 1977. "The Isawiya of Tunisia and Their Music". PhD dissertation, Seattle, WA, University of Washington

Kapchan, Deborah. 2007. *Traveling Spirit Masters: Moroccan Gnawa Trance and Music in the Global Marketplace*. Middletown, CT: Wesleyan University Press.

Karl, Brian. 2012. "Technology in Modern Moroccan Musical Practices", *International Journal of Middle East Studies* 44 (4): 790–93.

Klein, Debra L. 2007. *Yorùbá Bàtá Goes Global: Artists, Cultura Brokers, and Fans*. Chicago, IL and London: The University of Chicago Press.

Langlois, Tony. 1996. "The Local and Global in North African Popular Music". *Popular Music*, 15 (3): 259–73.

Langlois, Tony. 1999. "Heard but Not Seen: Music among the Aissawa Women of Oujda, Morocco". *Music and Anthropology: Journal of Musical Anthropology of the Mediterranean*, 4.

Largey, Michael D. 2006. *Vodou Nation: Haitian Art Music and Cultural Nationalism*. Chicago, IL: University of Chicago Press.

Magidow, Melanie Autumn. 2013. "Multicultural Solidarity: Performances of Malhun Poetry in Morocco". PhD dissertation, The University of Texas at Austin.

Magidow, Melanie. 2016. "Trending Classic: The Cultural Register of Moroccan Malhun Poetry". *The Journal of North African Studies*, 21 (2): 310–34.

Mann, Vivian B., Thomas F. Glick, and Jerrilynn D. Dodds (eds). 2007. *Convivencia: Jews, Muslims, and Christians in Medieval Spain*. New York: George Braziller.

Manuel, Peter. 1993. *Cassette Culture*. Chicago, IL: University of Chicago Press.

Marcus, Scott. 2001. "The Eastern Arab System of Melodic Modes in Theory and Practice: A Case Study of Maqām Bayyātī". In *Garland Encyclopedia of World Music, Vol. 6, The Middle East*, edited by Virginia Danielson, Scott Marcus, and Dwight Reynolds, 67–73. New York: Routledge.

Matory, J. Lorand. 2005. *Black Atlantic Religion: Tradition, Transnationalism, and Matriarchy in the Afro-Brazilian Candomblé*. Princeton, NJ: Princeton University Press.

M'Bokolo, Elikia. 1998. "The Impact of the Slave Trade on Africa". *Le Monde Diplomatique*. April 1998. Available at: https://mondediplo.com/1998/04/02africa#nb1.

McMurray, David A. 2001. *In & Out of Morocco: Smuggling and Migration in a Frontier Boomtown*. Minneapolis, MN: University of Minnesota Press.

McNeill, Rhashidah. 1993. "The Splendid Master Gnawa Musicians of Morocco". *RandyWeston. info*. Available at: www.randyweston.info/randy-weston-discography-pages/1992splendidmaster gnawa.html.

Meintjes, Louise. 1990. "Paul Simon's Graceland, South Africa, and the Mediation of Musical Meaning". *Ethnomusicology*, 34 (1): 37–73.

Menocal, María Rosa. 2002. *The Ornament of the World: How Muslims, Jews, and Christians Created a Culture of Tolerance in Medieval Spain*. Boston, MA: Back Bay Books.

Miller, Susan Gilson, Attilio Petruccioli, and Mauro Bertagnin. 2001. "Inscribing Minority Space in the Islamic City: The Jewish Quarter of Fez (1438–1912)". *Journal of the Society of Architectural Historians*, 60 (3): 310–27.

Moreno Almeida, Cristina. 2016. "The Politics of Taqlidi Rap: Reimagining Moroccanness in the Era of Global Flows". *The Journal of North African Studies*, 21 (1): 116–31. https://doi.org/10.1080/1 3629387.2015.1084101.

Moreno Almeida, Cristina. 2017. *Rap Beyond Resistance: Staging Power in Contemporary Morocco*. Cham, Switzerland: Palgrave Macmillan.

Morgan, Marcyliena and Dionne Bennett. 2011. "Hip-Hop & the Global Imprint of a Black Cultural Form". *Daedalus*, 140 (2): 176–96.

Munson, Henry Jr. 1993. *Religion and Power in Morocco*. New Haven, CT and London: Yale University Press.

Nabti, Mehdi. 2006. "Soufisme, Métissage Culturel et Commerce Du Sacré: Les Aïssâwa Marocains Dans La Modernité". *Insaniyat: Revue Algérienne d'anthropologie et de Sciences Sociales Insaniyat* 10 (32/33): 173–95.

Nabti, Mehdi. 2007. "La Confrérie Des Aïssâwa Du Maroc En Milieu Urbain. Les Pratiques Rituelles et Sociales Du Mysticisme Contemporain". PhD dissertation, Paris, France, École des Hautes Études en Sciences Sociales.

Nass El Ghiwane. 2009. *Musique du Monde: Chants Gnawa du Maroc*. Buda France. Audio CD.

Novak, David. 2013. *Japanoise: Music at the Edge of Circulation*. Durham and London: Duke University Press.

Oufkir, Malika and Michèle Fitoussi. 1999. *Stolen Lives: Twenty Years in a Desert Jail*. New York: Éditions Grasset & Fasquelle.

Page, Jimmy & Robert Plant. 1994. *No Quarter: Jimmy Page & Robert Plant Unledded*. Atlantic 82706-2. Audio CD.
Page, Jimmy & Robert Plant. 2004. *No Quarter: Jimmy Page & Robert Plant Unledded*. Atlantic. DVD video.
Pariser, Eli. 2011. *The Filter Bubble: How the New Personalized Web Is Changing What We Read and How We Think*. New York: Penguin Books.
Racy, Ali Jihad. 2003. *Making Music in the Arab World: The Culture and Artistry of Tarab*. Cambridge, UK and New York: Cambridge University Press.
Rasmussen, Anne. 2010. *Women, the Recited Qur'an and Islamic Music in Indonesia*. Berkeley and Los Angeles, CA: University of California Press.
Reynolds, Dwight F. 1995. "Musical Dimensions of an Arabic Oral Epic Tradition". *Asian Music*, 26 (1): 53–94.
Reynolds, Dwight. 2008. "Al-Maqqarī's Ziryāb: The Making of a Myth". *Middle Eastern Literatures* 11 (2): 155–68.
Rotana. 2010. "Haifa Wehbe Recites the Quran and Does Her Prayers". April 13, 2010. Available at: https://web.archive.org/web/20100421121956/http://rotana.net/news/Article.aspx?name=Haifa-Wehbe-Recites-the-Quran-and-Does-Her-Prayers.xml&AspxAutoDetectCookieSupport=1.
Sabry, Tarik. 2010. *Cultural Encounters in the Arab World: On Media, the Modern and the Everyday*. New York: I.B. Tauris & Co. Ltd.
Saghir Janjar, Mohamed. 1984. "Expérience Du Sacré Chez La Confrérie Religieuse Marocaine Des Isawa: Contribution à l'étude de Quelques Aspects Socio-Culturels de La Mystique Musulmane". PhD dissertation, Paris, France, Université Paris V – René Descartes.
Salois, Kendra. 2014. "Make Some Noise, Drari: Embodied Listening and Counterpublic Formations in Moroccan Hip Hop". *Anthropoloigcal Quarterly*, 87 (4): 1017–48.
Sayed, Omar. 2011. *Nass El Ghiwane*. Borgaro Torinese, Italy: Senso Unico Editions.
Schade-Poulsen, Marc. 1999. *Men and Popular Music in Algeria: The Social Significance of Raï*. Austin, TX: University of Texas Press.
Schaefer, John Philip Rode. 2015. "Middle Eastern Music and Popular Culture". In *A Companion to the Anthropology of the Middle East*, edited by Soraya Altorki, 495–508. Hoboken, NJ: John Wiley & Sons, Inc.
Schuyler, Philip D. 1984. "Berber Professional Musicians in Performance". In *Performance Practice: Ethnomusicological Perspectives*, edited by Gerard Béhague. New Haven, CT: Greenwood Press.
Schuyler, Philip D. 2002. "Malhun: Colloquial Song in Morocco". In *Garland Encyclopedia of World Music, Vol. 6, The Middle East*, edited by Virginia Danielson, Scott Marcus, and Dwight Reynolds, 495–500. New York and London: Routledge.
Shāmī, Yūnis al-. 1984. *Nūbāt Al-Ala Al-Maghribiyya: Al-Mudūna Bil-Kitāba Al-Mūsīqiyya (Nūba Ramal Al-Māya)*. Haqūq Maḥfūdha lil-Muʾalif.
Shāmī, Yūnis al-. 2009. *Al-Nūbāt Al-Andalusiyya: Al-Mudūna Bil-Kitāba Al-Mūsīqiyya (Nūba Al-Raṣd)*. Salé: Jamīʿ al-Haqūq Maḥfūdha lil-Muʾalif.
Shannon, Jonathan H. 2003. "'al-Muwashshahât' and 'Al-Qudûd Al-Halabiyya': Two Genres in the Aleppine 'Wasla.'" *Middle East Studies Association Bulletin*, 37 (1): 82–101.
Shannon, Jonathan. 2006. *Among the Jasmine Trees: Music and Modernity in Contemporary Syria*. Middletown, CT: Wesleyan University Press.
Shannon, Jonathan. 2011. "Suficized Musics of Syria at the Intersection of Heritage and the War on Terror; Or 'A Rumi with a View.'" In *Muslim Rap, Halal Soaps, and Revolutionary Theater: Artistic Developments in the Muslim World*, edited by Karin van Nieuwkerk, 257–74. Austin, TX: University of Texas Press.
Shannon, Jonathan. 2015. *Performing Al-Andalus: Music and Nostalgia across the Mediterranean*. Bloomington and Indianapolis, IN: Indiana University Press.
Shumays, Sami Abu. 2013. "Maqam Analysis: A Primer". *Music Theory Spectrum* 35 (2): 235–55.

Simour, Lhoussain. 2016. *Larbi Batma, Nass El-Ghiwane and Postcolonial Music in Morocco*. Jefferson, NC: McFarland & Company, Inc.

Stokes, Martin. 2009. "Abd Al-Halim's Microphone". In *Music and the Play of Power in the Middle East, North Africa and Central Asia*, edited by Laudan Nooshin, 55–73. Burlington, VT: Ashgate Publishing Company.

The Splendid Master Gnawa Musicians of Morocco Featuring Randy Weston. 1994. *The Splendid Master Gnawa Musicians of Morocco*. Antilles 314 521 587-2. Audio CD.

Thuburn, Dario and Najeh Mouelhi. 2011. "Tears and Joy as Tunisia's Revolution Rap Debuts". *Ma'an News Agency*. January 30, 2011. Available at: www.maannews.com/Content.aspx?id=355411.

Turino, Thomas. 2003. "Are We Global Yet? Globalist Discourse, Cultural Formations and the Study of Zimbabwean Popular Music". *British Journal of Ethnomusicology*, 12 (2): 51–79.

Walt, Vivienne. 2011. "El Général and the Rap Anthem of the Mideast Revolution". *Time.com*. February 15, 2011. Available at: http://content.time.com/time/world/article/0,8599,2049456,00.html.

Walser, Robert. 1993. *Running with the Devil: Power, Gender, and Madness in Heavy Metal Music*. Middletown, CT: Wesleyan University Press.

Weinstein, Deena. 2011. "The Globalization of Metal". In *Metal Rules the Globe: Heavy Metal Music around the World*, edited by Jeremy Wallach, Harris M. Berger, and Paul D. Greene, 34–62. Durham and London: Duke University Press.

Weston, Randy, and Willard Jenkins. 2010. *African Rhythms: The Autobiography of Randy Weston*. Durham and London: Duke University Press.

Witulski, Christopher. 2016. "Crossing Paths: Musical and Ritual Interactivity between the Ḥamadsha and Gnawa in Sidi Ali, Morocco". *Yale Journal of Music & Religion*, 2 (2): 175–94.

Witulski, Christopher. 2018a "Contentious Spectacle: Negotiated Authenticity within Morocco's Gnawa Ritual". *Ethnomusicology*, 62 (1): 58–82.

Witulski, Christopher. 2018b. *The Gnawa Lions: Authenticity and Opportunity in Moroccan Ritual Music* (Public Cultures of the Middle East and North Africa series). Bloomington, IN: Indiana University Press.

Ya Libnan. 2008. "Haifa Covers up Body to Sing in Bahrain". May 1, 2008. Available at: https://web.archive.org/web/20110322202219/http://yalibnan.com/site/archives/2008/05/haifa_covers_up.php.

Index

'Abbassid dynasty 10–11, 33
Abd al-Rzaq, Abd al-Rahim 61
activism *see* politics
Adil ('issawa muqaddim) 97, 99–100, 112–14
Africa *see* West Africa
ahl twat 106–7
Ajram, Nancy 29
al-ala *see* Andalusian music
al-Qarawiyyin 118–19; *see also* Fez
al-Qa'ida 39
al-unasa al-kabira 92–3
al-unasa al-saghira 91
Alaouite dynasty 45
Algeria 36–8
Amazigh 2, 10, 41–2, 141
Amrani, Abderrahim 79, 84–95, 107, 110, 131
Andalusia 9–13, 33; *see also* Andalusian music; heritage; nostalgia
Andalusian music 13–16, 49, 144; and healing 7–9; history 9, 11–12; innovations in 12, 16–17, 19; musical structures 17–20; poetry 14–15, 18; in relation to Arabic music 19–20; social and economic class 20–1; *see also* malhun
anthropology 32
Arab music 19, 32–4; *see also* Egypt; maqam
Arab Spring 25, 47, 53–6
Arabic language 31–2, 61, 141–2
Arabization 42
'ashiyya 63; *see also* gnawa: ritual practice
authenticity 3, 35

Balkani, Brahim El 71
banjo 44, 50
baraka 32, 82; *see also* "Moroccan Islam"; Sufism
Bekkas, Majid 71
bendir 51, 87–8, 103
Berber *see* Amazigh
bia' *see* innovation
blues 139
Boutella, Safi 43–4
Bowles, Paul 29
Burroughs, William 29
butshishiyya 84

Cairo 1
Calmus, Fredric 93–4
Casablanca 1, 43, 49
Chakara, Abdessadeq 34
Chiki, Ahmed 7, 16, 21–2
Christian rock 5; *see also* Christianity
Christianity 5, 52–3, 81; *see also* Christian rock
class 20–1, 55–6, 107; in music videos 30
collaboration 69, 71, 74, 110, 140; *see also* fusion
colonialism 26, 32, 35, 44–6, 49, 61, 119–20, 140–1
convivencia *see* Andalusia
Crosby, Stills, and Nash 28

dakhla 63, 65, 90
dance 101
dancing 116

159

Index

darbuka 16, 34; *see also* Arab music; rhythm
Dghughi, Sidi Ahmed 85–6, 91; *see also* hamadsha
dhikr 105
diversity 41
drari 63

economic class *see* class
economics 45–7, 138–9; *see also* class; colonialism; Morocco: history since independence
EDM (electronic dance music) 5, 139
Egypt 19, 34; media from 35; politics in 35; popular culture of 26
El Général 53–4
entertainment: music as 2; *see also* 'issawa; morality; popular music; weddings
Essaouira 65, 68–9, 139–40
Essaouira Gnaoua World Music Festival 140; *see also* Essaouira
ethics *see* morality
expectation 17

faith *see* religion
fatiha 91
festivals 43–4, 59–60, 139
Fez 77–8, 85, 102, 117–19, 140–1; geography 12; gnawa in 58; *see also* malhun: in Fez
Fez Festival of World Sacred Music 77–8, 110, 136n7, 139
Fikri, Saida 43–4
flamenco 34
Fnaïre 55
France 45, 49; *see also* colonialism
fusion 110, 116; *see also* popular music: fusion projects

gender 2, 63, 144; disparities in religious practice 30; female spaces 37; in rai music 40n9; in religious hierarchies 52
Ghania, Mahmoud 69, 71
gharnati 132
ghayati 80; *see also* ghita
ghita 80, 89, 90, 93, 98, 103
Ghumami 67
ginbri (gnawa instrument) *see* hajhuj
ginbri (hamadsha instrument) 87–9, 92–3
globalization 1, 25, 27–8, 33–4, 109, 142; *see also* mass media
gnawa 9, 84, 99, 107–9, 111–2, 122, 135, 140; changing status 72; commercial success 59–60; marginalization 65; relationship to Islam 96n3; representing slavery in ritual 61, 65; ritual practice 59, 61–8; spirits in *see* mluk
Gourd, Abdellah el- 74

guwwal 80, 87–8, 93–5
Gysin, Brion 29

H-Kayne 55
hadra 93–5
Hafez, Abd al-Halim 35
hajhuj 62, 65, 70
Hakmoun, Hassan 74
hal 83; *see also* Sufism
halal 75n2
hamadsha 79, 82, 106, 110, 131, 134; associated musical instruments 87–89; changing traditions 89–90; description of ritual 79–80; history 84–7; marginalization from mainstream Islam 80; rhythms 91–3, 95; ritual structure 90–5; *see also* Sufism: popular
Hamdush, Sidi Ali bin 80, 82, 85–6, 91; *see also* hamadsha
hammam 136n1
Hand of Fatima 38–9
harba 124
Harrison, George 28
Hassan II (king) 47
healing 7–9, 108
heavy metal 5, 27, 40n4; *see also* popular music
Hendrix, Jimi 28
heritage 20, 50, 121, 123–4, 126, 135–6, 144; *see also* tradition
heterophony 16–17
hip hop 27, 38, 40n4, 138; and politics 53–6; *see also* popular music
hizb 91

Ibn Khaldun 10
identity 137–40
ideology 27
imam 52
immigration 138
innovation 81, 102, 121–2, 123, 135–6; *see also* Andalusian music: innovations in
insiraf 125, 134
internet 3, 13, 29, 33, 44, 133
ISIS *see* Islamic State
Islam 9, 52; early history 10, 31–3; fundamentalism 81; and gender 30; globalization of 25–6; and gnawa practices 67; in modern life 26; as practiced in Morocco 30–3, 102; regional diversity 81; rejecting terrorism 39; Sunni and Shi'a split 32; under colonialism 45; *see also* "Moroccan Islam"; Sufism: popular
Islamic State 25
Islamization *see* Arabization
Israel 120; *see also* Jewish communities
'Issa, Muhammad al-Hadi bin 84, 101–2, 105–6

ʿissawa 92, 134; associated musical instruments 102–5; collaboration with malhun ensemble 115–6; description of a wedding 97–9; history 101–2; pilgrimage 84; poetry 105–6; ritual practice 105–9

Jamaaʿ al-Fanaʾ *see* Marrakech
Jewish communities 2, 40n8, 119–20
jihad 31, 144
Jil Jilala 123
jilala 106
Judaism *see* Jewish communities

Kasri, Hamid al- 70, 132
Khayat, Abd al-Hadi bil- 35–6
Khayat, Nadir 27
Kirouj, Abderrahman 50, 68–9, 110; *see also* Nass El Ghiwane

Lady Gaga 27
Lalla Aisha 79, 85–7, 89, 93, 108, 132
Lalla Malika 108
Lalla Mimuna 67
lila *see* gnawa: ritual practice; hamadsha: ritual structure; ʿissawa: ritual practice
Lyautey, Hubert 45

malhun 14, 106, 116, 121–5; in Fez 133–6; history 122; poetry 121; rhythms 124–5, 134–5; *see also* Andalusian music
maqam 19–20, 34–5
Marrakech 28, 58–61, 68, 139–40
marriage *see* weddings
mass media 3, 24–6, 29, 48, 69–70, 142, 144; representation 20; *see also* Egypt: media from; globalization; internet; popular music
Mawazine Festival 43–4; *see also* Rabat
Meknes 82–3, 101, 133, 140–1
Merchane, Abd al-Kebir 59
Merchane, Hicham 59
migration 138–9; *see also* urbanization
minorities 41–2
mizan 16–20
mluk 65–8, 108
modernity 26
morality 2–5, 45, 52; in popular culture 27, 29; *see also* religion
"Moroccan Islam" 32, 80, 126; *see also* Islam: as practiced in Morocco
Morocco: demographics 2, 46; history since independence 44–8; independence movement 46–7, 119; king as "commander of the faithful" 47, 53; rejecting terrorism 39; "Years of Lead" 47, 52, 56; *see also* Andalusia: history; Islam: as practiced in Morocco; "Moroccan Islam"

mudawana 47
Muhammad (Prophet) 31–2, 59, 101; in song texts 21–2
Muhammad V (king) 46–7
Muhammad VI (king) 39, 47
Mulay Brahim 59
Mulay Yaqub 115–7
muqaddim (hamadsha and ʿissawa) 79, 101
muqaddima (gnawa) 63, 68
music videos 1
musical taste 3–5, 90, 100–1, 109
mʿallem 63, 65

Nass El Ghiwane 43–4, 49–52, 55–6, 68–9, 110, 123, 141; membership 50
Nasser, Gamal Abdel 35; *see also* Egypt
nationalism 26, 35, 38–9, 59, 138, 140, 144
natures *see* tubuʿ
nay 34 *see also* Arab music
nfar 98, 103
nostalgia 17, 135–8, 144; *see also* heritage; tradition
nuba 17–18, 21; *see also* Andalusian music; tubuʿ

Oujda 36–7

Paco *see* Kirouj, Abderrahman
Page, Jimmy 71
patriotism 56–7
piety 53, 144–5
pilgrimage 82, 139; *see also* hamadsha; ʿissawa; Sidi Ali; Sufism
Plant, Robert 71
politics 34–5, 41, 53, 81, 138; *see also* hip hop: and politics
popular culture 137–8; *see also* mass media; popular music
popular music 3, 27–9, 35–40, 48–9, 109–10, 142, 144; fusion projects 55, 69–74
possession *see* spirit possession
poverty 20, 107
professionalism 100
protectorate *see* colonialism; France

qanun 16, 34 *see also* Arab music
qasba 51
qasida 106, 124
qiyas 128
Quran 21, 65–6, 91, 105
quraqeb 63, 104

rabab 15, 17; *see also* Andalusian music
Rabat 140; *see also* Mawazine Festival
racism 68
rai 36–8
Ramadan 14, 20, 102, 131–2

RedOne *see* Khayat, Nadir
religion 143–4; music influencing faith 2
rhythm: in Andalusian music 18–19; flali 134; *see also* hamadsha: rhythms; malhun: rhythms; mizan
riqq 34; *see also* Arab music
ritual *see* 'issawa; gnawa; hamadsha; Sufism
ruhiyya *see* sacred music
Ruicha, Muhammad 142
rural areas 45–6

sacred music 78, 100, 105, 109, 135–6
saf al-ginbri 93–5
sama'a 14
sama'i 18; *see also* Arab music
satellite *see* mass media
Shakira 4
Shankar, Ravi 28
Sheikh al-Kamil *see* 'Issa, Muhammad al-Hadi bin
shikhat 101
sh'abi 78n1, 99–101
Sidi Ali 83, 85–6
Sidi Brahim 67
Sidi Hamu 67–9
Sidi Mimun 67
Sidi Musa 66–8, 72
sintir *see* hajhuj
Slaoui, Houcine 48–9
slavery 58–9, 139; in Andalusia 11–12; slave trade 60–1; *see also* gnawa: marginalization; gnawa: slavery in ritual
social class *see* class
social media 26, 133; *see also* internet; mass media
Soussi, Muhammad 92, 115–7, 122, 133–6
Spain 10, 12, 21; terrorist attacks 39; *see also* Andalusia
spirit possession 63, 66–8; *see also* gnawa: ritual practice; hamadsha; 'issawa
Stitu, Abd al-Wahab 70
Sufism 9, 34, 52–3, 65, 81–2, 135, 143; among urban poor 121; in Morocco 20–1, 32; musical traditions of 21–2; poetry 82–3; popular 80–4; and popular music 100–1; *see also* hamadsha; Islam; 'issawa; "Moroccan Islam"
Sultan Mulay Abd al-Hafid 45
swissen 124

tabla 92, 98, 104; *see also* darbuka
Taha, Rachid 132

Tahir, Mulay al- 67
takht 34; *see also* Arab music
Tangier 28–9, 72, 99, 140–1
tar 16, 124; *see also* rhythm
tarab 34–5
tariqa *see* Sufism
tasliyya 92
taste *see* musical taste
tbal 63
technology 24–5; *see also* mass media
terrorism 25–6, 38–9, 75n1, 81, 95n1
The Beatles 28
tijaniyya 119–20
Toulali, Houcine 128–9
tourism 115–6, 139
tradition 17, 21, 55, 89–90, 122
trance 93, 102, 108, 112; *see also* spirit possession
tubu' 17–20; as personal nature 7–9; *see also* Andalusian music; maqam
Tunisia 53–4; *see also* Arab Spring
tushiyya 18
t'arija 87–8, 124

'ud 7, 11, 16, 21, 34 *see also* Arab music
'ud al-ramal 8, 11, 16
Umayyad dynasty 10–11, 33
Umm Kulthum 35
urban poor *see* poverty; urbanization
urbanization 46, 49, 68, 120–1, 140–1

ville nouvelle 46, 119–20
viola 16
violin 16, 34, 124; Andalusi playing style 131; *see also* Arab music

weddings 36–7, 99; *see also* 'issawa: description of a wedding
Wehbe, Haifa 30
West Africa 61; *see also* slavery: slave trade
Western Sahara 36
Weston, Randy 29, 71–4
Wooten, Victor 43–4
women 2, 49, 63, 144; *see also* gender; mudawana

Yâakoubi, Abdellah 97–9, 109–10
"Years of Lead" *see* Morocco: "Years of Lead"
youth 138
YouTube *see* internet

zawiya 21, 32, 65, 82; *see also* Sufism
Ziryab 11–13, 16; *see also* Andalusian music

Made in the USA
Monee, IL
01 July 2021